TAKE CARE OF FREEDOM AND TRUTH
WILL TAKE CARE OF ITSELF

*Cultural Memory*
*in*
*the*
*Present*

*Mieke Bal and Hent de Vries, Editors*

# TAKE CARE OF FREEDOM AND TRUTH WILL TAKE CARE OF ITSELF

*Interviews with Richard Rorty*

Richard Rorty

*Edited and with an Introduction by*
*Eduardo Mendieta*

STANFORD UNIVERSITY PRESS

STANFORD, CALIFORNIA

2006

Stanford University Press
Stanford, California

Printed in the United States of America on acid-free, archival-quality paper

Library of Congress Cataloging-in-Publication Data

Rorty, Richard.
   Take care of freedom and truth will take care of itself : interviews with
   Richard Rorty / Richard Rorty ; edited by Eduardo Mendieta.
       p.   cm. — (Cultural memory in the present)
   "Bibliography of Richard Rorty's writings."
   Includes bibliographical references and index.
   ISBN 0-8047-4617-6 (cloth : alk. paper)
   ISBN 0-8047-4618-4 (pbk. : alk. paper)
       1. Rorty, Richard—Interviews. 2. Liberty. 3. Truth. 4. Philosophers—
United States—Interviews. I. Mendieta, Eduardo. II. Title. III. Series.
B945.R524A5 2006
191—dc22

                                                                    2005013572

Original Printing 2006

Last figure below indicates year of this printing:
15  14  13  12  11  10  09  08  07  06

# Contents

## Acknowledgments

This book became a collection of interviews because Alejandro Sierra, the director of Trotta, the Spanish publishing house that published the Spanish version of this collection, was enthusiastic and supportive of my efforts to have Rorty translated. Without his support and patience this book would not have come together. I must also thank Helen Tartar, who took the project under her wing. I am sorry that she is no longer at Stanford University Press to see it published. In selecting, translating, and putting together these interviews, I have met, if only via e-mail, some wonderful individuals, whose support and work has been indispensable. I am especially grateful to James Ryerson, who granted me permission to use his profile and interview with Rorty from the now defunct *Lingua Franca*. Chronis Polychroniou shared with me two long interviews that he had conducted with Rorty, and allowed me full latitude in selecting what I thought would best fit this volume. I am extremely thankful as well to Edward Ragg for allowing me to include his excellent interview. The original table of contents of this volume included the lengthy interviews with Derek Nystrom and Kent Puckett, which had been published as a small pamphlet by Prickly Pear Pamphlets with the title *Against Bosses, Against Oligarchies: A Conversation with Richard Rorty*. While the publisher granted us permission to print a Spanish translation of it, we were not granted permission to include it in the English version. Still, I must thank the interviewers and the press for the rights to include it in the Spanish version. I am also grateful to the editors of the *Harvard Journal of Philosophy, Neue Rundschau, 2B: A Journal of Ideas*, and *Philosophy and Literature* for permission to reprint interviews from their journals. Gideon Lewis-Kraus, Richard Rorty's assistant, has also been indispensable, especially for the bibliography of Rorty's works. Cynthia Paccacerqua and Azucena Cruz helped me convert a lot of photocopies into an electronic manuscript. Azucena got me through the last steps of polishing the manuscript and kept me to the timeline. I also want to give special thanks to Norman Bussiere, a retired high school principal who took part of my Rorty seminar and kept me up with the latest Rortiana. Finally, this volume would not have been possible without Richard Rorty's willingness to be persuaded that such a book could be put together. But once he was persuaded, he gave me his full support, cooperation, and attention. I am certain that Richard Rorty is the most important living philosopher in the United States, and thus feel particularly honored to have been granted so much of his time. It is my hope that this book will allow many who dismiss him and deliberately misrepresent his views to consider how consistently Rorty has been on the side of democracy, a tireless defender of the dream of an America that we must keep striving for, because its "moral identity is still to be achieved, rather than needing to be preserved."

*Eduardo Mendieta*
*Stony Brook, New York, 2004*

# Introduction

### "Take Care of Freedom and Truth Will Take
### Care of Itself": Toward a Postphilosophical Politics

*Eduardo Mendieta*

## I

If Richard Rorty did not exist he would have to be invented. Americans, above all, would have to invent him. But philosophers, leftists, cultural critics, theorists, intellectual historians, novelists, preachers, politicians, apocalyptic soothsayers, lawyers, and even comics the world over would also have to invent him. Fortunately, Rorty exists. In fact, the existing Rorty has far outstripped what anyone could have dreamed up for the role of consummate critic, unnostalgic outsider, Socratic gadfly, irreverent demystifyer, perpetual noncontemporaneous dreamer, heroic prophet of the new dawns, ingenious mixer and masterful producer of modern bricolage, and patriotic critic of an unfinished country. He is a nemesis to many, and is claimed as a friend by only very few. His works are denounced everywhere across the country, in every discipline, and in each of the Ivy League universities. Yet he is one of the most read philosophers in the United States. Richard Rorty is a uniquely American anomaly. Amazingly, his work stands athwart most of what has come to represent America at the end of the "American century." His work is cosmopolitan, ecumenical, multilateralist, trans-American, anti-imperial, and confessedly ethnocentric, so that it can be critical of his moral community, both antischolastic and antidisciplinary. He is utopian, hopeful, and optimistic without being reckless, unrealistic, and antidemocratic.

Rorty's work is above all guided by two central virtues: respect and hope. His work is animated by profound respect for ordinary citizens. This respect is enshrined in the priority that he gives to the primacy of the agent's point of view. In turn, this respect is matched by his utopian hopefulness that social justice is a worthy project to devote our lives to, even if we have no guarantees that we will succeed and that our gains will not be rolled back.[1] In a country famously short on memory, Rorty's work always advocates the *long durée* of social movements and millennial intellectual traditions. His work, while deeply informed by the most recent developments in what is called Continental and analytic philosophy, is unabashedly antidisciplinary and postprofessionalization. One of the central aims of his writing has been to liberate philosophy from the ivory towers of the Ivy League, where it has been sequestered since Immanuel Kant began to turn philosophy into an academic discipline. Rorty's work is refreshingly new precisely because it has taken a stand against the kind of professional deformation that results in sterile forms of scholasticism—especially the esoteric writing that makes philosophy frivolous, irrelevant to the public life of a democracy. While he is dismissed, denounced, derided, and ridiculed by every major representative across the political spectrum, from the reddest of the left to the bluest of the right, he is still the most quoted living American philosopher. He has influenced and invigorated many fields within the humanities and social sciences. While he has been read by some as advocating the end of philosophy, his work has in fact led to the renewal of debates about the public role of philosophy. He is surely the most appealing and honoring public intellectual that the United States could have as a cultural ambassador, abroad and across the continental United States. In this age, in which the United States is perceived as an imperial Leviathan, stumbling blindly, rapaciously, and disastrously across the world,

1. I have benefited greatly from Mark Dooley's sympathetic engagement with Rorty's work. See in particular his "Private Irony vs. Social Hope: Derrida, Rorty, and the Political," *Cultural Values* 3:3 (1999): 263–90; "A Civic Religion of Social Hope: A Reply to Simon Critchley," *Philosophy and Social Hope* 27:5 (September 2001): 35–58. See especially his essay on Rorty and John Caputo, "In Praise of Prophesy," in *A Passion for the Impossible: John Caputo in Focus*, ed. Mark Dooley, 201–28 (Albany: State University of New York Press, 2003).

Richard Rorty's criticism of the recent administration's policies are all the more remarkable because it comes from someone who has also eloquently advocated an American patriotism and recalled for the American public the importance of Emerson's and Whitman's country, one that is still yet to be achieved.[2] Along with John Dewey, the philosopher of education and democracy, and John Rawls, the philosopher of justice and political liberalism, Richard Rorty will stand as one of the most important American philosophers of the twentieth century. Like Dewey and Rawls, he will also be remembered as a philosopher of what he has so beautifully called a "larger loyalty."[3] Like every major philosopher who is remembered by one or two philosophemes that embody the spirit of their philosophical quest and contribution, Rorty will be remembered by the words *irony, contingency,* and *solidarity.*

## II

Richard Rorty has pursued one philosophical aim over the past thirty years or so, namely, to demonstrate that pragmatism is not only one of the most important philosophical traditions to have emerged from the American experience, but that it synthesizes the philosophical and scientific advances made in the West over the past few centuries. In this sense, Rorty's work has been concerned mainly with the rehabilitation, rediscovery, and renewal of pragmatism. Many have accused Rorty of not interpreting the pragmatist canon correctly, arguing that he has not accurately understood the philosophers he has sought to rehabilitate.[4] Rorty's version of pragmatism is indeed unique and distinct, but pragmatism has always meant

2. I am thinking particularly of two pieces, "Fighting Terrorism with Democracy," *The Nation* (October 21, 2002), 11–14; and "Postdemocracy: Richard Rorty on Anti-Terrorism and the National Security State," in *London Review of Books* (April 1, 2004), 10–11.

3. Richard Rorty, "Justice as a Larger Loyalty," in *Richard Rorty: Critical Dialogues,* ed. Matthew Festenstein and Simon Thompson, 223–37 (Cambridge: Polity Press, 2001).

4. See the essays collected in Herman J. Staatkamp, Jr., ed., *Rorty and Pragmatism: The Philosopher Responds to His Critics* (Nashville: Vanderbilt University Press, 1995); and Robert B. Brandom, *Rorty and His Critics* (Malden, Mass.: Blackwell, 2000).

different things to different thinkers and philosophers. Even people who identify themselves as pragmatists, or who acknowledge that they share in the pragmatist approach to such a degree that they see themselves as part of a historical movement that aims to revive pragmatism, disagree on who are the central figures within the tradition and who are not. Thinkers of many persuasions and fields—Marxists, socialists, feminists, liberals, political conservatives, literary critics, legal thinkers, historians, philosophers, and so on—have called themselves pragmatists. Such individuals name John Dewey, Charles S. Peirce, Oliver Wendell Holmes, Alain Locke, Sidney Hook, George Herbert Mead, W. E. B. DuBois, William James, and Josiah Royce, to name some of the main figures in the pragmatist pantheon, as their predecessors and intellectual sources of inspiration. Richard Rorty has done more than any other contemporary U.S. philosopher to revive and reclaim the name and tradition of pragmatism. But he has also, more than anyone else, destabilized, blurred, jostled, and reinscribed the meaning of pragmatism. In Rorty's hands, pragmatism has not just been revived but also transformed into a formidable and venerable Western philosophical tradition.

To get at what Rorty means by pragmatism, I would like to split the difference between what he is against and what he approves of, and summarize what he advocates. In this way, we can outline how Rorty thinks we ought to be talking about what concerns human beings and their relations with one another, instead of giving a Rortian definition of pragmatism, and we can isolate what he thinks isn't worth our attention and concern.

Rorty's style is disarmingly chatty and colloquial, and what he says is expressed in terms of oppositions. The structure of his essays hinges on rhetorical and mnemonic devices; he does not demonstrate. He leads us to new insights not by syllogisms but through the force of narrative in his irreverent and original stories. Still, Rorty is anti-Platonist, that is, he rejects the appearance-essence, or contingent-eternal distinction that is fundamental to Platonism. He is anti-Aristotelian, that is, he rejects the convention-nature distinction. He is also anti-Thomist, that is, he rejects the natural law–human law, distinction. He is also an anti-Kantian, that is, he rejects the noumena-phenomena, analytic-synthetic, a priori–a posteriori distinctions. He is also anti-Cartesian, that is, he rejects the mind-matter, innate-acquired distinctions. He is anti-Hegelian, that is, he rejects the notion that there is a logic of history, and that this logic is the nature of reason, and that this reason is tied to freedom. He is also anti-Marxist, that is, he rejects the idea that all history is the history of class struggle, and the notion that the ruling ideas are the ideas of the ruling classes. All of this can be translated into anti-essentialism, antirealism, antimentalism, anti-subjectivism, anticognitivism, anti–historical materialism—in short anti-metaphysics and antifoundationalism. In Rorty's view, pragmatism is the name for the kind of philosophical approach that has sought to dispense with some of the most obdurate and entrenched philosophical obsessions and sacred cows.

Rorty's form of talking is also characterized by what it endorses. Each sentence that rejects a particular philosophical mythology or problematic is invariably followed by a sentence that puts forward some thinker and a particular argumentative breakthrough that allows us to dispense with what was rejected in the prior sentence. In this way, Rorty is able to split the difference between two extremes.[5] Thus, Rorty is avowedly pro-Humean, that is, he endorses Hume's emphasis of the education of moral sentiment over the alleged power of reason.[6] He is pro-Derridean, that is, he endorses the ways in which deconstruction is another name for jostling

5. I think that as one reads across Rorty's corpus, one notices that over the last decade or so, Rorty's early juxtaposition of Dewey and Heidegger has been replaced by the juxtaposition of Habermas and Derrida. I think that as Heidegger has become more suspect and untenable for Rorty, he has been replaced by Derrida, and as Dewey recedes in time, he has been replaced by Habermas. Furthermore, while Rorty has continued to attach names to the kinds of positions he espouses himself, it is quite evident that the extremes these two figures represent are the positions of, on the one hand, private irony or contingency, and social hope or solidarity on the other. Rorty writes as if he has read most everything important that has been published in the last hundred years, but only in order to achieve a kind of philosophical multilateralism.

6. Sociological analyses are not proofs for philosophical arguments. Yet, one cannot but side with Hume and Rorty in light of the 2004 National Endowment for the Arts report entitled *Reading at Risk*. The report is based on information mined from a survey conducted by the Census Bureau in 2002, "The Survey of Public Participation in the Arts." The report indicates that reading has declined in the United States; at the same time, it correlates the level of social engagement and reading habits. Thus, those who read more are also more likely to do volunteer and charity work. See Bruce Weber, "Fewer Noses Stuck in Books in America, Survey Finds," *New York Times* (July 8, 2004). I am thankful to Martin Woessner for bringing to my attention these articles.

and redescription, brilliant bricolage, and a form of polytheistic criticism. He is pro-Davidsonian, that is, he endorses the ways in which Davidson's view of language is a form of pan-relationalism, in which triangulation means submitting to the authority of reasons that are offered as justifications rather than as ways of finding something outside and beside what is merely human. He is also pro-Wittgensteinian, that is, he endorses the ways in which language use is tied to forms of life, and how changing ways of talking and describing the world entail changing practical relations. He is also pro-Heideggerian, but he endorses only the Heidegger who is interested in language as poetic novelty, the one who offers metanarratives that allow us to see how we may begin to be disenchanted with old mythologies and begin to articulate new languages and narratives. He is also pro-Habermasian, that is, he endorses the kind of shift from monological subjectivity to intersubjectivity and communicative rationality that Habermas has so eloquently described. Thus, Rorty advocates a pragmatism that is unequivocally and unwaveringly historicist, emotivist, deconstructivist, dialogic, linguistic, contextualist, and pan-relationalist.

Rortian discourse, not to be confused with either Heideggerianese or Derridean deconstructionism, both forms of language and description that began as heresies but which eventually became orthodoxies par excellence, generally includes a third type of sentence, after the rejections and endorsements, that articulates directly Rorty's own views.[7] Rorty's pragmatism is a form of thinking that is obsessively focused on the practical, or praxis, above theory or contemplation. The goal of philosophizing is not to discover eternal truths, or truths that can stand as ultimate alibis for theoretical claims, but rather, the instrumental character of ideas. Not whether ideas are right in accordance with something of which they are a copy or to which they refer, but instead whether ideas or narratives allow us to transform our world. In this way, Rorty's pragmatism is forward-looking and meliorative. Rorty's brand of pragmatism is profoundly antidogmatic; it is skeptical of received wisdom and canons, as well as of common sense. It is irreverent and suspicious of any authority, be it intellectual, philosophical,

7. The following list of positive goals that Rorty's type of pragmatism endorses was partly gathered from Richard A. Posner's description of the "pragmatic approach," in the introduction to his *Overcoming Law* (Cambridge, Mass.: Harvard University Press, 1995), 4–10.

or religious, especially if it has not been submitted to the test of the court of public justification. Rorty's pragmatism is polytheistic, or rather, it is a secularism to the nth degree. For the same reasons, Rorty's pragmatism is experimentalist and revolutionary. In this way, it is a form of thinking that gives primacy to the social over the natural and that therefore advocates the richest form of pluralism. In its political instantiation, this pluralism takes the form of political liberalism, or what Rorty has also called postmodern bourgeois liberalism.

From a third-person perspective, it may be tempting to describe Rorty's pragmatism in the following way. Epistemologically, it is antirepresentationalist; metaphysically, it is anti-essentialist; ethically, it is antifoundationalist, or anticognitivistic. Metaphilosophically, it is antiphilosophical, that is, it seems to advocate the end of professionalized philosophy. Politically, it is antinormative. While this may help the philosophical spectator place Rorty on the philosophical map, it would also misconstrue Rorty's unsettling and unorthodox views. He is not trying to rearrange the furniture within the edifice of philosophy. He wants the whole edifice to be opened up, aired out, and restructured. In fact, he wants philosophy to stop occupying the central role that has been given to it, a role that has been predicated on an elaborate misunderstanding of what philosophy is about, what it can deliver. Rorty does not so much want to reform as to transform philosophy. Philosophy can help transform the world only if it first transforms itself, and it transforms itself by ceasing to be deluded about its royal mission. In the end, Rorty's adamant skepticism and antidogmatism are simply ways to be anti-authoritarian and irreverently antifetishistic.[8] There is no supreme power that can offer an alibi, warrant, or proof for our claims and beliefs, nothing except fallible human authority. There is no supreme authority, other than the authority of human justifications and reasons, whose only power is the power of persuasion.

8. Rorty has provided an explicit and elaborate defense of this analysis in his 1996 Ferrater Mora lectures at the University of Girona, published in Spanish as *El pragmatismo, una version: Antiautoristarismo en epistemología y ética*, trans. Joan Verges Gifra (Barcelona: Ariel, 2000).

III

Rorty's articulation of his version of pragmatism has been fairly consistent since the early seventies, at least since 1974, when he published "Overcoming the Tradition: Heidegger and Dewey," an essay that anticipated many themes and approaches that would characterize Rorty's work.[9] It could also be argued that Rorty's call to transform, rather than to reform, philosophy was already announced in the introduction to the book he edited in 1967, *The Linguistic Turn: Recent Essays in Philosophical Method*.[10] In this introductory essay, entitled "Metaphilosophical Difficulties of Linguistic Philosophy," Rorty discusses the ways in which so-called analytic philosophy had driven itself into a cul-de-sac. The introduction begins with the sentence, "The history of philosophy is punctuated by revolts against the practices of previous philosophers and by attempts to transform philosophy into a science—a discipline in which universally recognized decision-procedures are available for testing philosophical theses." And then proceeds to argue that in the face of the recent debates that bare this prior affirmation, "one is tempted to *define* philosophy as that discipline in which knowledge is sought but only opinion can be had."[11] Rorty, however, came into the academic limelight with the publication of his major book, *Philosophy and the Mirror of Nature*, published in 1979,[12] an eloquent, carefully argued, and sweeping analysis of the origins and demise of

9. Richard Rorty, "Overcoming the Tradition: Dewey and Heidegger," in *Consequences of Pragmatism* (Minneapolis: University of Minnesota Press, 1982), 37–59. For an appreciative but critical engagement with this book, see Don Ihde, *Consequences of Phenomenology* (Albany: State University of New York Press, 1986). For a short but fairly accurate overview of Rorty's work, see the "Richard McKay Rorty" entry by Micahel David Rohr in the *Routledge Encyclopedia of Philosophy*, vol. 8, 352–56. Two excellent overviews of Rorty philosophy are David L. Hall, *Richard Rorty: Prophet and Poet of the New Pragmatism* (Albany: State University of New York Press, 1994); and Alan Malachowski, *Richard Rorty* (Princeton, N.J.: Princeton University Press, 2002).

10. Richard Rorty, ed., *The Linguistic Turn: Recent Essays in Philosophical Method* (Chicago: University of Chicago Press, 1967).

11. Ibid., pages 1 and 2, respectively.

12. Richard Rorty, *Philosophy and the Mirror of Nature* (Princeton, N.J.: Princeton University Press, 1979).

contemporary analytic philosophy.[13] This book offered a "quasi-Heidegg-erian" narrative of the origins and the flawed approach of most of modern philosophy. The book rejects realism, representationalism, subjectivism, and essentialism, all of which had plagued epistemologically obsessed analytic philosophy. In addition, Rorty argues that while Anglo-American analytic philosophy had made a linguistic turn, it had failed to follow through on what this meant for arguments about mind, statements, language itself, and most importantly, what this linguistic turn entailed for the very discipline of philosophy. What made this a crossover book in philosophy probably is part 3 of the book, simply entitled "Philosophy," which is composed of two chapters, "From Epistemology to Hermeneutics" and "Philosophy Without Mirrors." Here, Rorty lays out his famous distinction between systematic and edifying philosophy. Where the former is "constructive and offer[s] arguments" and builds for eternity, the latter is "reactive and offer[s] satires, parodies, aphorisms," and "destroy[s] for the sake of their own generation."[14] Whereas systematic philosophers seek to find a truth outside history and beyond human language, and thus seek to bring an end to philosophy by turning it into a science, edifying philosophers are simply "conversation partners," philosophers "who can never end philosophy, but they can help prevent it from attaining the secure path of a science."[15] The book ends with Rorty appropriating Michael Oakeshott's idea of the "conversation of mankind." With this appropriation, Rorty urges that philosophy should be rescued from its professional deformation at the hands of epistemologically obsessed academics. Instead, philosophy should become a partner in the conversation of humankind, and as such, Rorty concludes, the "philosopher's moral concern should be with continuing the conversation of the West, rather than with insisting upon a place for the traditional problems of modern philosophy within that conversation."[16] Philosophy contributes to this conversation not by insist-

13. One of my favorite reviews of this book remains Joe McCarney's in the British leftist journal *Radical Philosophy*. Joe McCarney, "Edifying Discourses," in *Radical Philosophy Reader*, ed. Roy Edgley and Richard Osborne (London: Verso, 1985), 398–405. See also the critical collection of essays on this book edited by Alan Malachowski, *Reading Rorty* (Oxford: Blackwell, 1990).

14. Rorty, *Philosophy and the Mirror of Nature*, 369.

15. Ibid., 372.

16. Ibid., 394.

ing on its problems, problems that turn out to be misunderstandings and misguided ways of understanding the relationship between humans, the world, and their languages. Instead, it contributes to the conversation of humankind by insisting on its edifying role, that is, by "finding new, better, more interesting, more fruitful ways of speaking."[17]

Rorty's next book was the now classic *Contingency, Irony, and Solidarity*, the publication that brought Rorty international attention.[18] Though published in 1989, this book is based on a series of lectures Rorty delivered in England in 1986 and 1987. The many memorable phrases in this book have been quoted and misquoted extensively. Essentially, it calls us to abjure the notions that have been associated with Western philosophy since the Reformation, the Enlightenment, and the French and American revolutions; notions that have to do with truths that are found and discovered, with fundamental human essence and real selfhoods, and with norms and principles that serve as foundations for our political institutions and moral practices. Rorty argues that we should abandon talk about discovering truths, heeding the call of human essence, and discerning the true logic and meaning of history. Such talk, such projects, such heedings are impossible, irretrievable, and intractably condemned to failure. Our staunch pursuit of these mirrors, fictions, and philosophemes only perpetuates our inattention to our own power, the power of human action, creativity, and solidarity. Truths, which are neither to be discovered nor found, ought to be replaced by compelling, transformative, generative narratives, or stories, in other words, that provide us with far more interesting ways of seeing ourselves, of reimagining ourselves in new personas, characters, goals, solidarities, and more expansive loyalties. For this reason, Rorty offers counternarratives that reinscribe and redescribe the ways in which we can and should understand those moments that have punctuated the moral and social evolution of the West. Instead of saying that the Reformation, the Enlightenment, and the American and French revolutions were about putting reason on a scientific grounding, discovering the norms and principles of rationality, and grounding our political institutions and moral practices on the unshakable ground of the truly good and just, we should see these historical events as a series of processes that have yet to be carried through

17. Rorty, *Philosophy and the Mirror of Nature*, 360.

18. Richard Rorty, *Contingency, Irony, and Solidarity* (Cambridge: Cambridge University Press, 1989).

to their conclusion. In this way, *Contingency, Irony, and Solidarity* is a major project of reinscription, a reinscription of Western intellectual history itself. Still, one of the central themes of the book is the contingency of our beliefs, whether they are moral or political. But this form of radical historical contingency does not result in ethical relativism. As Rorty wrote, "the fundamental premise of the book is that a belief can still regulate action, can still be worth dying for, among people who are quite aware that this belief is caused by nothing deeper than contingent historical circumstance."[19] But, if our beliefs have no other guarantee than the strength of our socialization into these beliefs, what holds society together? Rorty is jostling us so that we may begin to move away from obsession with the putative power of ethical norms and principles, to the actual power of solidarity that makes us act respectfully, morally, with empathy toward others. In this way, along with the radical historical contingency of our beliefs, Rorty's book articulates another central claim, namely, that "our responsibilities to others constitute *only* the public side of our lives, a side which competes with our private affections and our private attempts at self-creation, and which has no *automatic* priority over such private motives."[20] In other words, we must uncouple the private from the public life of citizens. Whereas in private life citizens pursue their dream of perfection, in public they are bound by solidarity, by mutual respect. If in our private lives we aspire to sublimity, in public we seek to "avoid cruelty and pain."[21] In this way, since there is no God, no history other than the one we make, and no real human essence, other than how we imagine humans to be creatures that suffer, all our beliefs are radically contingent, and thus disposable, or rather, transformable. In the face of this, the mature, inconsolably disappointed attitude of the citizen is to become ironic.

Irony is the name Rorty gives to the attitude that the only power our beliefs have is the power to inscribe us, make us see ourselves in a certain way. The ironist thus names "the sort of person who faces up to the contingency of his or her own most central beliefs and desires—someone sufficiently historicist and nominalist to have abandoned the idea that those central beliefs and desires refer back to something beyond reach of time and chance."[22] The ironist, therefore,

19. Ibid., 189.
20. Ibid., 194.
21. Ibid., 197.
22. Ibid., xv.

spends her time worrying about the possibility that she has been initiated into the wrong tribe, taught to play the wrong language game. She worries that the process of socialization which turned her into a human being by giving her a language may have given her the wrong language, and so turned her into the wrong kind of human being. But she cannot give a criterion of wrongness. So, the more she is driven to articulate her situation in philosophical terms, the more she reminds herself of her rootlessness by constantly using terms like "Weltanschauung," "perspective," "dialectic," "conceptual framework," "historical epoch," "language game," "redescription," "vocabulary," and "irony."[23]

Irony, however, is not the same as quietude, letting things be, passiveness, irresponsible and cruel derogation toward one's own and other people's final vocabularies. Irony reflects the power that we all have to reinscribe and redescribe. In this way, ironism is active, activist, critical, forward-looking. It is the power of irony that turns our confessed ethnocentrism into the imperative to create ever more critical pictures of what we have turned into and what we have failed to become. Irony, which is often seen as a form of cruelty, disdain, and derogation, is really linked to solidarity. Irony liberates us to a greater humanity. Irony grants us the power to abandon narrow, cruel, exclusivist, versions of our old and inherited "we." It grants us the power to create a larger "we," whose outer perimeter is drawn and redrawn from the perspective of marginalized people, from the perspective of those we have been socialized to think of as "they" rather than "us."

Rorty's next major work, based on the William E. Massey Lectures in the History of American Civilization he gave at Harvard, was *Achieving Our Country: Leftist Thought in Twentieth-Century America*.[24] Not unlike his earlier books, *Achieving Our Country* occasioned vociferous and animated criticism.[25] Unlike the earlier books, however, the theme of this book was not philosophical, but rather political and cultural. Paralleling the moves he makes in his earlier works, Rorty proceeds to reinterpret the role of the "left" in the United States. There is the old left, which he calls the "reformist left," one that was engaged with actual campaigns and movements, what Rorty sometimes calls the "real politics" of concrete po-

23. Rorty, *Philosophy and the Mirror of Nature*, 75.

24. *Achieving Our Country: Leftist Thought in Twentieth-Century America* (Cambridge, Mass.: Harvard University Press, 1998).

25. See John Pettegrew, ed., *A Pragmatist's Progress: Richard Rorty and American Intellectual History* (Lanham, Md.: Rowman and Littlefield, 2000).

litical goals. This socialist and social democratic left was engaged and immersed in everyday politics, not merely reflecting or contemplating social reality. Most importantly, this engaged and reformist left was not mired in self-loathing, for it sought to transform "America" precisely because it still had pride in the country whose moral character was not set but still to be made. While the reformist left actively sought to transform contemporary America, its eyes were on a future America, one which is yet to be achieved. For this reason, this left is the party of "hope." In contrast, the postsixties left, or what Rorty sometimes calls the "cultural left" and other times the "academic left," has eclipsed the modus operandi and also the spirit of the reformist left. This cultural left is caught in endless debates about identity, about cultural differences, about recognition and symbolic representation. It is overly theoretical, and most of its energy is consumed in theoretical or philosophical pursuits. Instead of storming city hall, it rushes for the English department or the dean's office. Its struggles are not labor struggles, but curricular debates. The cultural left has become spectatorial and thus disengaged from concrete campaigns and movements. In contrast to the reformist left, the cultural left has no pride in America. It is emotionally disengaged from it. In fact, it is motivated by a deep anti-Americanism and self-loathing. As Rorty put it elsewhere, "This over-philosophized and self-obsessed left is the mirror image of the over-philosophized and self-obsessed Straussians. The contempt of both groups for contemporary American society is so great that both have rendered themselves impotent when it comes to national, state or local politics. This means that they get to spend *all* their energy on academic politics."[26] Instead of aiming at a new America, this left is immobilized by its unsparing retrospective gaze. The racist, genocidal, imperial past of America weighs heavy on the cultural left. It cannot see what is worth preserving or achieving in this country. Rorty puts it succinctly in this way:

Insofar as a left becomes spectatorial and retrospective, it ceases to be a Left. I shall be claiming in these lectures that the American Left, once the old alliance between the intellectuals and the unions broke-down in the course of the Sixties, began to sink into an attitude like Henry Adams'. Leftists in the academy have permitted cultural politics to supplant real politics, and have collaborated with the Right

26. Richard Rorty, *Philosophy and Social Hope* (New York: Penguin, 1999), 129.

in making cultural issues central to public debate. . . . The academic Left has no projects to propose to America, no vision of a country to be achieved by building a consensus on the need for specific reforms.[27]

For this reason, Rorty calls for a "moratorium" on theory. Rorty admonishes that the academic and cultural left "kick its philosophy habit."[28] Just as importantly, Rorty urges the left to abandon its apocalyptic self-loathing and to become emotionally engaged in the nation by feeling, at the very least, shame.

You can feel shame over your country's behavior only to the extent to which you feel it is your country. If we fail such identification, we fail in national hope. If American leftists cease to be proud of being the heirs of Emerson, Lincoln and King, Irving Howe's prophecy that "the 'newness' will come again"—that we shall once again experience the joyous self-confidence which fills Emerson's "American Scholar"—is unlikely to come true. . . . A left that refuses to take pride in its country will have no impact on that country's politics, and will eventually become an object of contempt.[29]

*Achieving Our Country* is a masterful reinscription and redescription of the history of the left in America. It argues that the left, the reformist left, has inherited the ideals of the poets and great politicians of the country. As the party of hope it is on the side of an America that is yet to be made. It is emotionally engaged with the struggles of the country that have as their aim the spread of economic and social justice. Rorty is arguing that we should cease to attempt to make politics more philosophical, or to be guided by philosophy. Instead, he wants politics to be more concerned with the real lives of citizens. Rorty is thus advocating, as Rorty scholar Alan Malachowski notes, that instead of assuming a philosophical attitude toward politics we should assume an overtly political attitude toward politics.[30]

It is indeed difficult not to be moved by Rorty's eulogy of the leftist tradition in the United States.[31] Many specialists, of course, have con-

27. Rorty, *Achieving Our Country*, 15.

28. Ibid., 91.

29. Rorty, *Philosophy and Social Hope*, 254.

30. Alan Malachowski, *Richard Rorty* (Princeton, N.J.: Princeton University Press, 2002), 129.

31. See Richard J. Bernstein, "Rorty's Inspirational Liberalism," in *Richard Rorty*, ed. Charles Guignon and David R. Hiley (Cambridge: Cambridge University Press, 2003), 124–38.

tested the details of Rorty's counternarrative. Yet it is difficult not to appreciate Rorty's central point. The academic left has become so focused on theoretical and philosophical debates that it has become entirely alienated from the social reality of average Americans. The cultural left has made critical thought irrelevant to politics. In many ways, this book retraces similar steps to those Rorty made in *Philosophy and the Mirror of Nature*. If the systematic philosophers of analytic philosophy, the children of Plato, Descartes, Kant, and Husserl, have made philosophy so arcane and obtuse that it has become irrelevant to the ethical aims of the great conversation of humanity, the children of the countercultural sixties and poststructuralist turn of thought of the fifties have made philosophy so theoretical and self-obsessed that it no longer recognizes the concerns and needs of the American public. In *Achieving Our Country*, Rorty is urging us to move philosophy to the center of the public square, where its work can be of some use. The academization and professionalization of philosophy that got underway with Kant, and which achieved its denouement with the academic left of the postsixties generations of philosophers, has imprisoned philosophy in the ivory tower of the university. This call to transform philosophy is hardly a call to abolish or abandon it. For while Rorty has pursued engaged cultural and philosophical criticism, he has not ceased to produce analytically rigorous and encyclopedically expansive essays on current debates within professional philosophy. He has published in English three volumes of collected philosophical papers;[32] a fourth volume has appeared only in Spanish, as the Ferrater Mora lectures;[33] plus he has published *Philosophy and Social Hope*, a smaller collection of more popular pieces from the print media. This is hardly the output of a philosopher who wants to see the "end of philosophy." If we read Rorty as a reformer, a critic, and even a prophet who calls for philosophy's renewal and relevance to our social lives, we can see that his work resembles Marx's eleventh thesis on Feuerbach. Philosophy, as the thesis goes, is not about contemplation, interpretation, deconstruction, or description, but about transformation. Rorty's work aims at a similar redescription of philosophy. For as much as Rorty dismisses the Marx of "historical materialism," and the Marx of the

32. Richard Rorty, *Objectivity, Relativism, and Truth: Philosophical Papers I* (Cambridge: Cambridge University Press, 1991); *Essays on Heidegger and Others: Philosophical Papers II* (Cambridge: Cambridge University Press, 1991); *Truth and Progress: Philosophical Papers III* (Cambridge: Cambridge University Press, 1998).

33. Rorty, *El pragmatismo, una versión.*

"logic of history," he remains committed to the notion that philosophy can contribute to the utopia of social justice so long as it remains engaged with the world. In a passage that merits lengthy citation, Rorty places himself in this Romantic tradition:

The combined influence of Hegel and Darwin moved philosophy away from the question "What are we?" to the question "What might we try to become?" This shift has had consequences for the philosophers' image of themselves. Whereas Plato and even Kant hoped to survey the society and the culture within which they lived from an outside standpoint, the standpoint of ineluctable and change-less truth, later philosophers have gradually abandoned such hopes just insofar as we take time to think seriously, we philosophers have to give up the priority of contemplation over action. We have to agree with Marx that our job is to help make the future different from the past, rather than claiming to know what the future must necessarily have in common with the past. We have to shift from the kind of role that philosophers have shared with priests and sages to a social role that has more in common with the engineer or the lawyer. Whereas priests and sages can set their own agendas, contemporary philosophers, like engineers and lawyers, must find out what their clients need. . . . We can add that philosophy cannot possibly end until social and cultural change ends. For such changes grad-ually render large-scale descriptions of ourselves and our situation obsolete. They create the need for new language in which to formulate new descriptions. Only a society without politics—that is to say, a society run by tyrants who prevented so-cial and cultural change from occurring—would no longer require philosophers. In such societies, where there is no politics, philosophers can only be priests in the service of a state religion. In free societies, there will always be a need for their services, for such societies never stop changing, and hence never stop making old vocabularies obsolete.[34]

A society with politics, as opposed to a society whose politics would have been extinguished by a despot, would have philosophy as a dialogue part-ner in the great conversation about what that society should become. A philosophy that would seek to rule over politics, on the other hand, would betray not just politics but itself. Gary Gutting put it eloquently when he wrote, "What makes for poetry in the soul begets fascism in the city."[35] This

34. Richard Rorty, "Philosophy and the Future," in *Rorty and Pragmatism: The Philosopher Responds to His Critics*, ed. Herman J. Staatkamp (Nashville: Vander-bilt University Press, 1995), 197–98.

35. Gary Gutting, *Pragmatic Liberalism and the Critique of Modernity* (Cam-bridge: Cambridge University Press, 1999), 59.

is not a non sequitur. Philosophy has only poetry to offer, a type of inspirational jostling that foments a type of utopia that is generally expressed in literary terms. Philosophy's utopia is not unlike "Kundera's utopia [which] is carnivalesque, Dickensian, a crowd of eccentrics rejoicing in each other's idiosyncrasies, curious for novelty rather [than] nostalgic for primordiality."[36] When it is not instigating our moral and social imaginaries, trying to expand our loyalties, it is performing the humble job of clearing the pathways to a better society. Philosophy renders well its service to this political society by helping to retire obsolete vocabularies, ideas, and languages, and by dreaming up new, ever more appealing, ever more interesting vocabularies, images, and utopias. Philosophy can only do this, however, as a dialogue partner and not as a director or Führer. For "when it comes to political deliberation, philosophy is a good servant but a bad master."[37] Philosophy is a servant of the utopian dream of social justice, which can only be achieved by political means and not philosophical ones.

## IV

It would be tempting to say that the genre of the interview has come into its own, that it has finally become respectable and even acceptable as a scholarly vehicle and tool. Yet the interview is antischolastic. That it may

36. Anindita Niyogi Balslev, *Cultural Otherness: Correspondence with Richard Rorty*, 2nd ed. (Atlanta: Scholars Press, 1999), 114. This book, made up of a nice introduction by Balslev and the epistolary exchange between her and Rorty, is one of the most intimate and insightful looks at Rorty's work. It is particularly interesting when thinking about the imputation that Rorty is a hopeless ethnocentric and Eurocentric Pax Americana thinker. I think that there is no greater insight into what a global multicultural dialogue would look like, or sound like, than when Rorty writes: "My hunch is that our sense of where to connect up Indian and Western texts will change dramatically when and if people who have read quite a few of both begin to write books which are not clearly identifiable as belonging to any particular genre, and are not clearly identifiable as either Western or Eastern" (68). As Rorty and Balslev note, Salman Rushdie is an example of this type of writer who is neither/nor. Post-Orientalism is not just anti-Occidentalism. Nor is post-Occidentalism just pro-Orientalism. Beyond both pro- and anti-, a third evolves, something that is part of global culture, part each culture, but does not belong to any culture exclusively.

37. Rorty, *Philosophy and Social Hope*, 232.

have become an academic tool may also spell its death. Its fundamental inspiration and function is public dialogue and public debate. The interview is invariably conducted by a servant of open discussion and its audience is a broad public. Its role is not just to translate an arcane or potentially obtuse area of research. Its role is to register the zeitgeist and to instigate public debate. The interview is a barometer of the cultural life of a discipline and a nation. By agreeing to be interviewed the interviewee agrees to step outside his or her role as an expert and to speak *as a citizen*, outside an official role. Of course, he or she is being interviewed because of possessing authority in some area(s) of expertise. Yet, agreeing to be interviewed means agreeing to speak beyond the parameters of expertise. By agreeing to do this, the interviewee is put in a vulnerable position, speaking with authority but also humbly; allegedly objective and representing truth, but also speaking spontaneously and informally, caught in the evanescence of the moment. Like the diary, the interview is intimate and ephemeral, personal and temporally marked.

This collection of interviews with Richard Rorty spans more than two decades. The interviews were generally occasioned by the publication of one Rorty's books, but they were also brought about because of particular political events that some thought deserved Rorty's unique commentary. Although they are widely spread out in time, and over a fairly intense period of publishing and thinking in Rorty's philosophical itinerary, these interviews are also intensely focused. In Rorty's words, "they seem to say the same thing over and over." Although this is unfair and off the mark, it is not entirely inaccurate. They indeed tell us something about how consistently Rorty has taught and pursued his politics. They exhibit for us one of Rorty's central propositions: that the pursuit of private sublimity should be disengaged from the public pursuit of solidarity. Yet, as my remarks above should make evident, Rorty has been consistent in his views on politics, on the role of philosophy in politics, and on the role of politics in American society. If we are to believe Rorty's own autobiographical musings, his leftist views have been fairly consistent over the span of his life. What is also made patently evident in these interviews is that Rorty's postmodern bourgeois liberalism and postphilosophical politics are not motivated by either conservatism or anarchism. Nor are his views relativistic or frivolous. Rather, it is clear that Rorty's work is motivated by the hope and a utopia of social justice. There is a heroic dimension to Rorty's nominalist historicism.[38] He wants to hold on to the hope for social transformation, but without either a religious or historical alibi to guarantee either its success or its preservation.

Stories transform, and they transform us into tools of social transformation. Freedom, both economic and political, is indispensable if we want to allow stories to transform us. Stories thus need freedom. Above all, freedom is entwined with the narratives that allow us to weave a story about what we were and what we may become. The power to reinscribe, to redescribe, to say something new and different, something shocking and unexpected, unscripted and unimposed, is what Rorty is defending when he argues that "if we take care of freedom, truth will take care of itself." To take care of freedom means, as we read in these interviews and in most of Rorty's public and occasional pieces, giving priority to the political, for the political is the horizon of solidarity and where our expanded loyalties dwell. The political, understood in this way, is dependent on the power of stories to transform it, to keep it ever expanding and broadening. Rorty's democracy is indeed that of Thomas Jefferson, Walt Whitman, John Dewey, James Baldwin, and principally, I would say, that of Abraham Lincoln. In fact, Lincoln both embodies and illustrates Rorty's democratic pragmatism and postphilosophical politics. For Lincoln transformed America by regrounding it in a new narrative, a new proposition. On November 19, 1863, at the dedication of the cemetery at Gettysburg, Abraham Lincoln opened with the following words: "Four score and seven years ago our fathers brought forth on this continent, a new nation, conceived in Liberty, and dedicated to the proposition that all men are created equal." With barely two more paragraphs, and with a total of 272 words, Lincoln closed with these words:

It is rather for us to be here dedicated to the great task remaining before us—that from these honored dead we take increased devotion to that cause for which they gave the last full measure of devotion—that we here highly resolve that these dead shall not have died in vain—that this nation, under God, shall have a new birth of freedom—and that government of the people, by the people, for the people, shall not perish from the earth.[39]

38. David L. Hall, *Richard Rorty: Prophet and Poet of the New Pragmatism* (Albany: State University of New York Press, 1994), 14.

39. Garry Wills, *Lincoln at Gettysburg: The Words That Remade America* (New York: Touchstone, 1992), 263.

With these words, Lincoln performed a "stunning verbal coup," one that refunded and regrounded the nation in a new narrative and self-understanding. The great American historian Garry Wills, in his Pulitzer Prize–winning book *Lincoln at Gettysburg: The Words That Remade America*, articulated this verbal feat in the following way:

For most people now, the Declaration means what Lincoln told us it means, as a way of correcting the Constitution itself without overthrowing it. It is this correction of the spirit, this intellectual revolution, that makes attempts to go back beyond Lincoln to some earlier version so feckless. The proponents of states' rights may have arguments, but they have lost their force, in courts as well as in the popular mind. By accepting the Gettysburg Address, its concept of a single people dedicated to a proposition, we have been changed. Because of it, we live in a different America.[40]

Rorty's America is Lincoln's America, and what Rorty hopes to do with American pragmatism, and the party of hope, the American left, is not unlike what Lincoln did with the Declaration of Independence, namely, to provide us with new ways of reading it so that we could become a different America, one with more expansive and generous loyalties.

40. Garry Wills, *Lincoln at Gettysburg*, 147.

TAKE CARE OF FREEDOM AND TRUTH
WILL TAKE CARE OF ITSELF

# 1

# The Quest for Uncertainty:
# Richard Rorty's Pilgrimage

*James Ryerson*

The tranquil, hibiscus-lined eucalyptus grove in the UC-Santa Cruz arboretum is a nice spot for reflecting on philosophy's age-old questions. Fortunately for Richard Rorty, a nature lover with a distaste for those sorts of questions, it's also an excellent place for bird-watching. We have driven here on a bright California morning to do a bit of both. As we pass his binoculars back and forth, searching the grevilleas for hummingbirds, it's hard to believe that this shy, gentle-mannered sixty-nine-year-old Stanford professor is the same man whose ideas have been widely denounced for the past twenty years as cynical, nihilistic, and deeply irresponsible.

"I have even lost a friend in all of this," says Rorty of his fractious career as America's most famous living philosopher. "It was Carl Hempel, one of the best-loved figures in the profession and a model of moral character." Hempel, a teacher of Rorty's, had fled Hitler's Germany and symbolized all that was most inspiring about the scientific, social democratic, truth-seeking world of Anglo-American philosophy. "Hempel read my book *Contingency, Irony and Solidarity* and wrote me a letter saying, in effect, 'You have betrayed everything I stood for.' And he really didn't like me after that. I'm still very sad about it."

Rorty points to a bird flying overhead. "That's a kestrel," he adds without a pause, in his doleful, sighing voice, "the smallest American falcon."

The charge of betrayal is one Rorty has learned to accept over the years. Like his idol John Dewey, whom he credits with breaking through "the crust of philosophical convention," he has pursued twin careers as disciplinary bad boy and high-minded public philosopher. He has set out to deflate the aspirations of his profession—he rejects the idea of truth as an accurate reflection of the world—while placing his own unorthodox philosophical views at the center of an ambitious vision of social and historical hope. In recent writings especially, he champions an unlikely brand of "postmodern bourgeois liberalism" that has largely infuriated postmodernists and liberals alike.

A lucid writer with a penchant for dropping the names of virtually all the major thinkers in the philosophical tradition, Rorty has a knack for making his radical rejection of truth and objectivity seem an easy and agreeable shift of one's current perspective. Harold Bloom is not alone in judging him "the most interesting philosopher in the world today." But the success of philosophy's preeminent antiphilosopher has not come easily. Seemingly everyone who is impressed with one facet of Rorty's work harbors severe reservations about another. Those who share his admiration for analytic philosophers like Donald Davidson, Wilfrid Sellars, and W. V. O. Quine are angered by his opinion that analytic philosophy does not exist "except in some such stylistic or sociological way." Political theorists are dismayed by his proposal that their work be replaced by "genres such as ethnography, the journalist's report, the comic book, the docudrama, and, especially, the novel." Fellow enthusiasts of Hans-Georg Gadamer, Jacques Derrida, and Martin Heidegger aren't comfortable seeing their favorite Continental thinkers discussed in the frank, Anglo-American idiom in which Rorty was trained. And radical postmodernist fans of his assault on the idea of objective truth are disappointed to hear that his politics are "pretty much those of Hubert Humphrey."

In practice, this assortment of provocations adds up to one of the truly original personalities in academic life. A heavy-moving man with a snowy drift of hair and dark, impish eyebrows, Rorty embodies a rare blend of intellectual traits. The University of Chicago philosopher James Conant notes that "in certain ways he resembles a Parisian intellectual: He reads everything, he drops a lot of names, he's interested in very big questions." But as Rorty plods along the arboretum's dirt paths in his frumpy, oversized sweater, with binoculars resting on his thickset torso, he looks every bit the stereotype of the sober, diligent Anglo-Saxon scholar. He manages to combine genuine personal modesty with sweeping philosophical ambition, and calls on clear prose and sensible-sounding argument to unite a range of wildly adventuresome ideas. The result is exceedingly unusual in a specialized academic world: a "syncretist hack," in his own self-effacing words, who in style as well as substance melds the most impressive elements of two intellectual traditions.

But can the man who shattered philosophy's mirror of nature pick up the pieces? Over the past few years, Rorty has increasingly turned from the scholarly criticism of philosophy toward the public espousal of what he calls "social hope." In 1998 he left his longtime post at the University of Virginia and took a job at Stanford as professor of comparative literature—though he proposed the alternative title "transitory professor of trendy studies." That same year, he published a polemical work of intellectual history, *Achieving Our Country: Leftist Thought in Twentieth-Century America*, in which he encouraged a revival of national pride among the American left and disparaged cynical "cultural leftists" who rely on theoretical approaches to politics at the expense of practical, piecemeal reform. A year later, Penguin published *Philosophy and Social Hope*, a paperback selection of Rorty's most accessible writings, marketably packaged with a cover image by the German film director Wim Wenders. Its title alludes to the Deweyan notion that in politics we should "substitute hope for the sort of knowledge which philosophers have usually tried to attain." By Rorty's lights, a "postmetaphysical culture," in which we forsake the rhetoric of the true nature of the world, will help promote a classless, casteless, and egalitarian society in the long run. "The inculcation of antilogocentrism in the young will contribute to the strength of democratic societies," he asserts.

Rorty's critics charge that his blithe disregard for the notion of objective truth threatens to undermine the public's moral and intellectual integrity. The conservative cultural critic Neal Kozodoy complains that "it is not enough for him that American students should be merely mindless; he would have them positively mobilized for mindlessness." Others see in

Rorty a more promising example of intellectual conduct. Russell Jacoby, in his 1987 book, *The Last Intellectuals*, bemoaned the disappearance of "public intellectuals." But in a new edition of his book, Jacoby refers to Rorty as an all too infrequent exception—a university scholar who "represents an effort to invigorate a public philosophy." The distinguished UC-Berkeley intellectual historian David Hollinger concurs: "Being a public intellectual is an easy thing to do badly, and Dick is one of the few people who can carry it off with integrity."

Yet no matter how attractive it might sound, Rorty's message of hope will not hold up if his attack on the last two thousand years of philosophy as misguided and socially useless fails to persuade. In the recently published *Rorty and His Critics*,[1] Rorty goes head-to-head on this very matter with twelve of his most distinguished critics, including Jürgen Habermas, Donald Davidson, Hilary Putnam, Daniel Dennett, and Jacques Bouveresse. Despite Rorty's general disdain for the profession's ideals, the book suggests that his work has had a real impact on some important younger guns of the mainstream philosophical establishment. Still, the consensus among these friendly adversaries is that Rorty has gone too far with interesting ideas. "My own experience suggests that you can use Rorty as a great source on difficult thinkers like Heidegger or Sellars," says Dennett. "And if you multiply what he says by the number .673"—which Dennett playfully calls the "Rorty Factor"—"then you get the truth. Dick always exaggerates everything in the direction of the more radical."

Stauncher critics maintain that the Rorty Factor is considerably smaller. As the New York University philosopher Paul Boghossian remarks, Rorty faces the perilous task of rejecting the notion of objective truth while avoiding the charge that his own views are thus untrustworthy. "I just think he has never really pulled off the trick," Boghossian says. "I don't think that anybody has, but in particular I don't think that he has."

As a youngster, Rorty showed few signs of being an intellectual agitator in the making. "My parents were always telling me that it was about time I had a stage of adolescent revolt," he remembers. "They were worried I wasn't rebellious enough." James and Winifred Rorty set the bar high in that regard. Both were active members of New York City's anti-Stalin-

1. *Rorty and His Critics*, ed. Robert B. Brandom (Malden, Mass.: Blackwell, 2000).

ist, Trotskyite left—they had broken with the American Communist Party in 1932, a year after Richard was born. For years, James Rorty worked with the philosopher Sidney Hook on leftist causes like the anticapitalist, revolutionary American Workers Party; he later joined Hook in moving away from radicalism altogether. Winifred Rorty was the daughter of Walter Rauschenbusch, the legendary Social Gospel theologian, whom young Richard was raised to think of as "a sort of socialist hero." The Rortys typically spent half the year in rural Connecticut or New Jersey and the other half in Park Slope, Brooklyn, or the Chelsea Hotel in Manhattan. Surrounded by luminaries like A. Philip Randolph, Norman Thomas, Irving Howe, and Lionel and Diana Trilling, they epitomized the intellectually cosmopolitan lifestyle of the time, as depicted in books like Edmund Wilson's *Memoirs of Hecate County*.

Dragged in and out of various schools—and bullied at many of them—the timid, bookish Rorty was the sort of boy who sent opals as a gift to the Dalai Lama ("a fellow eight-year-old who had made good"), hunted for wild orchids in the mountains of northwest New Jersey, and worried that his love for those plants was incompatible with the Marxist criticism he had read of Walter Pater's aestheticism. At fifteen, he went off to the University of Chicago to get his bachelor's degree at the so-called Hutchins College, which permitted precocious students to enter in the middle of high school. There he studied a classical curriculum under scholars like Leo Strauss and Richard McKeon, alongside students like the future classicist and cultural scourge Allan Bloom.

Rorty decided to stay on at Chicago for a master's degree in philosophy, which was tantamount to a career choice. James Rorty was "rather surprised and dismayed" by the idea and asked his friend Hook to give his son advice. ("He wasn't encouraging," says Rorty of Hook. "He just said things like 'publish early and often.'") In 1952, Rorty moved to Yale for his Ph.D., and by 1956 he had quickly finished a dissertation on the concept of potentiality—too quickly perhaps. "I was drafted into the army because I stupidly didn't delay my dissertation until past my twenty-sixth birthday," he explains. "I have no idea why I was that dumb." After a two-year military stint in which he worked in the computer section of the Signal Corps (he was awarded a programming medal for persuading his higher-ups to adopt the more efficient Polish system of logical notation), Rorty taught at Wellesley College for three years and then in 1961 landed a job at Princeton, which had one of the most distinguished philosophy programs in the country.

At Princeton, the search for the foundations of knowledge was conducted in the forbidding and highly technical terms of analytic philosophy. By rigorously analyzing the meanings of words and the objects they refer to, Rorty's new colleagues hoped to reveal the structure and accuracy of our statements about the world. "My first years at Princeton I was desperately trying to learn what was going on in analytic philosophy," he confesses. "Most of my colleagues had been at Harvard, and you had to know what they were talking about at Harvard in order to be with it."

After about two years of fumbling about, Rorty got into the swing of the analytic approach and began to make a name for himself with innovative work in the philosophy of mind. He was especially intrigued by the ideas of Sellars, Quine, and, later, Davidson. These were thinkers inclined to tackle problems by tearing down chunks of philosophy that they felt were misconceived and focusing their attention on what remained. Rorty's predicament was that his favorite thinkers were often tearing down different aspects of philosophy. While Sellars questioned whether our sense perceptions really afforded a privileged form of knowledge, Quine wondered whether logical truths could be distinguished from empirical findings. Over a number of years, Rorty began to stitch together these various innovative projects in a creative way, for he was able to see more commonality than difference in them. The only problem was that if neither sense perception nor logic offered us the prospect of utter certainty, then how could we determine the accuracy of our claims in representing the world?

By the early seventies, Rorty had taken an even bolder turn: in part through his growing interest in the work of Derrida ("the cleverest man I'd read in years"), he was led to reread the work of Derrida's hero Heidegger. Reading Heidegger drew Rorty into the so-called hermeneutic tradition of Continental thought, which eschewed the project of breaking down language into its component parts in favor of an approach to knowledge more akin to literary interpretation than to scientific analysis. With a leg in both the analytic and Continental traditions, Rorty was positioned to see similarities among Heidegger, Ludwig Wittgenstein, and Dewey, three very different philosophers who nonetheless all asked what he called a "therapeutic" philosophical question: how can we avoid, rather than solve, the philosophical problems that bedevil us?

Rorty explored these highly controversial ideas in his 1979 classic, *Philosophy and the Mirror of Nature*, in which he argued that there was no sense in trying to give a general account of truth. "Granted that 'true' is an absolute term," he wrote in a later essay, "its conditions of application will always be relative." That is, whatever we may hope to mean when we call a belief "true," we use the word only when we feel our belief is justified—and justification always raises the question, "justified to whom?" To critics who would argue that the justification of our claims may always be relative to a particular audience but that truth is not, because it consists of accuracy to the way the world really is, Rorty had a frustratingly simple response: there's no point in saying that truth has anything to do with the way the world really is.

In the spirit of the earlier pragmatist tradition, Rorty argued that the notions of "truth" and "accurate representation" are nothing but compliments we pay to sentences that we find useful in dealing with the world. To say that science is useful in predicting and controlling nature because it describes the true nature of the world is, in Rorty's view, a tautology, for we have no criteria for whether we have described "the true nature of the world" other than success in predicting and controlling nature. And once we see that science is deemed successful only when it helps us achieve certain goals, he explained, we will realize that other forms of inquiry can be considered equally successful at achieving different goals—without ever having to ask whether one form of inquiry better describes the way the world really is.

As for the charge that he was ignoring the fact that there is a world beyond the confines of our thought, Rorty conceded that the world does shove us around. "Yet," he asked, "what does being shoved around have to do" with making claims about the world, which we always do in the terms of our language? Any attempt to square linguistic statements with the world is to compare apples and oranges, to try to climb out of our own minds and language to see the world as it is in itself, and Rorty saw no profit in it. Indeed, following his own pragmatist criteria, he did not suggest that he was offering an alternative view of the world; rather, he proposed that his way of talking about things was useful. Instead of spending valuable time asking whether various types of inquiry—science, political thought, poetry, alchemy—are better or worse at capturing the truth, we should ask whether there are new ways of describing and redescribing the world that better serve our variety of goals, with the understanding that "hope of agreement is never lost so long as the conversation lasts."

Rorty's colleagues were not pleased, though they were hardly surprised. "My recollection is that for the first ten years at Princeton, I was one of the boys," remembers Rorty. "But for the second ten years, I was seen as increasingly contrarian or difficult." In addition to philosophical differences, there were personal complications: "I got divorced and remarried, and because my first wife was a philosopher and a friend of my colleagues, there were problems. It was not a friendly divorce, and I didn't handle it very well."

Rorty made it known that he was interested in a job elsewhere, preferably a university professorship, so he could avoid the issue of how he was supposed to fit in with a philosophy department. In the early eighties, as *Philosophy and the Mirror of Nature* began to make waves throughout the academy, the University of Virginia made him the offer he wanted. "After years of thinking that what my colleagues were doing must be important," he recalls, "I began to think, maybe the analytic establishment is not the future of philosophy. Maybe it's just a bubble."

For all its audacity, *Philosophy and the Mirror of Nature* couldn't have appeared at a more opportune moment, and its ideas couldn't have been espoused by a better-situated academic. At the time it was published, legions of scholars in the humanities were inspecting the discourses of the past and seeking a theoretical warrant for assessing those discourses in ways—historical, sociological, and political—that didn't presuppose a timeless, universal notion of truth. "If you wanted nonfoundational-sounding stuff," Rorty concedes, "mine was as good as any."

Rorty's critics were quick to find something suspicious in his popularity with nonphilosophers. "One of the central morals of the book," says Paul Boghossian, who studied with Rorty at Princeton, "is that whatever there is that's still worth doing in philosophy is best done by literary critics rather than philosophers. This had tremendous, obvious appeal to those academics in the humanities who were already abandoning the study of literature narrowly conceived for much more general reflections on the relations between language, knowledge, truth, power, and society. Unfortunately, I don't think it's really possible to do good philosophy without a considerable amount of training in the subject."

Even some of Rorty's supporters have significant reservations about his views. The philosopher Daniel Dennett, who feels that Rorty's philosophy of mind is "just about perfect," nonetheless has qualms about Rorty's unwillingness to consider science a privileged form of inquiry and about his willingness to take seriously the philosophical views of thinkers like Derrida and Michel Foucault: "Dick Rorty has failed to discourage a lot of nonsense that I wish he had discouraged. It's an obligation of us in the field to grit our teeth and discourage the people who do the things that give philosophy a bad name. I don't think he does that enough."

Critics are also quick to pounce on some of Rorty's telltale stylistic quirks. Rorty's writings are littered with philosophical lists; for instance, many sentences will begin with a clause like "What Heidegger, Dewey, Cavell, Gadamer, Kuhn, Derrida, and Putnam are all saying is. . . . " It's a technique that may allow nonphilosophers to feel they have a handle on an extraordinarily diverse range of thinkers, but to most philosophers the implied comparisons sound forced, if not downright inaccurate. "Almost everybody I know who figures in one of these lists invariably wants to get off," notes Conant, "even though it's extremely flattering to appear on these lists, and Rorty has made some people quite famous."

Rorty sympathizes with those—like Thomas Kuhn, to take a prominent example—who have pleaded with him not to characterize their work in ways they find distorting or misleading. "It's a natural reaction," he says. "They think of themselves as having made a quite specific point, and with a wave of my hand I seem to subsume their specific point as part of some great cultural movement, or something like that. They think that it's a way of putting them in bad company and ignoring the really interesting thing they said, which my net is too gross to capture." Still, Rorty defends this tendency: "I don't see anything wrong with doing that. Regardless of how they feel about it, if you think there's a common denominator or a trend, then why not say so?"

Expelled from the mainstream philosophical community, Rorty took up ranks with those outside the discipline who had embraced his work. Given the widespread interest in Continental philosophy, the University of Virginia needed more professors to teach the material. So, Rorty explains, "I just picked up the slack." Teaching literature students was a relatively painless transition for him. "Princeton's got the best philosophy students in the country, so I missed that. I had to teach in a way that didn't allude to Quine's criticism of the analytic-synthetic distinction," he muses. "But it didn't matter much. By that time, I wasn't teaching in a way that required students to keep up with philosophical journals."

His scholarly interests, too, grew increasingly alien to the work done in academic journals. Though he continued to publish in those journals, picking "the same highly professionalized nits" that he picked in *Philosophy and the Mirror of Nature*, Rorty moved on to themes of more general concern, such as how to think about morality, liberal democracy, and a private self in a world without the possibility of objective truth. He addressed these issues in his 1989 book, *Contingency, Irony, and Solidarity*.

In his adolescence, Rorty had admired William Butler Yeats's ideal of holding "reality and justice in a single vision." Indeed, the desire for an all-encompassing perspective on the world had driven his intellectual curiosity. "I desperately wanted to be a Platonist," he admits, "to become one with the One, to fuse myself with Christ or God or the Platonic form of the Good or something like that." In *Contingency*, Rorty rebuked that objective. Morality, he felt, was not the voice of some inner part of ourselves that we needed philosophical reflection to discover; rather, it was simply the practical effort to work with other members of a community to find some mutually acceptable code of self-protection. Art, by contrast, involved the individual's efforts at "self-creation."

As for the liberal tradition of political thought, Rorty agreed with "ironists" like Foucault that liberalism's supposedly timeless balance of rights and duties is a mere historical contingency; at the same time, he agreed with "liberals" like Habermas that liberal democracies are worth fighting passionately for. The absence of any universally valid notions of human rights or individual liberties was no reason to find fault with the well-functioning institution of liberal democracy itself. The sole factor responsible for keeping liberal democracy alive, Rorty argued, was the hatred of cruelty and a solidarity with those who suffer. He offered books like George Orwell's *1984* as examples of how writers can redescribe the world in ways that cultivate this sort of solidarity. When faced with opponents who don't share our worldview, Rorty explained, we cannot hope to refute them, but we can concretely elucidate our worldview in the hope that it will make their worldview look untenable. "There is no answer to a rede-scription," he pronounced, "save a re-re-redescription."

Alongside this talk of incremental redescription, one could detect signs of a grander vision. At stake was nothing less than the progression of Western culture into its next stage of maturity. The first stage of this mat-uration, in Rorty's eyes, was overcoming the pre-Enlightenment religious outlook, which required humans to appeal to something nonhuman and divine for moral guidance and truth when in fact they should have been seeking moral guidance among themselves. Many thinkers acknowledge the freedom that this aspect of the Enlightenment has brought. But Rorty regrets that few of them see a parallel between overcoming the dubious re-ligious idea of a nonhuman divine Other and overcoming the dubious sci-entific idea of conforming our inquiry to the way the world really is.

Such metaphysical pretensions, Rorty believes, are the traces of un-profitable ways of talking about the world, and if philosophers can per-suade people to stop talking as though our worldview describes things as they really are, they can make a substantive contribution to the de-diviniz-ing of the world. Rather than assuming that our inquiry can cease when it hits the hard bedrock of truth, Rorty wants people to realize that the goals of inquiry continually evolve and are best met by an enduring commit-ment to experimentation, novelty, poetic creativity, and pluralism.

So are philosophers useless, or do they have a world-historical role to play in dispelling deep metaphysical superstitions? Rorty acknowledges this tension: "You're right. I wobble on that point." But he draws a distinc-tion between the day-to-day irrelevance of worrying about truth and the epochal significance of learning to talk in ways that sidestep the ideal of certain knowledge. "Just because world-historical movements are happen-ing doesn't mean you can apply that knowledge in everyday practice."

As Rorty turned toward political and cultural questions, he had less and less patience with his postmodernist colleagues in the humanities. In particular, he disliked their politics. "I was surrounded by what seemed to me an idiot Left in the literature departments," he explains, "people who claimed to be politically involved but who, as far as I could see, weren't." In *Achieving Our Country*, Rorty responded by excoriating what he described as a "spectatorial, disgusted, mocking Left." He laid the charges of compla-cency and political impotence on academics who had permitted "cultural politics to supplant real politics." He lamented the disappearance of the "reformist left," Americans such as Eugene Debs and Franklin Roosevelt, who "between 1900 and 1964 struggled within the framework of constitutional democracy to protect the weak from the strong."

In *Rorty and His Critics*, Rorty comes as close as he ever has to an apology for throwing his philosophical weight behind literary scholars who used his work for suspect political ends. When he arrived at UVA to teach Continental philosophy, Rorty confesses, he "did not foresee what has actually happened: that the popularity of philosophy (under the sobriquet 'theory') in our literature departments was merely a transitional stage on the way to the development of what we in America are coming to call the Academic Left." These leftists, Rorty asserts, "have convinced themselves that by chanting various Derridean or Foucauldian slogans they are fighting for human freedom. . . . The political uselessness, relative illiteracy, and tiresomely self-congratulatory enthusiasm of this new Academic Left, together with its continual invocation of the names of Derrida and Foucault, have conspired to give these latter thinkers a bad name in the United States." He concludes: "I am, I must admit, chastened. But I am not ashamed. . . . There are other things to do with Foucault and Derrida than are currently being done with them by the School of Resentment, just as there are other things to be done with Nietzsche than to use him as the Nazis used him."

But has Rorty articulated a politics any more practical than that of the academic left he disdains? Though he has made specific proposals in *The Nation* in favor of campaign finance reform, universal health care, and the more equitable financing of primary and secondary education, many critics find his views too much those of a relatively uninformed outsider. At a City University of New York lecture on public intellectuals in May 2000, the judge and libertarian economist Richard Posner attacked Rorty's conception of politics for its indifference to the workings of actual economic or socioeconomic policy. Rorty's political outlook, Posner charged, is "unworldly," "pessimistic," and "almost Spenglerian," with a whiff of "nostalgia for the militancy and class struggle of the old labor movement."

Meanwhile, leftists like the New School political philosopher Richard Bernstein have attacked Rorty for his complacent disregard of the more sinister overtones of his pro-American stance, calling his views on politics "little more than an ideological apologia for an old-fashioned version of

Cold War liberalism dressed up in fashionable 'post-modern' discourse."
Even the economist Robert Kuttner, a figure whom one might expect to
be more sympathetic to Rorty's strain of redistributionist-minded liberalism, has attacked Rorty's call for eliminating Social Security benefits for
the wealthier elderly. In *The American Prospect*, Kuttner called Rorty's *New
York Times* op-ed piece in March on this topic "so politically innocent and
self-defeating that one didn't know whether to laugh or to cry."[2] Kuttner
explains his irritation: "I was annoyed at the Social Security Op-Ed because I thought, and still think, that Rorty simply missed the logic of social
solidarity: the greater security and equality for have-nots that is inherent in
universal social programs. And this from a professed egalitarian."

If Rorty has met with mixed reactions in the public realm, he has,
ironically, enjoyed a small revival in the philosophical world he left behind.
Several of the most highly respected thinkers within contemporary Anglo-
American philosophy—John McDowell, James Conant, and Rorty's former student Robert Brandom—have expressed their intellectual debt to
Rorty. In the preface to his seminal 1994 book, *Mind and World*, McDowell acknowledged that he sketched out his initial ideas "during the winter
of 1985–6, in an attempt to get under control my usual excited reaction to a
reading—my third or fourth—of Richard Rorty's *Philosophy and the Mirror of Nature*." He added that it should be "obvious that Rorty's work is in
any case central for the way I define my stance here."

As McDowell explains in his essay "Towards Rehabilitating Objectivity" in *Rorty and His Critics*, Rorty's greatest accomplishment has been
to help us escape from the idea that we need philosophy to bridge the supposed gap between our knowledge and the world. ("It was largely from
him," McDowell says, "that I learned to think like that.") But McDowell
feels "a piece of mere sanity" is missing from Rorty's account. Like Rorty,
McDowell emphasizes that we cannot get outside our particular perspectives or worldviews. But unlike Rorty, he does not conclude that this means
we must give up our notions of truth and objectivity altogether. To preserve a distinction between a truth that consists of consensus and a truth
that consists in getting things objectively right, McDowell argues, "is not
to try to think from outside our practices; it is simply to take it seriously
that we can really mean what we say from within those practices." Indeed,

2. "Making the Rich Richer," *New York Times* (March 6, 2000), op-ed page.

he asks, what would it mean to have a worldview if, à la Rorty, we avoid the idea that our statements are true in light of the way the world is in our view of it?

In an exceedingly rare statement of self-doubt, Rorty replies: "Sometimes McDowell almost persuades me that I should back off from my highly unpopular attempt to replace objectivity with solidarity. . . . Sometimes I think that I really must have the blind spot he diagnoses." But in the end, though he finds "about 90 percent of *Mind and World* very appealing indeed," Rorty cannot figure out why McDowell refers to consensus as "mere consensus." If one norm of inquiry, consensus, can fully capture the sense in which our knowledge is in touch with the world, then why does McDowell insist on the need to add a second, perhaps more commonsensical but metaphysically heavier, norm of inquiry—that of getting things right about the world? "Here again," says Rorty, "the question is whether we have a difference [between choosing one norm of inquiry or two] that could ever make a difference."

James Conant believes he can show Rorty the difference. In his essay in *Rorty and His Critics*, "Freedom, Cruelty, and Truth: Rorty Versus Orwell," Conant claims to demonstrate that Rorty's pragmatism cannot satisfy its own requirement of being useful—which, after all, is the only reason that Rorty adheres to it. In *Contingency, Irony, and Solidarity*, Rorty championed Orwell's *1984* as a model of how literature can create greater awareness of suffering. But Conant worries that Rorty himself offers the individual no resources with which to condemn a world of Orwellian thought control. In the totalitarian scenario of *1984*, the protagonist, Winston Smith, remembers having seen airplanes in his childhood, before the Party took power. And yet, since the Party took power, everyone but Winston has been brainwashed into believing that the Party invented the airplane. When Winston says, "the Party did not invent the airplane," by Rorty's standards he does not make a knowledgeable statement, because he cannot bring about the consensus of his peers. Isn't this a case where McDowell would be right in suggesting that an appeal to a second, nonconsensus norm of inquiry makes a difference? "If Winston tries to do everything that Rorty thinks he can do," explains Conant, "then he'll quickly come to the conclusion: 'The Party invented the airplane.' But if he tries to do something that is left out of Rorty's theory of justification, which is to try to get it right, trusting his memories and so on, then he has reason to think that the Party didn't invent the airplane."

Rorty's response to Conant is straightforward and bleak: "The difference between myself and Conant is that he thinks that someone like Winston, trapped in such a society, can turn to the light of the facts. I think that there is nowhere for Winston to turn." For Rorty, the way to prevent a situation like this from coming about in the first place is not to reclaim the notion of objective truth, but rather to promote what he calls "truthfulness"—namely, the freedom to say publicly what you believe, even when it is disadvantageous to do so. If we take care of making sure people can say what they believe, he argues, "truth" will take care of itself.

For Conant, though, it is unclear if Rorty can speak of truthfulness without having a notion of objective truth. Indeed, he points out that in *1984*, part of the horror is that Winston's fellow citizens have been encouraged to cultivate a high degree of "doublethink"—that is, to believe they speak the truth even though they are not saying anything that is true. Conant believes that such doublethink satisfies—indeed, perversely resembles—Rorty's prescription of "truthfulness."

"Rorty's quite right that consensus is a necessary condition of justification," Conant says. But Conant feels there's room to balance that insight with the idea of truth as getting things right—all without succumbing to the traditional philosophical idea that getting things right involves capturing the world as it is apart from our view of it. "It's an overly restricted set of options that causes Rorty all his trouble," Conant concludes. "The right things to say in philosophy are much more delicate than that."

Why is Rorty—the advocate of pluralism, of not knowing things for sure, of openness and variety—not more comfortable with the balancing act that philosophers like McDowell and Conant want to pull off? For all the important mysteries about Rorty, his colleagues call attention to one seemingly insignificant aspect of his personality: his voice. Rorty's voice is, as Daniel Dennett notes, "sort of striking—these firebrand views delivered in the manner of Eeyore." When philosophers talk about Rorty, few can resist trying to imitate his distinctively somber delivery. Of Rorty's mode of presentation, the British philosopher Jonathan Rée says: "There's a tremendous kind of melancholy about it. He tries to be a gay Nietzschean, but it's an effort for him." For Conant, hearing Rorty speak for the first time was something of a revelation. "It's easy to read his writings in a register of excitement and a heightened, breathless voice," he explains. "But the note that I heard when he was reading these sentences in his own cadences and rhythm was—for want of a better word—depression. I thought, this is the voice of a man who feels as if he's been let down or betrayed by philosophy." Jürgen Habermas concurs that Rorty's antiphilosophy "seems to spring from the melancholy of a disappointed metaphysician." And for Conant, this melancholy goes far in explaining the intransigence with which Rorty holds to his pluralistic philosophy of dialogue and playfulness. "It's as though he's been let down by philosophy once, and he's not going to let it happen again," Conant says.

But how are we to square this vision of philosophical depression with the explicit role that hope plays in Rorty's philosophy? For David Hollinger, Rorty's somber intellectual mood is not one of depression, but rather one of hope wisely tempered by experience. "I think Dick is rightly concerned about the legacy of naive optimism that Dewey is constantly being assaulted for," he says. "There's this idea that the children of the Enlightenment were smug and Panglossian; they felt they had renounced God and could go forth on a Promethean basis. In contrast to this, Rorty injects a sober realism about the evils of the world: Do you know about the Holocaust? Do you know about the atomic bomb? There is a feeling in Dick that this Enlightenment inheritance is basically right, if only we could be a little bit more chastened about it. Dick really does see himself in world-historical terms. And he is one of the few people who can do this without being pretentious about it."

Conant, though, insists that there remains a strong tension between Rorty's disenchanted philosophical views and the place that hope has in his public philosophy of late. "Part of the reason that the concept of hope plays such a central role," he says, "is that he's trying to give us hope without giving us a great many of the things that used to allow for the possibility of hope. So the concept of hope itself becomes important, and he wants to supply it, and so it has to go on the title page, because any of the things that might have brought us hope in their wake—truth, beauty, humanity—have been left out."

Rée, too, senses Rorty's apparent need to push forward with a positive vision and social message despite his disappointment with philosophy.

"Rorty found his distinctive voice in the shock of a kind of bereavement," he says. "Long ago, truth must have been a god to him." But though Rée, as a Gadamer scholar, thinks Rorty's philosophical stance may be unimpeachable, he is not sure that humankind can master its own future the way Rorty seems to believe. "One possible picture of metaphysics," he explains, "is that it's rooted not in the studies we make as students but in the ways we try to make sense of ourselves starting from earliest infancy. Our notions may not withstand a Rortyan scrutiny—they may not be not justified in any way. But nevertheless they're not arbitrary. We've grown to be the people we are because of them. It's more than a matter of will that we came by them, and it's more than a matter of will to change them."

Has Rorty really rejected his one-time ideal of holding reality and justice in a single vision? Or is he merely passing it off in another guise? After all, though he encourages pluralism and not knowing, he puts forth a view that settles many questions, and settles them once and for all. He suggests that the single measure for assessing all vocabularies is whether they are useful. Has he, contrary to his own intentions, simply created another kind of metavocabulary—a general way of assessing all ways of talking?

Achieving the proper sort of uncertainty may be hard to do, but it is critical to Rorty. When reflecting on his early days at Princeton, he begrudges the intellectual climate there. "Analytic philosophy was correlated with intellectual talent," he remembers. "Exposing the hidden assumptions and unclear terms in arguments: That was the only skill that was valued." Rorty confesses that he wasn't "good at it, wasn't sharp enough." But he regrets the inability of his sharper colleagues to second-guess their teachers or their own most basic assumptions. For Rorty, the most pernicious idea in that intellectual atmosphere was that technical clarity in problem solving was the chief intellectual virtue. "That's a recipe for scholasticism if I've ever heard it," he says, shaking his head disapprovingly. "What about imaginative virtues? If you don't allow people to be unclear, intellectual progress grinds to a halt. It's the vague people who are the pioneers."

# 2

# From Philosophy to Postphilosophy

*Interview Conducted by Wayne Hudson
and Wim van Reijen*

*Question*: Professor Rorty, you have recently written a book, *Philosophy and the Mirror of Nature*, which has aroused comment throughout the English-speaking world. In it you argue that the analytical movement in philosophy has run its course and that a more hermeneutical kind of philosophy is now required. Could you perhaps say something about your way into philosophy, the main stages in your development, and the tendencies in your own thinking which you have had to struggle against most?

*Richard Rorty*: As an undergraduate I went to the University of Chicago, to a university with a curriculum devised by a philosopher, where you were given the impression that anyone worth anything would study philosophy. I stayed on for graduate work at Chicago. My teachers there were Rudolf Carnap, the logical positivist; Charles Hartshorne, a disciple of Whitehead; and Richard McKeon, an historian of philosophy. I worked with Hartshorne on speculative metaphysics and wrote a lot about Whitehead. After getting my master's degree I went to Yale, where there were the same alternatives: Carl Hempel in place of Carnap, Paul Weiss in place of Hartshorne, and Robert Brumbaugh in place of McKeon. There I wrote a thesis comparing Aristotle on *dunamis* with the seventeenth-century rationalists on the notion of possibility. It was a very McKeonite, comparative piece. My interests until 1960 were historical and metaphysical. Then I got a job at Wellesley, a small college near Boston. My colleagues there explained to me that I was behind the times and ought to find out what was going on in the world of philosophy. So I read the then fashionable Oxford philosophers (Austin, Ryle, Strawson). Earlier I had read the logical positivists but not liked them much. I also read Wittgenstein's *Investigations* for the first time, and that made a great difference. So I changed from being an old-fashioned philosopher to being an up-to-date analytic philosopher partly as a result of pressure from my peers. When I got a job at Princeton after having been at Wellesley for three years, even more pressure was applied. There were certain things one had to know. I then spent about ten years trying to do things with Sellars and Wittgenstein within the framework of contemporary analytic philosophy. In the early seventies I got sick of that and tried to do something larger in *Philosophy and the Mirror of Nature*, which was very much the old McKeonite trick of taking the larger historical view. The tendencies which I have had to struggle against most have been, on the one hand, the temptation to avoid contact with contemporary discussion and just be historical, and, on the other, the temptation to become so immersed in contemporary discussion that I just write journal articles.

*Q*: Have your views changed since you wrote *Philosophy and the Mirror of Nature?*

*RR*: The main change I'm aware of is getting considerably more respect for the late Heidegger. I used to think of Heidegger as having a brilliant grasp of the historical tendencies which led to what he thought of as the late Nietzsche, and what I think of as pragmatism. But I thought that his view of the Greeks was merely nostalgic. I now think I was wrong and that the late Heidegger had a much subtler view. I am now trying to write a book called *Heidegger Against the Pragmatists* to give an account of how Heidegger managed to see Nietzsche's quasi pragmatism as dialectically correct (in the sense that if you were in the Western tradition Nietzsche was where you were going to end up) but nonetheless as a reductio ad absurdum of that tradition.

*Q*: What faults do you now detect in *Philosophy and the Mirror of Nature?*

*RR*: I think that what may be wrong with the book is that I take the positivistic therapeutic enterprise of clearing away pseudoproblems terribly seriously. Sometimes I think I've overdone it. The book has been read by nonphilosophers as blowing the whistle on analytic philosophy and all it stands for, whereas it seems to me to be an attempt to carry out the positivists' original program.

*Q*: Are you worried that the effect of your book may be different from that which you intended?

*RR*: Yes, I am. The book should not be read as an attack on analytic philosophy. What I was trying to say was that there is a dialectical strand within analytic philosophy which fulfils itself in the American philosophers Quine and Sellars in a way which leads back to Dewey and the American pragmatists. Of course, Quine and Sellars don't like what I make of their work. They don't want to see analytic philosophy as veering back to Dewey.

*Q*: Many people will want to ask you why Dewey? What can we still learn from him?

*RR*: I think Dewey and James are the best guides to understanding the modern world that we've got, and that it's a question of putting pragmatism into better shape after thirty years of superprofessionalism.

*Q*: But such a reformulated pragmatism might differ considerably from your own views. What, for example, do you make of Dewey's theory of experience?

*RR*: I regard that as the worst part of Dewey. I'd be glad if he had never written *Experience and Nature*.

*Q*: But if, as you suggest, philosophers give up the idea of truth as accurate representation, then might not a theory of experience be important for philosophy which had abandoned both the attempt to find foundations and the search for a theory of knowledge?

*RR*: I'd prefer *discourse* to *experience*.

*Q*: How far are you worried by the charge that at the end of *Philosophy and the Mirror of Nature* you fail to provide an adequate account of the form which future philosophy should take?

*RR*: The sense that people have at the end of the book that I should have answered the question "What should philosophy do now?" is probably my fault. The way I hoped they would react was to say that maybe the notion of philosophy as a discipline or a distinct sector of culture had run its course. Philosophy as we understand it was something invented by the German Idealists between about 1780 and 1830, as a candidate for the leadership of culture. After that, no one believed in it anymore. Since then it's just become another academic discipline, but with pretensions. I agree with the late Heidegger that the science/poetry/philosophy distinctions we have lived with are outmoded, and, in particular, the notion of philosophers as the people who can provide the rest of culture with a framework. It seems to me that the demand that there be something for philosophy to be is unfounded. It assumes that there is some normal, necessary, human activity called philosophy.

*Q*: Nonetheless, isn't the sense of intellectual parsimony which pervades the book to some extent a legacy from ideas which imply that there is something for philosophy to be?

*RR*: In *Philosophy and the Mirror of Nature* I was perhaps in transit. I now think that what I should have tried to do at the end of the book was to make a transition from philosophy as a discipline to a larger and looser activity.

*Q*: One could question whether that would have been enough if, as you suggest, philosophy is now coming to an end and we are entering a period of postphilosophy. You say in one of your articles that pragmatism is the philosophical equivalent of literary modernism. Isn't modernism a rather old trick to bring out at this stage?

*RR*: Not in philosophy, which in this respect has lagged behind. I agree that in the culture as a whole it looks a little stale.

*Q*: You are conspicuous among contemporary analytic philosophers in your positive reassertion of the postphilosophical significance of creative imagination. To what extent do you think that we need a greater awareness in philosophy of the effectivity of stories?

*RR*: Surely what the French philosophers and the Yale literary critics are doing is helping us to see how we live in story after story after story.

Perhaps the Yale literary critic Harold Bloom does it best. He's currently writing a huge book on Freud which just might provide us with a way of reading Freud as a figure in the Romantic tradition. People like Derrida and De Man [another Yale literary critic], on the other hand, still seem to me to have too much respect for philosophy.

Q: Have you particular criticisms of contemporary French philosophy?

RR: What I find disturbing about the fashionable French is that they aren't utopian. They hold out no hope. I think that their position is an overreaction. I have written a comparison between Dewey and Foucault, in which I argue that Foucault's stuff on truth as only being available as a product of power is simply saying what Dewey said: that discourse and truth are made possible by community life. Of course, calling it power sounds more pejorative. But Dewey was a utopian thinker who tried to create a culture in which setting up heroes was a natural form of cultural advance. Whereas Foucault doesn't want any heroes. Almost as though philosophers have no right to have heroes.

Q: Did Heidegger have any heroes?
RR: Hölderlin. The poets of the past.

Q: If you recognize the need for a degree of utopianism in philosophy, shouldn't you make more methodological provision for it? Isn't there a contradiction in your work between the tough-minded eliminative side, which is largely continuous with the old analytic philosophy, and the more tender-minded side where you want philosophy to do things for which you don't provide adequate methods?
RR: I don't see that.

Q: Perhaps it is another way of asking you if your position is not really too conservative. If you are really not still too close to old-style analytic philosophy. Take the philosophy of psychology. In *Philosophy and the Mirror of Nature* you attack the Cartesian understanding of human beings which implies that we have minds as well as bodies. You speak instead of persons without minds. That is in the old negative tendency of analytic philosophy. But couldn't you approach it differently? Couldn't you ask how far persons can change what they can become by ascribing to themselves counterfactual properties?

*RR*: But the human ability to change character by redescribing oneself is not an attempt to discover the nature of the mind. It's an attempt to create something that did not previously exist.

*Q*: But then isn't the distinction which you draw in your work between empirical description and moral deliberation too dualistic? Doesn't it perhaps reflect the influence of the *Geisteswissenschaften* tradition which you yourself criticize Charles Taylor for advocating?

*RR*: I agree that you could read some passages in my writings without ever realizing that most moral deliberation does take the form of finding new forms of self-description. So I guess that I made too much of that dichotomy.

*Q*: One of the most interesting things in your work may be that you suggest that analytic philosophy is watered-down Kantianism, which should now abandon its transcendental project or the attempt to construct a single neutral matrix in terms of which all questions can be judged. Could you expand on this?

*RR*: The fundamental mistake of transcendental philosophy, it seems to me, is to take one form of discourse and to say that it has been so successful that there must be something in it through which we can discover the secret of rationality. I think that analytic philosophy is a recent variation on this transcendental theme, which, in so far as it is a Kantian transcendental enterprise, has the faults of all such enterprises.

*Q*: But you don't see this as going to the methods used by analytic philosophy?

*RR*: No. I think that analytic philosophy can keep its highly professional methods, the insistence on detail and mechanics, and just drop its transcendental project. I'm not out to criticize analytic philosophy as a style. It's a good style. I think the years of superprofessionalism were beneficial.

*Q*: Aren't there passages in your work which suggest that you yearn for another style? That philosophy should acquire a new vocabulary?

*RR*: In philosophy as therapy, as in psychoanalysis, no special vocabulary is useful. Philosophy as a free-floating criticism of culture does not require a special vocabulary. It's continuous with the kind of writing you get throughout the academy. If you think of Skinner and Dunn in England, Foucault in France and Clifford Geertz and Lionel Trilling in the United States, they really are or were in the same business. Although some of them are philosophers and some of them are not.

*Q*: If you think that philosophy should be social and cultural criticism because the more ambitious tasks which it has set itself simply cannot be performed, would you want to argue this, not simply in terms of the competence of philosophy as a discipline, but in terms of a doctrine of the radical finitude of man? Are you, after all, influenced by Kant?

*RR*: Certainly by Heidegger's book on Kant. The late Heidegger finds words to express this finitude. I think it's a question of conserving the realization of it, rather than of attempting to turn it into another theory.

*Q*: As a pragmatist you tend to evaluate doctrines in terms of their historical success. Doesn't that make it difficult for you to maintain a rationally justifiable critical approach to the way things turn out? To the path which historical tendencies take?

*RR*: I agree that there is something conservative about pragmatism. Nonetheless, it seems to me that devotion to concrete historical contents is something one loses at one's peril. One then falls into utopianism in the bad sense, when people begin to kill each other for abstract principles.

*Q*: But you don't have a stronger notion of utility than historical tendency, how things worked out?

*RR*: No, I don't. I think it's a trap to be avoided. It leads to setting up entities above history.

*Q*: But does that leave you with an adequate position in moral philosophy? How, for example, can one know who acts well or badly?

*RR*: As Kantian individual selves we could not do it. As members of a community we do it all the time. Those who act badly are those who behave contrary to the project which makes us the community we are.

*Q*: If, however, you take the pragmatist approach here, in what terms would you develop a moral criticism of current social rules?

*RR*: The only way we can criticize current social rules is by reference to utopian notions which proceed by taking elements in the tradition and showing how unfulfilled they are.

*Q*: Would you think that the only way one could criticize a Nazi guard in a concentration camp was by reference to utopian notions?

*RR*: By reference to what to him would seem utopian notions. Given his education, it would be a question of saying that there is a picture of Europe very different from yours, in which all this wasn't necessary. Moral criticism is too easy here. It's as easy to say that someone is doing wrong as it is to kill him. What is difficult is to say why we aren't doing it too.

*Q*: You once edited a very influential anthology called *The Linguistic Turn*. Do you now think that in some areas the turn to language in analytic philosophy made the real philosophical issues more difficult to see? For example, in the philosophy of psychology?

*RR*: I see what you mean in the case of Gilbert Ryle or Norman Malcolm. But do you think it affects a philosopher like Daniel Dennett? At the moment I'm trying to persuade the people in Heidelberg that in the philosophy of psychology Dennett is all anyone needs.

*Q*: Despite your enthusiasm for pragmatism, your own approach to psychological questions is neobehaviorist rather than pragmatist. What do you make of the psychological doctrines of William James?

*RR*: I confess that I never finished his book on psychology. I think that in his philosophical books he was defending his father's religious views against nineteenth-century positivism.

*Q*: There is a lot of interest currently among philosophers in the essentialist logical doctrines of Saul Kripke, who is also at Princeton. What is your attitude to Kripke?

*RR*: I find his views arguable. He seems to me to be saying: take all the intuitions you can think of which are antipragmatic and I'll give you a philosophy of language which matches those intuitions. But how one could argue whether one *wanted* these concepts I can't imagine. I have the same reaction to Thomas Nagel, who was at Princeton until recently. Nagel has a deep sense that the problems of philosophical realism are the problems to work on, and his work is getting more and more interesting—especially toward the end of his new book, *Mortal Questions*, where he emphasizes that the traditional philosophical problems are not just historical, but still relevant. He and Kripke fit together beautifully. But I don't think either of them has much in the way of arguments.

Q: What do you make of Donald Davidson and the contemporary philosophy of action, which has been taken very seriously on the Continent?

*RR*: I never found it very interesting. It seems to me to be a hangover from the problem of free will. I'm afraid that after reading Hume on the compatibility of free will and determinism I never looked back. Unlike some German writers, I don't see it as having much to do with moral philosophy.

Q: And the work of the Oxford philosopher Michael Dummett? Are you worried by the problem of intuitionism? Some philosophers might say that, as a matter of fact, the giving of grounds often comes to an end with an appeal to intuitions, such as when we say "I see that" or "It's not clear."

*RR*: I don't see a problem. Either one refers to what we all intuit or to what we all normally do. It doesn't make much difference.

Q: Are you worried by the charge that there is a contradiction between the idealism of your metaphysical views and the materialism of your psychological views?

*RR*: Idealism as a metaphysical view is pointless: the old idealist attempt to find some phenomena which the materialist cannot explain fails. But I think, as Sellars shows, that you can have all the advantages of both materialism and idealism if you just make a few distinctions. So be a materialist if you want to, but realize that being a materialist is simply putting a bet on what the vocabulary of the predictive disciplines will turn out to be.

Q: So the doctrine that creates the impression of tough-mindedness doesn't have much tough content. Would you take the same approach to scientism? Do you think that the only reliable, valid knowledge we have is scientific knowledge?

*RR*: That way of putting it presupposes that knowledge is a natural kind. I think it's better to say that there are lots of different justifiable assertions, including not only scientific assertions but aesthetic and social judgments. One end of the spectrum has an elaborate machinery for establishing the norms behind it, just as there are experts at one end of the spectrum, the other not. But the two kinds of enterprise are one. So there is really no need to worry where knowledge stops because the distinction between where you go to explain something and where not is not a distinction between knowledge and opinion. It's a sociological distinction.

*Q*: Nonetheless, you do cling to a form of scientism?

*RR*: I think of myself as stealing the point from Sellars that one's categories in metaphysics should be the categories of the sciences of one's day. But that's simply to say what a boring subject metaphysics is.

*Q*: Can we end on the problem of your approach to history. You began as a McKeonite comparativist taking the larger historical view, and have now returned to it. Yet your philosophical training does not really help you all that much with the problem of how to influence future historical developments. It does train you in the art of destruction, and you could be seen as attempting to destroy philosophy as the theory of knowledge just as Adorno attempted to destroy social philosophy. But such destructions often have unintended effects. How can you envisage them, let alone take responsibility for them? In sum, you don't have a theory of history?

*RR*: No, I don't. I'm not a historicist in Popper's sense.

*Q*: But you are perhaps an historicist in the sense of one who holds that history is all-important, and that it is usually helpful to take careful account of changing historical circumstances and exact processes of historical genesis. Could you perhaps say something about your relationship to the British philosopher of history R. G. Collingwood?

*RR*: I read Collingwood a long time ago in my twenties and forgot most of it. I now realize that I may have recently taken up things which I originally read in Collingwood. We have to take history seriously. I see postphilosophy continuing the conversation of mankind in that context.

# 3

## Postphilosophical Politics

*Interview by Danny Postel*

*Question*: Professor Rorty, what do you mean when you say that analytic philosophy has "transcended and canceled" itself?

*Richard Rorty*: What I mean is that it worked itself out of a job: It started with notions of logic, language, analytic truth, conceptual analysis—which it then criticized. So the effect of its analyses was to analyze away its own tools.

*Q*: How, as you see it, did Wittgenstein, Quine, and Sellars contribute to this?

*RR*: What's common to them, I think, is holism—that is, the notion that you can't dissect words or sentences and their relation to the world in isolation, that you have to understand words and sentences in the context of an entire linguistic practice. Once you see this, the empiricist image which lay behind logical positivist polemics can't be sustained.

*Q*: Allan Bloom's *The Closing of the American Mind* has caused quite a sensation both in the intellectual community and in the public culture generally. To what is this to be attributed?

*RR*: I still don't understand the book's popularity. It was half a polemic against the mores of contemporary student life in America and half a polemic against the philosophical convictions of most contemporary

American intellectuals. My criticisms were largely of the latter, while I think the book's wider audience was interested mainly in the former.[1]

*Q*: His book did give you occasion to express some of your own views on the politics of higher education.[2] You wrote that higher education "should be a matter of inciting doubt and stimulating imagination, thereby challenging the prevailing social consensus."

*RR*: What I had in mind is that the American colleges and universities have been centers of leftist political thought in our century. And this seems to me their most important social role. They've served to help the country realize that it was committing an injustice, that it was in danger of becoming too greedy, too selfish.

*Q*: And do you support this function of theirs?

*RR*: Sure. It's this kind of contribution to society for which universities principally exist.

*Q*: Do you think students should be critical of the ties that link universities to the military-industrial complex? Many students are now taking action—calling for their institutions to end research for the military, to divest from corporations damaging the environment, to ban the CIA from recruiting on campus, and so on. Do you support this movement?

*RR*: I don't think it can do any harm, but doubt it has any great effect. Like getting the ROTC units off campus during the sixties, it at least expresses concern. It didn't change the army to get the ROTC units off—and you probably can't change the companies—but it can't hurt.

*Q*: You've asked in your writings what a "postphilosophical" culture would look like, suggesting that we are moving toward being one. What would it mean to be living in such a culture?

*RR*: What I mean by a postphilosophical culture is one doesn't have any surrogate for God. Think of a philosophical (secularist) culture as a successor to a religious culture, as the Enlightenment thought of itself. That philosophical culture still had notions like Nature, Reason, Human

1. See "That Old-Time Philosophy," review-article on *The Closing of the American Mind*, by Allan Bloom, *New Republic* (April 4, 1988), 28–33.
2. See "Education Without Dogma," *Dissent* 36:2 (Spring 1989): 198–204.

Nature, and so on, which were points of reference outside of history by reference to which history was to be judged.

*Q:* In *Contingency, Irony, and Solidarity* you draw not only from the work of such analytic thinkers as Wittgenstein, Quine, and Sellars, but also from the writings of Continental figures like Derrida, Heidegger, Nietzsche, and Freud. You argue that thinkers such as these allow us to see ourselves as historical contingencies. Can you talk about that?

*RR:* Seeing yourself as an historical contingency is the opposite of seeing yourself as linked to something fateful like Reason, Nature, God, or History. Thinking of yourself as a contingency means thinking of what matters most to you as mattering most for no deep reason, but simply due to the kind of parents you happened to have, the kind of society you grew up in, and so on.

*Q:* How have Freud, Nietzsche, and Derrida helped us along in this respect?

*RR:* Freud, I think, is very good at making us see how our sense of importance is relative to the accidents of upbringing. Nietzsche and Derrida are very good at criticizing the theological or metaphysical notion of a reference point outside of language or outside of history.

*Q:* Interestingly, while you draw from the criticisms Foucault has offered of these Enlightenment notions, you seem not to share his rejection of the social arrangements and political institutions that derive from and rest upon Enlightenment ways of thinking about the world. Why is that?

*RR:* I don't see what Foucault had against bourgeois liberalism, except that in the France of the fifties and sixties it just wasn't respectable to be a bourgeois liberal. I don't think he has any arguments against it or anything better to suggest. So, I'm inclined to think that his opposition to liberalism and reformism was merely a contingent French fashion.

*Q:* What about other arguments against bourgeois liberalism—Dewey's for example? Didn't Dewey see the need for far-reaching structural change in the basic institutional arrangements of American society?

*RR:* Yes, Dewey was what in Europe would have been called a social democrat. He was the inspiration for a good deal of what we think of as the left wing of the Democratic Party.

*Q*: Given the enormous problems we're seeing—the specter of an ecological crisis rooted in an economic system that produces obscene social inequalities, threats to the planet and its inhabitants caused by uncontrolled economic growth, and an international system that's choking the Third World—wouldn't a Deweyan be calling for some serious changes in the order of things?

*RR*: I'm all for social changes, but I would prefer them to be reformist rather than revolutionary. I don't see that it's liberalism that is to blame for America's willingness to let the ghettos crumble and let black kids grow up without hope. You can blame the American voters for not being liberals, but I don't think you can blame liberalism.

*Q*: I'm suspicious of the old distinction you invoke in *Contingency, Irony, and Solidarity* between the public and private realms of life. Given your praise for what you see as Dewey's having overcome this kind of Western distinction (fact/value, subject/object, theory/practice, etc.), why reassert the dichotomy of the public and private spheres?

*RR*: I guess I don't see this as the kind of distinction Dewey sought to overcome. Maybe I just haven't read the right things in Dewey, but I can't see what he'd have against it.

*Q*: Hasn't feminism awakened us to the danger of separating the public and private realms?

*RR*: I guess I don't see the relevance of feminism here. The kind of private/public distinction the feminists mostly talk about is the distinction between who stays home and does the dirty work with the cooking and kids, and who gets out of the house into the great world outside. That has nothing to do with the distinction I'm trying to draw between individual self-creation and public responsibility.

*Q*: You don't see politics as something that permeates all realms of human life?

*RR*: With luck, politics doesn't permeate all realms of human life. It does in countries like China. But in countries that are better off, it often doesn't, and I don't see why anybody would want it to. I think of the aim of liberal politics as leaving as much space for privacy as possible.

*Q*: Can you talk about the political theme of the book: solidarity? You argue that solidarity should be our social goal.

*RR*: As I'm using the term, it's a sense of other people and ourselves being "we"—we feel that what affects them affects us because we, to some extent, identify with them. I was trying to describe social progress in a way borrowed from Wilfred Sellars: the expansion of "we" consciousness, that is, the ability to take in more and more people of the sort fashionably called "marginal" and think of them as one of us, included in us. The argument I make is that this is mainly done by going into concrete details about marginal lives rather than by having theories about what all human beings have in common.

*Q*: Would you say that it's a practical rather than a philosophical matter?

*RR*: I think of it as a matter for novelists rather than theorists.

*Q*: Why don't you think theoreticians should attempt to, say, speculate about the human condition or reflect critically on the problems of the times—or even suggest how solidarity might become a more vital part of human interaction?

*RR*: I think there's a long record of them trying to give theoretical arguments for greater human solidarity, and I don't think anything much came of it. It's not that I have a high a priori argument against theory—it's just looking at the track record of the novelists and the track record of the theorists.

*Q*: What about the work of Jürgen Habermas? You often seem to be drawing from his thinking, and yet his project has been that of finding a philosophical grounding for a commitment to social solidarity.

*RR*: Absolutely, and he and I are always arguing about this. He thinks of me as some kind of relativist, and I think of him as some kind of transcendentalist.

*Q*: He has been active in the current debates over Martin Heidegger's Nazism, arguing that a deep connection exists between Heidegger's fascism and his philosophy. Others, such as Derrida, have downplayed the connection. Where do you stand on that question?

*RR*: I think Heidegger's philosophy and his politics can be explained on the basis of some of the same biographical facts. But I don't think the politics contaminate the philosophy. You can explain Sartre's Stalinism by reference to the same biographical facts that gave rise to *Being and Nothingness*, but I don't think that book is contaminated by the Stalinism.

*Q*: Sidney Hook's death marks the end of a chapter in the history of American pragmatism. Hook took himself to be Dewey's philosophical and political heir, while he championed the cause of the Cold War and failed to criticize the United States for its atrocities from Vietnam to Central America. Once a leading Marxist revolutionary, he became a supporter of Ronald Reagan and an apologist for American power. Do you think he carried Dewey's political project through faithfully?

*RR*: Yes, though I disagreed with him about Vietnam and voted Democratic while he voted Republican. Our disagreements were on political tactics rather than on overall strategies.

# 4

# After Philosophy, Democracy

*Interview by Giovanna Borradori*

*Question*: Europe always searches for well-rounded philosophers who are versatile and engaged in public debate. Accordingly, you have been assigned the role of "teacher of neopragmatism," a sort of reincarnation of John Dewey.

*Richard Rorty*: Dewey was the dominant intellectual figure in America in my youth. He was often called the philosopher of democracy, of the New Deal, of the American democratic intellectuals. If one attended an American university any time before 1950, it would have been impossible not to be aware of him. I think that he was a remarkable man. He started out as an Evangelical Christian, then he became a Hegelian, then he read Darwin and he sort of dropped Christianity to try to put together Darwin and Hegel. His philosophy is a kind of naturalization of Hegel—Hegel without the split between nature and spirit. Just as Hegel's philosophy was a kind of secularized Christianity, so Dewey's was a sort of Christian social hope combined with a Darwinian way of looking at human beings.

*Q*: But what can Dewey contribute to a philosopher like you, approaching the end of the millennium?

*RR*: What I find attractive about Dewey, now that I'm older, is his criticism of Platonism, of Cartesianism, of Kant, of the whole tradition of metaphysics that Derrida and Heidegger oppose. His criticism, however, sprang from an optimistic social perspective, since he didn't think that the end of metaphysics was a matter of despair or nihilism. He thought that ending metaphysics could be done gradually, in the way we have gradually got rid of theology. Dewey thought that liberating culture from theological considerations and from metaphysical dualisms was a good idea. He was aware that it would take a long time to accomplish, and that it would be the final stage in the secularization of culture.

*Q*: How would you define the difference in perspective between Deweyan pragmatism and your neopragmatism?

*RR*: I don't think there is any great difference in fundamentals. I pay close attention to the philosophy of language, while Dewey did not. It is a matter of intellectual context, and I was brought up on analytic philosophy, particularly the philosophy of language. Within analytic philosophy, Dewey's themes—or, better yet, Dewey's attacks on traditional dualisms—have been persuasively presented in the form of doctrines in the philosophy of language, particularly by Quine and Davidson. I don't think this adds anything much to Dewey: it is just adapting what Dewey said for a different audience, for people with different expectations.

*Q*: When was your first encounter with logical analysis?

*RR*: I was briefly a student of Carnap and of Hempel, but they were not my principal teachers. My training had been predominantly historical. My encounter with analytic philosophy took place at Princeton, when I was already teaching. It was an exciting period. Wittgenstein's later work was just being assimilated, and Quine and Sellars were writing their most important material.

*Q*: What was Wittgenstein's role in the analytic realm in the United States?

*RR*: I first read Wittgenstein in the late fifties, as a sort of relief from Reichenbach. Wittgenstein played the role of a pragmatist within the philosophy of language, decentralizing philosophy of language itself. Wittgenstein was a threatening figure because he contributed substantially to detranscendentalizing and deprofessionalizing philosophy. Hence, academic philosophers in America and England always had an ambiguous reaction to him. On the one hand, he is obviously the greatest figure in the field; on the other, he is a danger to the profession. All this aside, Wittgenstein has a great appeal for me. As Stanley Cavell says, what's remarkable about the two great philosophers of the twentieth century is that Wittgenstein writes as if he had read nothing, while Heidegger writes as if he had read everything.

*Q:* Why did American philosophy open itself with such enthusiasm to European émigrés between the two wars?

*RR:* Americans simply had not produced anything in philosophy for a long time. Dewey's best work had been written before 1925, hence for twenty-five years not much had happened in American philosophy—though Dewey was still alive and revered. In the thirties, the German and Austrian émigrés began coming over—people like Carnap, Hempel, Tarski, Reichenbach—and, after the Second World War, they simply took over American philosophy departments. They were an explicitly antihistoricist movement, attempting to make philosophy scientifically, rather than historically, oriented.

*Q:* What was the reason for this opposition to historicism, so quickly assimilated by American philosophy?

*RR:* The logical positivists thought that fascism was associated with antiscience, and that respect for science and scientific method was the mark of antifascism in philosophical thought. Heidegger's identification with the Nazis was important for Carnap because he saw Heidegger's "historicity of Being" and his Nazism as somehow connected. When Carnap came to the United States he imported the belief that philosophy had to be defended from historicism and Nazism by avoiding thinkers like Plato, Hegel, and Nietzsche. Karl Popper presented the same view in his book *The Open Society,* which was an extremely influential book in America. Popper thought that Plato, Hegel, and Marx were totalitarian thinkers, and that we had to avoid their style of thought and embrace a more modern, up-to-date, and scientific way of thinking. This was a very powerful ideological rhetoric, still believed by most American philosophers, who are convinced that political and moral decency is a matter of respect for scientific rationality.

*Q:* Do you believe that the same fate lies in store for hermeneutics in the United States? I refer mainly to the hermeneutic historicism of Gadamer, who is at the center of a great part of the European debate.

*RR*: I don't think so. Hermeneutics isn't a term we use much in America: we prefer to talk about "Continental philosophy," which includes everyone from Gadamer to Lyotard. However, I do not think that the term *hermeneutics* has a uniform interpretation in Europe either. In the sixties and seventies it was widely discussed in France and in Germany; today it has been replaced by poststructuralism.

*Q*: If you had to write a history of American philosophy, when would you locate its beginning?

*RR*: I would certainly emphasize the sharp break of the fifties, the development of analytic philosophy, which is a different kind of philosophy. The question of where to locate its beginning is still open. Many American philosophers—Royce and Santayana—have not left a school of followers.

*Q*: What about Emerson?

*RR*: Emerson was never read by philosophers as a philosopher. Before Heidegger, Nietzsche also wasn't considered a philosopher. Only recently have people like Stanley Cavell and Cornel West tried to bring Emerson into the philosophical canon. Emerson and Thoreau were considered literary figures in the tradition of American eccentrics.

*Q*: Dewey appears to be an exception in the American panorama: he left a school; he reconciled, so to speak, the logic of the monastery with that of the city, reawakening in American thought an interest in questions of an ethico-social order.

*RR*: American culture is essentially political. America was founded upon an ethical concept of freedom. It was founded as the land of the freest society, the place where democracy is at its best, where the horizons are open. There is a kind of national romance about a country that says, "We are different from Europe because we made a fresh start. We don't have traditions, we can create human beings as they are supposed to be." I think that the romanticism about America runs through from Emerson to Dewey. Unfortunately, it has been lost. It's been lost quite recently, around the time of the Vietnam War.

*Q*: You identify the intellectual identity of the United States as an interrupted "national romance." But what is happening today?

*RR*: Old socialists, like Sidney Hook, are among the few American intellectuals involved in this sort of social romanticism. I think that the romance of American life had a lot to do with our sense that we were the country of the future. Then it gradually turned out that this was the end of American dominance and that we were no longer the biggest, richest country. Suddenly, it was as if the intellectuals turned sour and had been deceived.

*Q*: Why should it have been interrupted with the Vietnam War?

*RR*: There had been two previous wars fought by Americans: the Mexican-American War and the Spanish-American War. These wars were denounced by intellectuals because it looked as if we were becoming merely European, that is, just one more imperialist power. The intellectuals looked favorably upon the First and Second World Wars because they were fought to defeat the forces of evil. Hence, after the Second World War, the American intellectuals could feel very proud of their country's historical role: things like the Marshall Plan gave a sense of a better world to come. The Vietnam War changed all that. This was a completely unjust war. It wasn't even imperialism. We were simply trying to take over a country for the sake of its natural resources—we were killing people in a mindless way. Somehow we never recovered from it. Also, it was the first time we had ever been defeated in war. We were sort of defeated in the Korean War, but not intellectually. For the first time in two hundred years we had lost a war, and the people started to think that we were not God's country after all.

*Q*: Do you believe that religion has played an important role in the national self-determination of the United States?

*RR*: At times, but not dominantly. Thoreau and Whitman weren't religious. Surely, religion became important at the beginning of the twentieth century, the time of the so-called social gospel, a sort of social-democratic Christianity. The Protestant churches in the north took the lead in social reforms. It resurfaced in the sixties with the civil rights movement and Martin Luther King.

*Q*: Let's now try to switch places, and to look at Europe from the United States. Who is the "Continental" author who has had the most influence on your philosophy?

*RR*: I would say, Martin Heidegger. I first read him in the late fifties because I was curious about what was happening in Europe.

*Q*: Which Heidegger interested you most: the existential Heidegger of *Being and Time*, or the hermeneutic Heidegger of *Holzwege*?

*RR*: At the beginning, the only work we knew about was *Being and Time*. Until the early sixties, even in Europe, Heidegger meant *Being and Time*.

*Q*: In Italy today, some philosophers, like Gianni Vattimo, tend to unite the two phases of Heideggerian thought into a single curve, thereby incorporating the existential Heidegger into a new postmetaphysical perspective. What do you think?

*RR*: I agree. I prefer to think that Heidegger struggled all his life to reach one objective: self-overcoming. The *Letter on Humanism* repudiates *Being and Time* in the same way that *What Is Thinking?* repudiates the *Letter on Humanism*. This is significant for the "Heidegger case" and his relationship to Nazism. The fact is that between European and American philosophy there is no continuity. American intellectuals forgot about philosophy until the sixties, when people like Habermas, Gadamer, Foucault, and Derrida reminded them. However, that does not mean that there was an actual interaction.

*Q*: Why do you attribute this role to Derrida, Foucault, and Habermas, and not to Marcuse and Adorno? That is to say, to the preceding generation, which, aside from immigrating to the United States, also regularly taught here?

*RR*: They were here and they weren't here. They were here in body, but not in spirit, since they never noticed America, and the things they used to say about America were just absurd. They lived here in exile without really believing that this was a real country. I think that to get caught up on Adorno and Marcuse one has to take Marx more seriously than he has ever been taken in America. Derrida, Foucault, and Heidegger don't ask you to take Marx all that seriously. Before the sixties we had no Marxist tradition; in the United States people simply didn't read Marx, people still don't read Marx.

*Q*: Among the authors of so-called French poststructuralism, Foucault seems to be the one you have identified with most.

*RR*: He was a remarkable man, he had a great imagination, and he wrote memorable books. Foucault has been the most influential figure on the culture of the American left, but his influence has been dangerous. The result has been the "disengagement" of intellectuals: the idea was to resist the biopower exercised by capitalist society, but without any political notion of how to resist, without any political program, without any political utopia. Foucault's effect on the American intellectual community has been one of profound resentment.

*Q*: In Italy, Foucault's influence has been remarkable both in the intellectual debate and in the major institutional reforms that revolutionized psychiatry in the sixties, and, more generally, the structure of mental hospitals.

*RR*: We also closed our mental hospitals, but not because of Foucault. He's read by the literary intelligentsia, not by the medical people. Doctors don't take him seriously.

*Q*: Marx has been of fundamental importance for all the French poststructuralist authors: Lyotard, Deleuze, Virilio, and also Foucault. Have you ever read Marx?

*RR*: My parents' home was full of Marx. They read him, so I read him as a kid, but not as a philosopher. I still can't read him as a philosopher.

*Q*: Does this have any influence on your reading of Habermas and on his recent American assimilation into the postmodern perspective? I'm thinking of Fredric Jameson, in particular, and about his idea of a "political unconscious" in the consumer society.

*RR*: When Habermas says that he is a Marxist, I can't imagine how or why, since he does not sound like one. He sounds like an ordinary Deweyan liberal. There is a kind of piety in European thought, by which you must not turn your back on Marx. You must find something good in Marx, somewhere, if only in the early manuscripts. This has never been the case in America. I mean, nobody cares whether you have read Marx—not even Fredric Jameson.

*Q*: Marxism, then, is simply a distinctly European heritage?

*RR*: There are two barriers dividing American and European thought. The first is that Americans have read fewer history books and know less about the history of ideas than Europeans. The other is the American reception of Marx.

*Q*: The optimistic thrust of your philosophy clashes with the crepuscular, decadent, and somewhat nostalgic tone of our Continental *esprit du temps*. In fact, philosophical hermeneutics, trans-avant-gardism, and neoromanticism in music, are all movements that attribute a new centrality to memory and citation, understood as a privileged channel of access to history.

*RR*: If in hermeneutics you include "weak thought," which I am familiar with, we have to be clear about it. Neither Dewey nor weak thought imply that history is on our side, or that there is any necessary force that's going to cause a good outcome. On the contrary, there are nine chances out of ten that things will go to hell. However, what is important is the hope that they might not end badly, because they are not fated to go one way or the other. There is not just one Hegelian story of progress, or one Heideggerian story of nihilism to be told.

*Q*: One of your most debated definitions, that of postphilosophical culture, reproposes the problem of transdisciplinarity, both at the theoretical and institutional level.

*RR*: This problem is a reaction against the scientific notion of philosophy. Philosophy is not a quasi-scientific discipline: once you think of philosophy as continuous with literature you give up disciplinary segmentation. It seems to me that Europeans have been reading philosophy as continuous with literature for a long time. Valéry and Sartre could wander back and forth between the two as they wished. This is a desirable situation, not to have to worry about whether you are writing philosophy or literature. But, in American academic culture, that's not possible, because you have to worry about the department you are in.

*Q*: In defining the postphilosophical perspective, it seems to me that you want to link the dissolution of the barrier between philosophy and literature to the notion of narrative. What do you mean by this?

*RR*: I relate it mainly to the difference between Kant and Hegel, between the *Critique of Pure Reason* and the *Phenomenology of Spirit*. It seems to me that in the *Phenomenology*, and in Hegel's early writings, there is a kind of philosophical writing that is narrative in form; it is basically a story about the history of human nature. I believe that's become the dominant mode of philosophical thought, except in the academy. In the universities you can't write narratives, you have to pretend to be studying some subject—the nature of a text, the nature of signs, the nature of science. This strikes me as somewhat phony.

Q: Yet in your last book, *Contingency, Irony, and Solidarity*, you state that authors like Derrida, who is not an analytic thinker, write books that are limited to a reading public of philosophers because others would lack the necessary points of reference to understand them.

*RR*: Not exactly philosophers, but people who haven't read the previous history of philosophy. If you have gone to a gymnasium, the Italian *liceo* or the French *lycée*, where philosophy is part of the ordinary curriculum for at least three years, you will be able to follow a philosophical argument. But I write for an English-speaking audience, and, typically, well-educated English and American people won't be able to follow what Derrida is talking about, because they can't catch the allusions.

Q: The problem of writing stories on philosophy, of writing about philosophy as an author, then translates itself into the problem of the reader: whom do we write for?

*RR*: That's okay. Hegel's audience was limited too. People will always read Plato and Nietzsche, and they will also read Derrida on Plato. At least some people . . .

Q: Still on Derrida, how do you evaluate the success of "deconstruction" in America? Paradoxically, in Europe, where it was created, it occupies a much less central position.

*RR*: I think that deconstruction is an American product. God only knows what it is, it is a very loosely used term. It really applies more to Paul de Man than to Derrida, but a de Manian literary criticism, as far as I know, simply does not exist. However, because we have a hundred thousand professors of English in America, it is part of the training in graduate school.

*Q*: How would you define the difference between *deconstruction* and *textualism*, the very successful term you coined in *Consequences of Pragmatism*?

*RR*: I used textualism as a sort of lowest common denominator between de Man and Derrida, but it is not a term that should be pressed very hard. It is a way of doing with signs what used to be done with ideas.

*Q*: What is the relationship between the notion of text, from which textualism is derived, and your concept of *narrative*?

*RR*: Narrative means telling a story about something, like the world spirit, or Europe, man, the West, culture, freedom, class struggle. It is the story of some big thing like that, in which you can place your own story.

*Q*: Then, the purpose of these stories is to allow culture a dialogue, more than communicating a comprehensive vision of the world.

*RR*: I think that the purpose of constructing such narratives is to give sense to the author's existence. It is a way of relating himself or herself to the great men of the past. When you read Plato, Cervantes, or Dante, at some point you ask yourself what your connection is with them, and you tell yourself a story.

*Q*: Is there an element of the monumental in what you are saying?

*RR*: Sure. Because you have to think about great heroes, freedom, class struggle, as the great monuments of one's story.

*Q*: In your last book you speak about "liberal utopia." What are you alluding to?

*RR*: Nothing very new. I mean the ordinary notion of equality of opportunity, what Rawls describes in his book *A Theory of Justice*, the idea of a society in which the only reason for inequalities is that things would be even worse if they did not exist.

*Q*: And what does the figure of the "ironic liberal" refer to?

*RR*: If you speak about society in terms of this liberal utopia of equality of opportunity, and you don't have a philosophical backup such as the laws of history, or the decline of the West, or the age of nihilism, then you are in a position to be what I call an ironist. An ironist is someone who says that a liberal utopia isn't something that expresses the essence of human nature, the end of history, God's will, but is simply the best idea people have had about the object for which they work. Ironism, in this context, means something close to antifoundationalism.

Q: In the artistic avant-garde, but also in the philosophical tradition from Socrates to Voltaire, the concept of irony is not simply a descriptive modality, but contains a subtle element of transgression.

RR: In my use, it does not. The kind of irony I have in mind doesn't care about transgressing, because it doesn't think there is anything to transgress. It is just a sort of attitude, the way you feel about yourself, a form of life.

Q: Where do you place existential themes such as death and anguish?

RR: I don't believe that philosophy has one particular object. Some people spend a lot of time thinking about death, others about sex or money. I don't think that one of them is more philosophical by nature than any other.

Q: I find your indifference to existentialism curious, and it brings me back to talking about your first approach to Heidegger. What were you looking for in Heidegger at the end of the fifties?

RR: I was trying to understand what had happened after Hegel; the answer turned out to be Nietzsche. Hegel is such an overpowering figure that you wonder what there was left to do in philosophy after him. I think that I read Heidegger to find out what people who read Hegel were saying about him; I read Kierkegaard for the same reason.

Q: You told me that your mother and father were old-time socialists. Was there any conflict in looking to Dewey instead of Marx?

RR: Marxism always struck me as a perfectly reasonable criticism of capitalism, imbued with a lot of philosophy. But compared to Hegel and Heidegger, Marx seemed to me third-rate. Marx was good for economics. I had the same problem with Kolakowski. It seems very hard to read Marx without Lenin or Stalin.

*Q*: How does the philosophy of science figure in your perspective?

*RR*: Originally it meant empiricist epistemology; when Carnap and Reichenbach used this term, it was an attempt to repeat what the British empiricists had done in terms of sense perception. After Kuhn's *The Structure of Scientific Revolutions,* and the work of Feyerabend, the distinction between science and nonscience began to be blurred. It meant rethinking the nature of scientific endeavor in general.

*Q*: Do you think that philosophy should assume a "critical" function with respect to science?

*RR*: I don't see philosophy as criticizing anything. When people refer to philosophy as "critical," they seem to say, "scientists or politicians use the vocabulary of some other philosopher, they shouldn't use that vocabulary, they should use mine!" When people say that philosophy criticizes science, or other areas of culture, all it comes down to is that it's criticizing the residues of past philosophies, as they appear in cultural practice.

*Q*: I am having a hard time understanding how you tie together the liberal perspective and the idea of a philosophy totally estranged from social criticism.

*RR*: We do not need philosophy for social criticism: we have economics, sociology, the novel, psychoanalysis, and many other ways to criticize society. Take the very powerful critic Foucault. His best work does not strike me as particularly philosophical. The most interesting parts of his work are the details about the culture of the insane asylums, of prisons, of hospitals. Foucault was also a great philosophical mind, but he made a social difference not as a philosopher, but as someone who looked at particular things harder than anybody else.

*Q*: Then, what is philosophy? A testimony to the survival of a community of readers of philosophical texts?

*RR*: I don't think one should ask that question. The reason I write philosophical books is all the other books I have read, and my reaction to those books. I react to some books and not others. Every once in a while you get an original poet, or sociologist, or philosopher, but it is a very bad idea for a discipline to say that it has a mission.

# 5

## Toward a Postmetaphysical Culture

*Interview by Michael O'Shea*

*Question*: What is a "postmetaphysical" culture?

*Richard Rorty*: A poeticized, or postmetaphysical, culture is one in which the imperative that is common to religion and metaphysics—to find an ahistorical, transcultural matrix for one's thinking, something into which everything can fit, independent of one's time and place—has dried up and blown away. It would be a culture in which people thought of human beings as creating their own life-world, rather than as being responsible to God or "the nature of reality," which tells them what kind it is.

*Q*: Do you see us tending toward that kind of culture?

*RR*: I think that since the time of the Romantics, there have been strains in European and American culture that have gone in that direction. There are Emerson and Whitman in America, and various other lingering Romantic influences in Europe.

How long this can last, I don't know. It seems to be the product of a wealthy, leisured elite which has time to worry about this kind of thing, time to imagine alternative futures. The world may not permit the existence of this kind of elite much longer.

*Q*: Could the ironic, poetic worldview characteristic of this elite ever become the property of the masses?

*RR*: Yes. I think that the success of secularization in the industrialized democracies suggests that. The sixteenth- and seventeenth-century notion that man would never be able to let go of religion has turned out to be wrong. The promise of the Enlightenment came true: that you could have a society which had a sense of community, without any religious agreement, and indeed without much attention to God at all. If you can secularize a society like that, you can probably de-metaphysicize it also.

*Q*: Given their training in metaphysics and similar fields of thought, what purpose could our current professors of philosophy serve in such a culture?

*RR*: I think that the main purpose they've served in the past has been to get past common sense, past common ways of speaking, past vocabularies; modifying them in order to take account of new developments like Enlightenment secularism, democratic governments, Newton, Copernicus, Darwin, Freud.

One thing you can count on philosophy professors doing is what William James called "weaving the old and the new together," in order to assimilate weird things like Freudian psychology with moral common sense. Thomas Nagel wrote a good article in the *New York Review of Books* on how Freud's thought has become a part of our moral common sense. I think that illustrates the process nicely. Philosophers have helped with that process.

*Q*: So philosophers are professional renderers of coherent worldviews?

*RR*: Yes, and the reason they'll probably always be around is that there will always be something exciting happening [in culture] that needs to be tamed and modified, woven together with the past.

*Q*: Do you see the de-transcendentalization of culture as an inducement to political involvement? Jürgen Habermas and others have seen it as the opposite.

*RR*: I do see it as an inducement to involvement, and I think that Dewey did too. Dewey is saying: suppose you're a pragmatist about truth— that is, you think that truth is what works. The obvious question, then, is whom does it work for? This is the question that Foucault raises. You then ask political questions about whom you want it to work for, whom you want to run things, whom you want to do good to—questions which come prior to philosophical questions. Then let democratic politics be what sets the goals of philosophy, rather than philosophy setting the goals of politics.

Whereas Habermas seems to think that if you don't have philosophy out there as point man, telling society and politics where to go, then you're somehow stuck.

Q: Do you have doubts about the same things that people like Habermas do, namely, that the sort of large-scale discourse about values that is needed in a democratic state can go on without an extralinguistic norm of rationality, a "master narrative"?

RR: Not really. I don't see why Habermas thinks it can't go on. He has this view that every assertion is a claim to universal validity, and that if you give up thinking of assertions in that way, you won't be able to take yourself seriously, or take communication seriously, or take democracy seriously. I just don't see the reasoning there. It's something like what [Hilary] Putnam thinks, when he claims that we need a "substantive" notion of truth. I never got that one either.

Q: Perhaps such notions are meant to capture the idea of a certain responsibility that attaches to our utterances.

RR: Yes, but that seems an unnecessary detour in the attribution of responsibility. I think we ought to be able to be responsible to our interlocutors without being responsible to reason or the world or the demand of universality or anything else.

Q: Is there a way to change current patterns of education and acculturation in order to bring this sense of responsibility about?

RR: I don't know. But I think that a lot of that change has been accomplished by the gradual emergence of literature as the primary alternative to science. Philosophy, at the moment, is sort of occupying a halfway position between the sciences and literature. But just for that reason, it's tending to fall between two stools and to be ignored by intellectuals. Philosophy in the English-speaking world is simply not a big deal to most intellectuals, and the reason is that the weight of nonscientific culture has been thrown over to literature. The philosophers, in turn, are viewed by most as being nostalgic for the days when science was the name of the game.

*Q*: What, then, do you find problematic about contemporary attitudes toward physical science?

*RR*: There's still a tendency to want somebody to occupy the social role formerly held by the priests. The physicist tends to be nominated for that role, as someone in touch with the nature of reality, with, as Bernard Williams puts it, reality apart from human needs and interests. This tendency to need a priest-figure is unfortunate; it seems to me a form of self-abasement. But I'm not sure how serious that science worship is anymore. You still find a little of it in contemporary debates, in Searle's debate with Jacques Derrida, for instance.[1]

*Q*: Is the situation changing in philosophy?

*RR*: Not that I can notice, at least in the English-speaking countries. It's going to be very difficult for analytic philosophy, given its professional self-image, ever to outgrow its association with the so-called hard sciences. That association really doesn't exist in non-Anglophone philosophy, and that's why I think it's going to be hard for the two [traditions] ever to merge.

*Q*: Hilary Putnam, analyzing parts of your critique of reason in his *Renewing Philosophy*, declares that "relativism á la Rorty is rhetoric." Are you comfortable with this evaluation of your work? What role do you intend your work to play?

*RR*: Primarily persuasion. I don't much care whether it's called rhetoric or logic. I think of my work as trying to move people away from the notion of being in touch with something big and powerful and nonhuman. The reason I prefer Donald Davidson's work to Putnam's is that Davidson's views on philosophy of language and mind go further in that direction than Putnam's.

1. The reference here is to John Searle's debate with Jacques Derrida, reiterated in Derrida's book *Limited Inc.*, ed. Gerald Graff and trans. Jeffrey Mehlman and Samuel Weber (Evanston, Ill.: Northwestern University Press, 1988), about the philosophy of J. L. Austin.

*Q*: Is yours the kind of work that creates a foundation that someone else could build upon? Could it found a school?

*RR*: I would hope not. Founding a school is relatively easy. You can set up a problematic within which a generation can happily pursue professional activity, but you can never quite tell whether you've actually done something useful, or simply encouraged further, decadent scholasticism.

One of the things I rather like about people like Derrida is that they have no real disciples. Derrida has a lot of American imitators (none of whom, I think, is any good), but he really is inimitable. There's no such thing as a "Derridean problematic." He doesn't give anybody any work to do—nor does Harold Bloom. And I admire that.

*Q*: It might be argued that while your work has helped to dismantle a number of traditional philosophical dualisms, the ironist worldview you espouse seems itself to culminate in a strict dualism of the public and the private. You say that we should read some authors (Nietzsche, Derrida) in order to enrich our private, poetic existences, but others (Rawls, Mill) should be read in order to make ourselves better citizens of a liberal democracy. Is this distinction tenable? If our private beliefs are prevented from informing the social sphere, then what substance do they have?

*RR*: I don't think private beliefs can be fenced off [from the public sphere]; they leak through, so to speak, and influence the way one behaves toward other people. What I had in mind in making the distinction was this: the language of citizenship, of public responsibility, of participation in the affairs of the state, is not going to be an original, self-created language.

Some people, the ones we think of as poets or makers, want to invent a new language—because they want to invent a new self. And there's a tendency to try to see that poetic effort as synthesizable with the activity of taking part in public discourse. I don't think the two are synthesizable; but that doesn't mean that the one doesn't eventually interact with the other.

When people develop private vocabularies and private self-images, people like Nietzsche, Kierkegaard, and Derrida, it's very unclear what impact, if any, this will ever have on public discourse. But over the centuries, it actually turns out to have a certain impact.

*Q*: If a reader of Heidegger, for example, is struck not only by the idiosyncratic, "world-disclosing" accomplishment of his writings, but is also attracted by his vision of responsiveness to Being as the fundamental aim of man, how will this attraction show up in public behavior?

*RR*: I don't know, but I think it pays to bear in mind that during the fifties and sixties Heidegger managed to grab hold of the imaginations of all the interesting people in Europe. When Habermas, Foucault, and Derrida were in school, Heidegger was "their" philosopher. What they each made of him was, God knows, very different, but it's clear that we won't be able to write the intellectual history of this century without reading Heidegger. Just as there were sixteen different ways of reacting to Hegel in his day, there were sixteen different ways of reacting to Heidegger; and I think it's pointless to ask what was the "true" message of either Hegel or Heidegger—they were just people to bounce one's thoughts off of.

*Q*: But you have written in *Contingency, Irony, and Solidarity* that "as a philosopher of our public life," Heidegger is "at best vapid, and at worst sadistic." Is the sense of using Heidegger that you were discussing there a different sense than the one we're talking about here?

*RR*: I think that attempts to get a political message out of Heidegger, Derrida, or Nietzsche are ill-fated. We've seen what these attempts look like, and they don't succeed very well. Hitler tried to get a message out of Nietzsche, and Nietzsche would have been appalled by it. And people who attempt to get a political message out of Derrida produce something perfectly banal. I suspect it isn't worth bothering.

But that's not to say that these figures will always be publicly useless. Having a great imagination and altering the tradition in insensible ways is going to make a difference in public affairs somewhere down the line. We just don't know how.

*Q*: Given your view that our epoch is one of increasing secularization, what do you make of the existence in this country of a fundamentalist, religious right that does have a noticeable effect on public policy? This seems to show that traditional religion and other forms of nonironic belief are alive and well in the public sphere.

*RR*: I think it's what happens whenever you have a middle class that gets really scared and defensive. It starts to look around for ways of dividing society into sheep and goats, in order to scapegoat somebody. The

American middle class has excellent reason to be scared about its economic future, and the economic future of the country. The more there is of this fear, the more you'll see cults, quasi-fascist movements, and things of that sort, all the stuff we classify as the "crazy right."

*Q*: What is there to stave that off, beside economic recovery?

*RR*: My hunch is that the normal cycle of boom and bust doesn't matter much, as long as the long-term average income of the middle class keeps going down, and the gap between rich and poor keeps growing. I don't think there's anything that's going to reverse that. I don't have any optimistic suggestions.

*Q*: Are you then a pessimist about the future?

*RR*: I'm not confident enough in economics to say anything, but all the predictions about how the globalization of the labor market will affect the standard of living in the industrialized democracies seem to me fairly convincing. I think that as long as the standard of living of the middle class in the democracies is in danger, democratic government is in danger.

*Q*: You once described yourself as a "postmodern bourgeois liberal." Given that self-designation, how do you see the contemporary academic left, a left alternately informed by the Frankfurt school thinkers and the French poststructuralists?

*RR*: That designation ["postmodern bourgeois liberal"] was supposed to be a joke. I thought it was a cute oxymoron—but no one else seemed to think it was funny.

I think there are really two lefts. The Frankfurt school, for example, is an attempt to modulate Marxism down into plain, social democratic, reformist left politics. And I think of myself as belonging to that left—it's the same as the so-called "old left" in America, the anti-Stalinist, social-democratic left centered around *Dissent*. Irving Howe and people like that.

There's also what I regard as a pretty useless, Foucauldian left, which doesn't want to be reformist, doesn't want to be social democratic. Fredric Jameson is a good example of that sort of left. I can't see it as having any sort of utility in America; it seems merely to make the left look ridiculous.

*Q*: What do you think has been the effect of the contemporary, Foucauldian academic left on American universities? Do you agree with the criticisms often leveled against left-leaning academics these days?

*RR*: The Foucauldian left is about 2 percent of the faculties at American universities, and it isn't very important, except that it gives the right a terrific target. It's enabled the right to generate an enormous amount of hostility against the universities because it can point at these few.

*Q*: Where is the political center of gravity of the humanities faculty at a typical American university?

*RR*: It's still the same sort of intellectual—left-liberal, social democratic, reformist—but the Foucauldians make a whole lot more noise.

*Q*: In the fall of 1994, you wrote an editorial about the Virginia Senate election, in which you analyzed the candidacy of Oliver North as a symptom of a crisis of values among Virginians. Is the flight toward the sort of old-style, "manly" virtue that people find in Oliver North analogous to the kind of cultic flight that you see in the contemporary American middle class? Is it born of the same fears?

*RR*: Yes. The fundamentalist preacher and the military officer become figures of strength and purity more or less simultaneously. They're both seen as people with no time for moral weakness, or any other weakness, and therefore no time for the bad people—the liberals. They're strong guardians of virtue against the weak, bad people.

*Q*: What resources does American pragmatism offer us today?

*RR*: Among the philosophy professors, in the form of Davidsonian philosophy of language and mind, it offers a way out from the boring realism versus antirealism issue, which I think has been done to death. Davidson gives us a way of getting out from under the dogmatism/skepticism oscillation that's plagued philosophy since Kant. I see Davidson as rewriting in terms of language the same things that James and Dewey did in terms of experience.

Actually, I've just finished reading John McDowell's book [*Mind and World*]; and he thinks that Davidson will actually keep the oscillation going—because no one will ever accept Davidson's view that beliefs are mostly veridical. As a sociological point about the philosophy professors, this may be right. But I don't see why they won't accept it.

Outside of the philosophy profession, I think that pragmatism is just a continuation of the idealistic, onward-and-upward Emerson-Whitman tradition of viewing American democracy as the greatest thing ever invented, and the source of all good things.

*Q*: The sort of "Emersonian theodicy" that Cornel West talks about in his history, *The American Evasion of Philosophy*?

*RR*: Yes. I think West gives a very good description there of the politico-spiritual dimension of pragmatism.

*Q*: You have often spoken of Anglo-American philosophy professors' reluctance to accept a vision of philosophy that doesn't break down along fixed problematics. Do you have an idea about how to reform undergraduate and graduate education in order to change this?

*RR*: Not really, because I think the philosophy professors are in a bind in the English-speaking world. The undergraduates would really like to hear more about Nietzsche and the other Europeans, but the professors feel that this is bad for the poor kids, that it will tempt them toward irrationalism, literature, unscientific thought, and things like that. If [the professors] can't get over that block, I think they're going to paint themselves into a corner.

So philosophy departments in the English-speaking world are cutting themselves off from the rest of the university in a way that will eventually prove debilitating. And I wish they'd stop.

*Q*: In *Consequences of Pragmatism*, you suggested that we might end up with two different disciplines being taught under the rubric *philosophy*: Continental thought and literary criticism on one side, and science-oriented analytic philosophy on the other. Does that diagnosis still hold?

*RR*: Yes. I don't think the issue is as much an involvement of literary criticism, as it is of historical orientation. Outside of the English-speaking world, training to be a philosophy professor is pretty much training in the history of philosophy. In Europe, you're a good philosophy professor just insofar as you have a good story to tell about [that history] which relates it to the present.

That kind of professional training is so different from the professional training you get in the English-speaking world, where you're supposed to keep up with the "preprint culture," and spend your time getting in touch with the hot new problems in the field, that it's hard to imagine the two ever coming together. What the [two groups of] kids are trained to do in graduate school doesn't have anything in common. And by the time they're done with graduate school, each group hasn't the slightest idea what the other is worrying about.

*Q:* What part of your own philosophical education have you found most valuable?

*RR:* The historical part, mostly acquired at the University of Chicago, where history of philosophy was practically all there was. The department was dominated by a historian of philosophy, Paul McKeon, and he kept your nose to the grindstone. You couldn't get a master's degree there without being able to rattle off an awful lot of history. If I hadn't been forced to read all those authors, I never would have been able to read Hegel or Heidegger, and I would have regretted that.

On the other hand, if I hadn't gotten a reasonable background in what we now call analytic philosophy, I wouldn't have been able to appreciate Wilfrid Sellars and Donald Davidson, and I would have regretted that, too.

# 6

# There Is a Crisis Coming

*Interview by Zbigniew Stanczyk*

*Question*: What is the role of contemporary philosophers?

*Richard Rorty*: By accident they might have some importance. Dewey in America, Habermas in Germany, Kolakowski in Poland: these are intellectuals who are important for the life of their countries. They happen to be philosophy professors, but if they had been historians or sociologists, they could have done about the same thing. Being a philosopher as opposed to an historian or a literary critic is not all that essential; it's being an intellectual that matters.

*Q*: Would the role of a philosopher be more that of a guardian of ideas than that of a producer?

*RR*: I'm not happy with either notion. People read books and then write books in response to the books they read, and we could call this producing ideas if you want to, but that's a little too fancy for me.

*Q*: Do you see yourself as producing ideas?

*RR*: Well, I guess so. I do write books.

*Q*: How would you react if you found you were attracting a group of followers?

*RR*: It would just be an inconvenience. Philosophers such as Dewey or Habermas, who do have national importance, don't really want to form a school of followers. For me it's not likely, and it would be a nuisance if it happened. One doesn't want to talk to a school; one wants to talk to the public.

Q: Yet you still have to relate to other philosophers.

RR: Not necessarily. Dewey and Habermas are sort of my heroes, and they always had two conversations: one with their professional colleagues on technical issues that only philosophy professors care about, and another conversation with the public. And it was the latter that made them important. I have a debate with Habermas in *Deutsche Zeitschrift für Philosophie* that concerns the nature of truth and is completely without interest to anyone who is not a philosophy professor. No one else would ever care. [*Laughter.*] But, you know, it is interesting for us.

Q: The idea of truth is still basic to any conversation, isn't it?

RR: Yes, but not the kind of thing we talk about. The difference between me and Habermas is really technical. It just isn't the kind of thing that the public should get interested in.

Q: How could we define truth in terms of function in public life?

RR: There are two questions here. I think that what people really worry about is truthfulness. They think they are being lied to all the time, and usually they are right. They are being lied to. And they wish that people would tell them the truth. But what they mean here is not a question of the nature of truth. They just want people to say what they believe, governments to say the same things to the public that they say to other governments, and so on. Truth as a philosophical problem is a question of whether true statements are representations of reality, or whether the notion of representation applies to statements, and so on. This is really technical.

Q: What is the role of truthfulness in the international public sphere or on the platform where discussions take place?

RR: It is a question here of making democracy work by having information freely available. That's why people put such hopes in the Internet. If one wants to know how many people are out of work in a given country, or what the average wage level in the country is, one can find it. One won't be lied to. And that, of course, is terribly important, but it's not the kind of thing a philosopher has anything to say about. My slogan is that if you take care of freedom, truth takes care of itself. A true statement is just one that a free community can agree to be true. If we take care of political freedom, we get truth as a bonus.

*Q*: What are the significant ideas produced in this, the twentieth century?

*RR*: They are just the same ones that were important in the eighteenth and nineteenth centuries. The Christian idea of human brotherhood, the democratic idea of constitutional, representative government. I don't think that the twentieth century has come up with any improvements on the nineteenth.

*Q*: Haven't "deconstructive ideas" become the specialty of this century?

*RR*: I don't think of them as ideas. I think of Marxism and fascism just as conspiracies, not as ideas. I don't think they should be given any intellectual dignity.

*Q*: For some, the twentieth century has also brought great moral achievements.

*RR*: The most obvious thing is voting rights for women. And increasingly religious tolerance; I mean that religion is not as much of an issue as it was in 1900. There is more sexual tolerance, too. Things are better for homosexuals now. The sexual revolution of the seventies helped to overcome the churches and the clergy. In the twentieth century, people did learn not to take sex as seriously as the churches had told them before, and that was a good thing.

*Q*: The caesura of 1989, when communism in Eastern Europe unexpectedly collapsed, is seen by many people as a moment of great liberation on the one hand, and as the beginning of a great ideological void on the other. Does the downfall of the pre-1989 ideologically bipolar world mean entering a vacuum?

*RR*: No, in 1989 much of the world got out from under a gang of criminals, of some gangsters who had been ruling Poland, Russia, Romania, and so on. It wasn't that those opposed to them lacked ideas. The dissidents had kept the good old ideas of the Enlightenment alive, and these ideas were still lying around waiting to be used. I don't see that there has been a vacuum.

What is still happening in Eastern Europe can be seen as a struggle between the gangsters and the intellectuals, and I have no idea who is going to win in which country. The astonishing thing that happened in Russia, it seems to me, is that the entire property of the state was stolen within a couple of years, [*laughter*] and now everything is privatized which means that the *nomenklatura* owns it privately. I think of the Russian communists as simply having taken the entire wealth of the country and put it in individual Swiss bank accounts for themselves. I don't know whether democracy can survive that kind of gangsterism. And I just don't know whether the same problem exists in Poland, Hungary, and so on.

In general, I don't think communism contributed anything. Marxism was simply an excrescence of socialism. Suppose Lenin had lost, Kerensky had not been overthrown by Lenin, there never had been a Bolshevik revolution. Gorbachev said recently that it would have been so wonderful for Russia if Kerensky had won, because we might then have had a social democracy in Russia, instead of gangsters. That seems right to me. I don't believe that Marxism has any more importance than the so-called philosophy of National Socialism. It was just an excuse for the gangsters to rule, the way certain parts of Catholic theology were an excuse for the priests to rule.

*Q*: Did you know that Kerensky was a Hoover fellow?[1]

*RR*: Yes, and my father was slightly acquainted with him. One day I was with my father when he bowed to someone. I asked who it was, and he said, "That was Kerensky."

Did you see the *New Yorker* interview with Gorbachev by David Remnick? It was called "The First and the Last," an interview with the last general secretary of the Communist Party of the Soviet Union. Gorbachev was saying that Lenin was a horrible, cruel man, a complete disaster. [*Laughter.*] Of course while he was still in office he couldn't even allow himself to think such thoughts.

1. Zbigniew Stanczyk's talk with Rorty took place at the Hoover Institute.

*Q*: After the collapse of communism, do you see any new trend emerging, something that would constitute a political basis for the coming century?

*RR*: Just ordinary liberal democracy is all the ideology anybody needs. Yet, liberal democracy works in times of economic prosperity and doesn't work in times of economic insecurity and, since I think we're entering a time of economic insecurity, I don't have much faith that we can keep liberal democracy going. But that's not for lack of ideas, that's for lack of money. When there is prosperity, there is not that much distance between the people and the intellectuals—the liberal democratic liberals. When things are bad, then you get cults, fundamentalists, churches, fascist movements, all kinds of weird things. I tend to think of it as a reflection of economic circumstances rather than a current of ideas that has its own strength. Therefore, I expect we'll get more dictatorships in the future. It's difficult to imagine liberal democracy arising in China. It's quite possible that there will be a counterrevolution in Russia, which will reestablish a dictatorship in Moscow. I don't have much hope that this can be avoided. Within Europe and North America I suspect that right-wing fascist movements are going to make more and more progress. I am inclined to say that the West may have to try to close itself off from the rest of the world. But even if it does, I don't think that this will work because I don't think that individual nation-states will be able to effect economic decisions after the economy has become globalized. The globalized economy may prevent the existence of individual democratic nation-states.

*Q*: In your recent *New York Times* essay, you wrote about new cultural trends—ones based on feelings of fraternity and of solidarity—that would become prevalent in the next century.

*RR*: It wasn't really cultural trends, it was just economic trends that would have a bad impact on democratic politics. It seems to me that Europe, North America, Japan, and South Korea are in the same situation. They need a bourgeoisified working class; that is, they need a working class that doesn't live too differently from the middle class. However, they're not going to get it, because they are going to lose all the jobs to Thailand, Africa, Slovakia, and so on. There is a crisis coming for all the old industrial democracies. I don't think culture and ideas have much to do with it. The idea of solidarity of which I wrote—that was just an optimistic scenario about how America might eventually get itself back together again after a fascist revolution. For all I know, this time the fascists will win; the dictators will be there forever.

As to the very concept of solidarity, I see it as people thinking of themselves first and foremost as members of a trade union or citizens of a country, or members of an army, people engaged in a common effort, so that if the effort fails, identity is in trouble. If the revolution doesn't succeed, if the union can't be organized, if the country doesn't survive, if the war isn't won, then the individual is crushed. Solidarity is just what exists in such movements. It is accepting reciprocal responsibility to other members of the group for the sake of a common purpose. In that sense the Communist Party of the Soviet Union had solidarity, the Nazis had solidarity, Mao's cultural revolutionaries had solidarity. The bad guys can have solidarity too. [*Laughter.*] Solidarity is morally neutral, so to speak. It's like self-respect. It's for groups what self-respect is for individuals. America once had a sense of solidarity. At the time of the victory over Hitler, for example, there was a sense of America as a coherent nation with a purpose in the world and a meaning. That's what we don't have anymore.

Q: If not a feeling of solidarity, then perhaps some revival of religious values—ones that shaped Western society—might become a remedy.

RR: I can understand the return to the Church in Eastern and Central Europe, where so many people used to have the welfare state and now the state isn't going to do anything much, so they still have hope for the Church. They're bound to be disappointed—I don't believe the Church is going to take the place of the state.

Similarly, I don't think religion is going to be very important in America, where religious tolerance is fairly well established, and the difference between Christians, Jews, and Muslims is not essential. What is important is the contrast between fundamentalist religions and nonfundamentalist ones, because it is the difference between fanatics and nonfanatics, fascists and democrats. The members of the fundamentalist churches in the U.S. tend to be fanatically prejudiced and fanatically violent, and they are just not trustworthy citizens of the country. Theirs is a return to the churches as a way to establish a sense of identity that excludes infidels, nonfundamentalists, and nonbelievers. In this respect, the churches are functioning to exclude rather than include: they're not functioning as apostles of brotherhood, they're operating as ways of dividing society further. As long as fundamentalism is on the increase as a result of economic insecurity in America, religion will be important in the U.S. I don't think that world-wide antagonism among Catholicism, Orthodoxy, Protestantism, and Islam is of any importance—we've been distracted by the example of Bosnia.

*Q*: Within the landscape that you are drawing, is there any space left for our utopia of human brotherhood?

*RR*: No, there isn't. The socialists and the Marxists were perfectly right, that countries tend to divide into the rich and the poor, and brotherhood isn't possible. In America it looked as if we were solving the problem up until 1973. We were, as it were, bourgeoisifying the proletariat fairly steadily through the first six decades of the century, and then everything turned around. The gap between the rich and the poor in America was getting smaller for the first decades, and it's been getting wider for the past thirty-five years. The equality of opportunity is much less in the U.S. now than it was thirty years ago, so there's a good deal less brotherhood. Affirmative action might be the only hope, but I don't think that it will happen because the taxpayers in the suburbs aren't willing to pay taxes to support people who don't live in the suburbs, so we're dividing into the suburbs and the rest of the country.

Yet, the most important fact about American society is that the globalization of the labor market is driving down U.S. wages and it's producing not exactly unemployment, but employment at a starvation wage. If a husband and wife in America both work for the minimum wage, they take home about twenty thousand dollars a year, but no one can raise a family in the U.S. on twenty thousand dollars a year. For the people who work for minimum wage, which is going to be more and more of America, there is no future. Sooner or later there will be a populist upheaval, probably from the fascist right.

*Q*: Will this eventually lead to an antagonism between America and the rest of the world?

*RR*: No, it will be an antagonism of the American working class and the American middle class. There was already some attempt to focus American antagonism on Japan, and in the next century they will try to focus it on China. I can imagine a fascist president making war on China to satisfy the American people. If that happens, it will be merely an attempt to get out of the impossible socioeconomic inequality in America.

*Q:* As the tension between mainstream American society and its peripheries—poor immigrant minorities—increases, will race become more of a factor than income differences?

*RR:* Yes, but race would not matter if it were not for the income inequality. If there were lots of good jobs, the black/white issue and the Hispanic/white issue wouldn't be important. There isn't enough money to pay a working class decently, and so we're importing immigrant labor and then refusing to give such immigrants social benefits. It's an incredibly cruel system. California, for example, needs cheap immigrant labor, so the border is in effect open, and if you are a Mexican, you can get in somehow, if you want to. But once you get here, you'll be treated like dirt.

*Q:* Is there any unifying element in American culture around which a new social consensus might be reached?

*RR:* I don't think so, because the economic gap is too great, and a common culture isn't possible if one group is either enslaved or condemned to do the untouchable jobs. We tried to make the blacks into a hereditary cast of servants, and that isn't sharing a common culture.

*Q:* Some analysts point to a lack of strong ideologies in America, in contrast to Europe, that has made the U.S. economically prosperous in the twentieth century.

*RR:* I don't think America prospered because it lacked ideologies. It prospered for accidental economic reasons. I myself don't have much use for the notion of ideology. There were promises made by dishonest politicians. Some of them were called communists, some of them were called fascists. These promises didn't come true. There were fewer of these promises made in the U.S. because constitutional democracy was working more or less all right in America. The reason we didn't have the ideologies was because we didn't have the kind of extreme economic crises as occurred elsewhere. I think America produces as many ideas as any other country, but none of them has been used the way Hitler and Stalin put their ideas to use.

*Q*: There is an opinion that "great ideas" have always come to the U.S. from the outside.

*RR*: I'm not sure that there is much difference between European, American, and Japanese ideas. I don't think that there will be any big intellectual revolutions from now on. The educated political classes of all countries are going to be thinking in the terms of the European Enlightenment, and civilization is going to be Eurocentric. The politicians in places like China, Burma, and Singapore will try to prevent this from happening, and they might succeed, but if communication remains really free, then the European Enlightenment might win.

*Q*: Considering the technological advantage of the U.S. over the rest of the world, doesn't this state of technology, including the Internet, dictate who will have the last word?

*RR*: By now the upper middle class of Europe, Japan, Australia, Canada, and the U.S. is pretty much the same. It's a cosmopolitan middle class, and America doesn't have any particular dominance. Where it is dominant is in music and movies: it produces endless garbage that has nothing to do with the reality of American life, just the manufacture of endless fantasy. That seems to be what people want. In the U.S. we used to have social novels, novels of protest, films of protest, and music that told the truth about America, but we don't have them any more. Therefore, someone in Africa or Asia who looks at what comes out of Hollywood will have no sense of America at all. It is not exactly communication between the two countries. It's just that America happens to own the place where the world's fantasies are manufactured.

As to the Internet, unless the politicians get in the way of its use, the Internet is much more hopeful than television as a means of international understanding and also a means of educating the world's children. Educational computer programs, because they can be interactive—because the computer can respond to the child's questions and correct its answers and so on—are more efficient educational instruments than television shows. It seems to me that if we were doing things right, we would just abolish institutions like UNESCO, for instance, and use the money we spend on sending intellectuals to conferences toward putting Internet connections all over the world, so that computer terminals would be available in any village, any town. If that happened it would be good for political liberty, because you would know that if certain messages were not coming through any more from a certain place, the politicians had cracked down and were suppressing the population in that part of the world. The Internet really could create a global village, but I think the politicians will prevent it from doing so.

# 7

# Persuasion Is a Good Thing

This interview was conducted in Munich in May 1998 by Wolfgang Ullrich and Helmut Mayert.

*Question*: You have recently accepted an offer from Stanford University, where you will teach in the Department of Comparative Literature. Does this academic change from philosophy to literature have a more substantive, programmatic sense?

*Richard Rorty*: In Princeton, I was a professor of philosophy, but I didn't get along particularly well with my colleagues, and I thought that things might be easier if I could find a teaching position that was outside of a philosophy department. The University of Virginia, where I taught for the past fifteen years, gave me precisely what I wanted—a teaching position not linked to a department, but rather what we in the United States call a university professorship. When one holds such a professorship, one is exempt from department meetings and can teach whatever one likes.

At the University of Virginia, I ended up teaching mostly nonanalytic philosophy (Nietzsche, Heidegger, Derrida, etc.) to students of literature, and I shall be doing the same thing at Stanford. In my first year there, I shall be giving a course about Nietzsche and William James, one about Heidegger and Derrida, and another about Foucault and Habermas. That I will be in the comparative literature department rather than the philosophy department has no particular significance. Nonanalytic philosophy is, in America, more frequently taught outside of philosophy departments than within them, and that is the case at Stanford.

*Q*: You have written repeatedly that literature is, from many perspectives, more important than philosophy.

*RR*: Literature is more important for moral progress, because it contributes to the widening of the moral imagination. It makes us more sensitive by deepening our understanding of the motivations of, and of the differences among, our fellow humans. Philosophy is useful for summarizing previous moral insights in the form of moral principles, but it doesn't do much creative work. For example, philosophical reflections did not do much to eliminate slavery, but narratives about the lives the slaves were living contributed a lot.

*Q*: What were your first great experiences with literature?

*RR*: There were two sorts of books that especially impressed me: on one side socialist novels by authors like Upton Sinclair, Sinclair Lewis, James Farrell, Émile Zola, and Theodore Dreiser, and on the other, *Bildungsromane* [novels of education and moral formation], above all those of Proust and Thomas Mann.

If you think that literature is more important for moral education than philosophy, doesn't this redescription indicate a kind of demotion, as well? In your last instance, literature has been made into a mere tool, a useful means to expose exploitation or establish solidarity and identification.

I don't mean to say that the only thing literature does is to increase our sensitivity toward the needs of others. Its achievements are many, and it's impossible to make a complete list of its functions. One function, of course, is entertainment. Another is to give us the same sort of overall *Weltanschauung* as do philosophical systems; Wordsworth and Coleridge gave us something of that sort. Another is to give us the chance to make the acquaintance of very unusual people, such as Blake or Whitman.

*Q*: But you distinguish between the kind of literature that fulfills private needs—of edification and self-development—and the kind that is important for social interests.

*RR*: There is no bright line of separation between the different functions, but there is a spectrum. Zola is more likely to be placed on the public end, and Proust on the private.

*Q*: You put the poets and writers close to the engineers and technicians: both succeed, you have written, in getting us nearer the goal of the greatest possible happiness for the greatest number of people. Could you expand on this?

*RR*: Utilitarians and pragmatists like myself do not hope that human beings will become more religious or more rational. We hope instead that human beings will come to enjoy more money, more free time, and greater social equality, and also that they will develop more empathy, more ability to put themselves in the shoes of others. We hope that human beings will behave more decently toward one another as their standard of living improves.

The engineers and scientists contribute to improving our material life, while the poets and novelists help us become friendlier and more tolerant. Those are obviously not the only things that either do, but they are what constitute their respective contributions to moral progress.

In comparison, the philosophers don't have much to offer. If the source of morality were indeed what philosophers have sometimes said it was—something like what Plato called recollection of the Idea of the Good, or what Kant called the abiding presence of the moral law within our souls, then philosophers might perhaps have had something more useful to say. But the problem with such metaphysical conceptions of the origin of morality is that the voice of conscience says one thing to some people and another thing to others. Think of the religious fundamentalists who persecute members of other faiths because, they say, their conscience tells them to do so. Reflection on history and anthropology forces us to think of what Kant called the voice of conscience as an internalization of historically contingent social traditions. Once we hold that view of conscience, it is hard to see what special moral expertise philosophers are supposed to have.

The scientists and engineers who are concerned with making our lives less dangerous and threatening, like the novelists who expand our range of sympathy, do not appeal to something deep and hard-wired inside us. They just help us make ourselves us into better people, people better able to treat each other decently.

*Q*: Since you juxtapose literature and philosophy, how do you distinguish between them?

*RR*: As I see it, a philosopher is somebody who thinks and writes with constant reference, implicit or explicit, to the problems formulated by Plato and Kant. This is not a very precise definition, but I cannot give a better one. If one does not have an opinion on how to interpret these two authors, and on what they got right and what they got wrong, one does not count as a philosopher. This criterion accords with our practice of putting Nietzsche and Kierkegaard on the philosophy shelf in the library, but not Proust and Mann.

That is to say, the "pragmatic" answer is this: what relates to a determined canon of texts is defined as philosophy.

That definition at least lets one exclude a series of candidates: religious mystics, wise-cracking aphorists, megalomaniacal natural scientists who, having received the Nobel Prize, think that they are now in a position to straighten the philosophers out, and various other people who sometimes claim the title *philosopher* for themselves. My suggested definition puts nonanalytic philosophers like Odo Marquard, Hannah Arendt, and Hans-Georg Gadamer in the same box with analytic philosophers like John Rawls, Peter Strawson, and Donald Davidson. All these people read Plato and Kant at some point in their lives, and developed an interest in the questions these books presented to them. Anybody who can't make sense of what Plato said about the Forms or what Kant said about the distinction between phenomena and noumena will not be much interested in the writings of the six contemporary thinkers whom I just mentioned. Even antimetaphysical analytic philosophers like Russell and Carnap began where Gadamer and Arendt did. Nobody would bother to conduct a campaign against metaphysics if Plato and Kant had not, at some point, intrigued them.

*Q*: You once wrote that Western culture would lose its uniqueness if the polemic between literature and philosophy were to come to an end. Would this be a loss?

*RR*: My thought was that at the center of philosophy there is an effort to find an order among the things that are already familiar to us, whereas literature provides us with new things. Seen in this way, philosophy aspires to beauty, to agreeable and harmonious arrangements of already known entities. Literature, instead, strives toward the sublime. It wants to say things never said before. The tension between philosophy and literature is the tension between the known and the unknown.

The litterateurs have, for example, expanded our language using metaphors that later on became established in usage. Insofar as philosophers pride themselves on clarity, and forbid themselves the use of metaphor, they are necessarily conservative. The philosophers pride themselves on skill in argumentation, but the poets suspect that philosophical arguments merely rearrange what is already on the table, whereas the poets themselves put something new on the table.

*Q*: Do arguments also possess aesthetic qualities for you?

*RR*: I imagine that Plato was the sort or person for whom a proof in Euclidean geometry is an authentic source of aesthetic pleasure. He, like all philosophers who take delight in constructing complex and convincing arguments, practiced a form of art. Romantic poets practice another form of art. The two complement one another nicely.

*Q*: Is this the sense in which many mathematicians speak of the beauty of equations?

*RR*: Yes. We also speak of the beauty of Newton's unification of the movements of the planets and the movements of projectiles. We say that the discovery of DNA offers us a "beautiful" way to explain processes of biological evolution. The sublime, by contrast, neither integrates nor unifies. It transcends.

*Q*: Then in what sense are arguments "merely" rhetorical?

*RR*: Some philosophers see an important difference between logic and rhetoric, or between "convincing" and "persuading." I do not. There is of course a difference between good and bad arguments, but this is a matter of the audience to which the argument is directed. An argument is good only for a public that accepts its premises. There is also a difference between arguments put forward sincerely and arguments put forward even though the propounder does not herself find them convincing. And, of course, there's a distinction between deductive arguments that are formally valid and those that are not. But, given those three distinctions, we do not need an additional distinction between logic and rhetoric.

*Q*: Your distinction between poetry and philosophy represents a type of division of labor within culture. The poets expand our vocabularies and ways of seeing in previously unforeseeable ways, and the others—among them the philosophers—have to take care of returning to order.

*RR*: Yes. When we say, for instance, that Plato and Hegel are more poetic than Aristotle and Leibniz, we mean that they were more willing to use words in ways in which they had never before been used. They re-shaped the old language to make it fit the new uses they had in mind. (Think of the metaphorical use that Plato made of the word *idea*, or of Hegel's use of *concept*.) Aristotle is less metaphorical, and thus closer to common sense. Plato's metaphors gave us a whole new game to play, but Aristotle mostly just moved the old pieces around.

*Q*: In your great appreciation of poetry and literature, is there also a bit of the old jealousy of philosophers?

*RR*: I envy the poets, just as analytic philosophers like Quine envy natural scientists. One of the differences between analytic and nonanalytic philosophy has to do with the object of the philosopher's envy. I cannot imagine being envious of a physicist or a mathematician, any more than of an accountant or a lawyer—no matter how talented or how socially useful. I am not sure that Quine could have imagined being envious of a Blake or a Rilke.

*Q*: This brings us to Harold Bloom, to whom you make reference often, and to the description that he gives of the "strong poet" (the influen-tial, original poet). For Bloom, the poets rise to heroic heights by distanc-ing themselves from, and asserting themselves against, tradition.

*RR*: I find Bloom's claim that poets attempt to overcome their pre-decessors in the same the way that adolescents attempt to supersede their parents very persuasive.

*Q*: Is Bloom's whole dramatic scenario necessary to have arrived at this fairly modest conclusion?

*RR*: Perhaps Bloom dramatizes too much, but I think that his way of thinking is illuminating in regard to both poetic and philosophical prog-ress. Blake wants to use Milton, but he also wants to go beyond him. Marx wants to use Hegel, but he also wants to supersede him. Davidson asks himself: "How can we clarify Quine's premises in such a way that we can go beyond Quine's conclusions?" Everyone wants to surpass the teacher from whom they learned most, just as sons want to surpass beloved fathers.

*Q*: How can we relate the idea of the heroic poet with the liberal ironic figure whose model we ought to emulate?

*RR*: In my book *Contingency, Irony, and Solidarity*, I defined *irony* as recognition of the contingency of one's "final vocabulary."[1] This is simply consciousness of the fact that the deepest convictions one holds are the result of past poetic and creative achievements. This goes along with the recognition that there never will be a final poem. There will always be space for self-creation, because no previous act of self-creation can be ratified as final by some nonhuman authority.

When it comes to philosophy, however, it doesn't always make sense to call the supersession of one poem by another a victory. Sometimes, within philosophical traditions, problems aren't solved—they, along with the ways in which we formulate them, are simply forgotten. In Nietzsche's words, "Philosophical problems are not solved, they become frozen."

Nietzsche is completely right. Russell made the same point when he said that nobody had refuted Bergson, but everybody had become bored with him. Philosophical problems are transitory, as are the vocabularies with which they are formulated. For this reason, there will always be a tension between the clarity of the old languages and the crudeness and roughness of new suggestions about how we might speak.

*Q*: There is, therefore, no *philosophia perennis*. But couldn't one claim that there are certain philosophical problems that should not be forgotten—not because one insists on finding an ultimate "solution," but instead because there is value in their elaboration and because of the potential for refinement of our modes of description?

*RR*: One can describe very abstract problems, such as "the One and the many," and maintain that they have always been discussed and always will be. But no philosopher really works at such a high level of abstraction. So I doubt that it is fruitful to claim that we possess methods more refined than those of the Greeks for resolving the problems they discussed. Still, it doesn't matter much whether we say that the problems discussed by Plato

1. Richard Rorty, *Contingency, Irony, and Solidarity* (Cambridge: Cambridge University Press, 1989), 74–75.

and Aristotle are the same as those discussed by Wittgenstein. There are many similarities and many differences.

*Q*: To return to the ironist: he is defined by his prudence and modesty, but on the other hand, you speak with great emotion of the heroes of poetry. How do these hang together?

*RR*: We who are not heroes are made modest by the presence of the heroic. Hegel, Wordsworth, Blake, and Schiller are heroic figures. They renewed and transformed our vocabularies and our thinking. Each new generation ought to acknowledge the greatness of such figures, and aspire to follow their example, even while knowing that the vast majority of such attempts will be futile, and perhaps even ludicrous.

To speak of heroes is surely a problem for Germans. The word is burdened.

After Hitler there was an entirely natural tendency to say: enough with the veneration of heroes, let us return to reason. But the fact that a country once venerated a mad tyrant is not a reason to renounce hero worship, It would be absurd if, because of Hitler, the Germans stopped venerating the heroes of German social democracy.

*Q*: Does rational discourse consist merely in making existing argumentative moves back and forth, in using dead metaphors? Does it never give rise to something new?

*RR*: As Hegel saw, this back and forth movement is a source of moral and intellectual progress. Some of our heroes (Václav Havel, Martin Luther King) are heroic because they spoke the simple truth to a public that was trying to deceive itself. But others are heroic because they expanded our imagination, our consciousness of what might be possible. Nietzsche and Marx are heroes of this second sort. Progress needs both types of heroes.

*Q*: Here in Germany, the heroic and the sublime—when used politically—are looked at with distrust . . .

*RR*: I can understand why people distrust the sublime. Politics should not strive after the sublime. Lyotard was wrong to criticize Habermas for thinking that politics cannot be sublime, but merely beautiful. In politics what is usually needed is compromise, clever utilization of the tools at hand. A compromise can be beautiful, but not sublime.

However, can one really distinguish sharply between private preferences for the sublime and public, political instrumentalization?

It seems to me that we constantly distinguish between private sublimity and public beauty. Believers do this when they distinguish between their relation to God and their dealings with their fellow human beings. The private piety of a Catholic legislator is directed toward something that goes beyond mere beauty. But as a politician working within a democratic system, she has to be content with compromises—possibly beautiful ones.

Rawls said that we learned from the wars of religion the importance of separating private visions of the good from public affairs. It took us a long time to grasp that people from different religions, or with different opinions about the meaning of life, can be loyal citizens of the same nation-state. The Romantic suggestion that we see religion as a form of poetry helped us see that a democratic society can and should tolerate people who make up their own religions—as Blake and Joseph Smith (the founder of Mormonism) did.

Kant took off from the idea that the sublime can awaken a consciousness of the ideal of reason and that, in this way, it actualizes uniqueness—and demonstrates the greatness of man before nature. This actualization of the idea of reason can also create a type of solidarity among men, a consciousness of the human species as a whole: all human beings are united with one another through their reason.

Kant's idea of justifying human solidarity by reference to "pure ideas of reason" was a good try. But I don't believe it worked. It was no more plausible or implausible, no more useful or useless, than the attempt to justify human solidarity by saying that we are all children of the same divine father. This also didn't work. Neither attempt contributed much to the elimination of the cruelty with which human communities treat one another.

Something that has actually worked, instead, is identification across boundaries by imaginative projection—by coming to acknowledge that the members of a despised group are very much like the members of one's own. *Uncle Tom's Cabin* worked fairly well, and so did stories by Alan Paton and plays by Athol Fugard about the lives of blacks under the apartheid regime in South Africa. If we really believed that all human beings are brothers, or that they are tied together by the pure ideas of reason, then we wouldn't allow the poor to suffer as much as we do. The rich sometimes help the poor, not because of abstract philosophical or religious convictions about human solidarity, but because the rich sometimes feel sufficiently secure to be able to share part of their wealth, and because they have enough imagination to grasp what it is like to be poor.

In other words, it is not a matter of finding something that is common to all, but of understanding that existing differences (among blacks and whites, heterosexual and homosexuals) are less important than we used to think. An increased acknowledgment of this unimportance is not the result of having heard better philosophical arguments.

*Q:* But can't religious convictions at least contribute to bringing us closer to the goal of reducing cruelty against other human beings?

*RR:* Sometimes religious convictions have decreased cruelty, but sometimes they have increased it. Think of the attitude of the Dutch Reformed Church in South Africa toward blacks, or of the Southern Baptist Conference in the United States toward homosexuals and feminists.

For example, marriages between members of different communities are essential to break down the kind of distrust that leads to cruelty. But religious organizations have typically vehemently opposed such marriages.

Solidarity among humans can be strengthened through religious convictions, as it was in the civil rights movement in the United States, but it can also be weakened by such convictions. Religious convictions, like philosophical doctrines, are tools that can be used either to include or to exclude.

*Q:* Let us return to your conception of philosophy. Does the reading of philosophical texts have therapeutic effects for you? What does knowledge of the philosophical tradition, and in particular of analytic philosophy, contribute?

*RR:* Philosophy can have as diverse effects as literature. It can inspire or depress, excite or bore, encourage or discourage. Some people find analytic philosophy inspiring and encouraging, especially Europeans who are recovering from overdoses of Lacan or of Heidegger.

As I see it, analytic philosophy does not possess any special historical importance or significance. Some analytic philosophers (for example, Donald Davidson, Daniel Dennett, Annette Baier, Robert Brandom) have made intellectual advances. But the fact that, in the Anglo-Saxon countries, philosophy is almost exclusively analytic has done some harm— mainly by causing philosophy students to neglect the history of philosophy and therefore to take too seriously the problems discussed in current journal literature.

Students who study analytic philosophy typically do not spend enough time asking where those problems come from. Had they spent more time studying the transition from Kant to Hegel, for example, they might be more inclined to be suspicious. Their education is such that, unlike students in Germany, they are not invited to perform for themselves the movement from Kant to Hegel—the movement that leads from the thought that all human beings will always be hard-wired with the same conceptual repertoire to the thought that concepts are born and die in the course of history.

Analytic philosophy took two steps backward and then three forward. Wittgenstein's *Tractatus* was a step backward, but his *Philosophical Investigations* was a triumphant overcoming of himself. Carnap represented a fall backward into an antiquated form of philosophical atomism, but the radical holism of Quine and Davidson provided vigorous and useful reformulations of the old arguments against atomism.

*Q:* Wittgenstein defended the idea of a therapeutic function of philosophy.

*RR:* The later Wittgenstein helped analytic philosophers to understand that many of Locke's and Kant's problems did not have to be taken seriously. But Hegel and Nietzsche had reached that conclusion long before. The neglect of Hegel and Nietzsche in Anglophone philosophy circles contributed to the fact that Wittgenstein appeared more important and original than he was. In other countries, philosophy was able to distance itself from Kant sooner than philosophy in the Anglo-Saxon world did. The English-speaking philosophers let themselves be distracted for a long time by the linguistified version of Kantianism that was dreamed up by Russell, Carnap, A. J. Ayer, and C. I. Lewis in the twenties and thirties.

For Anglophone philosophers, these people were as bad as Husserl was for their Continental counterparts. But the young Heidegger, Sartre, and others made it possible for French and German philosophy to shake off its debt to Husserl relatively quickly. English-speaking philosophers, alas, kept right on boring each other with discussions of sense data. Even today, Anglo-Saxon philosophy is only slowly linking up with the rest of the philosophical world. Anglophone philosophers need more therapy than their colleagues in other parts.

*Q*: You've written a lot about American pragmatism and a lot about Heidegger and Davidson, but don't tend to write much in detail about Wittgenstein. Why?

*RR*: I've written a few papers on Wittgenstein. In my opinion, he can be read in two ways. One can say that the late Wittgenstein liberated us from the harmful quasi Kantianism of people like Russell, Carnap, and Wittgenstein's own early self. Alternatively, one could argue that that he did something much more important, something less historically limited, something like modifying our understanding of philosophy itself. Stanley Cavell prefers this second reading. I prefer the first.

*Q*: But how can you define the later Wittgenstein only in terms of the metaphysics of the *Tractatus*, when he also spoke more generally of the therapeutic functions of philosophy?

*RR*: The later Wittgenstein offers effective therapy for people who are trapped in a specific complex of ideas. But imagine saying to Gadamer, "Hey, listen, you ought to try some of this fantastic new Wittgensteinian therapy! He can show you how one might escape from the fly bottle in which you are buzzing about." That would be pointless, because Gadamer never got into that bottle. There's nothing that Wittgenstein could have taught him. He had never let himself be held captive by the images that kept the young Wittgenstein prisoner.

*Q*: One could formulate it in this way: everything one might need from Wittgenstein can also be found in the more "superficial" Ryle? When his book *Concept of Mind* was published, Wittgenstein supposedly said that the way in which Ryle treated problems made them "lose their magic."

*RR*: That's more or less the situation. When one is persuaded by Ryle (or O. K. Bouwsma or Wilfrid Sellars), one no longer needs the great- er part of the treatment that one undergoes in reading *Philosophical Investi-*

*gations.* I could have written my book *Philosophy and the Mirror of Nature* without having read any Wittgenstein; I could have gotten everything that I needed from Ryle and Sellars. I am grateful to Wittgenstein for many reasons, but I just don't consider him a titanic figure. I think of Wittgenstein as one of those thinkers that did something that Dewey, Bergson, the early Heidegger, and many others also did: he helped us distance ourselves from Descartes, Locke, and Kant.

*Q*: But doesn't philosophical therapy have its own point of departure? The idea is that so-called "common sense" shows itself to be just more metaphysics when you push the issue far enough.

*RR*: What Wittgenstein showed, it seems to me, was that "common sense" is nothing more than the web of linguistic practices common to a certain community. These practices are constantly being modified. When you set something called "common sense" against something else called "philosophy," you're not opposing reality to metaphysical illusion. Rather, you are raising the questions: Do these philosophers do anything really useful? Do they accomplish anything positive for our self-image or our practices? When Thomas Reid appealed to "common sense" against Hume, or when J. L. Austin made the same move against A. J. Ayer, they were really just asking: who needs that stuff?

The idea that "common sense" embodies some fundamental truth is as wrong as the idea that philosophical systems do. It is . . .

*Q*: Only a *façon de parler*?

*RR*: Yes. Consider, for example, the claims that "common sense" affirms both free will and determinism, thus showing itself to be inconsistent. That claim is, as Hume pointed out, ridiculous. Obviously, one can construct an opposition between the two, but this requires philosophical acuity. "Common sense" doesn't conceal philosophical problems or contradictions within itself, but it does provide the material out of which a Leibniz or a Sartre or a Descartes can construct such problems.

*Q*: Do you think that engaging with the classic problems of the philosophical canon has any value at all?

*RR*: Well, philosophy students cut their dialectical teeth discussing the tension between free will and determinism, or the question of the existence of the material world. But these problems should be treated as pedagogical devices, not as serious issues. The students have to read books like Descartes' *Meditations*—but not because Descartes raised good questions.

*Q*: But why should they read these books?

*RR*: If they don't read these books they run the risk that they themselves will write them. There's a famous remark by George Santayana: those who do not study the past are condemned to repeat it. The more influential old books one reads, the more prudent one becomes, because the sources and histories of contemporary ideas become clearer. There's a difference between reading these books with the hope of finding profound truths, and reading to figure which fly bottles to stay out of.

*Q*: And this is how one becomes a liberal ironist?

*RR*: Exactly. Part of being an adult means understanding that no book will reveal to us the secret of the universe or the meaning of life. It means realizing that all of these wonderful old books are only rungs on a ladder that, with a bit of luck, one day we may be able to do without. If we stopped reading the canonical philosophy books, we would be less aware of the forces that make us think and talk as we do. We would be less able to grasp our contingency, less capable of being "ironists," in the sense in which I use the expression.

*Q*: How can we distinguish between more important and less important books, if all we're doing is playing descriptions off of one another?

*RR*: There is a process of natural selection. People return again and again to Plato, the Bible, Cervantes, Goethe, Hegel, and Proust, regardless of how many other books they've read. Professors speak in class about books they love, and they hope their students will come to love them, as well. Over time, however, some books begin to decay, while others continue to flourish. Cultural evolution is like biological evolution: no one can really predict the paths either will take, but it can be very exciting to observe the process. If you're still looking for something other than the play of reciprocally countervailing descriptions, you're still hoping for what religion and philosophy have traditionally attempted to provide: a fixed point in a changing world, an unmovable pivot. But, since Hegel and Darwin, we tend to have become more content to do without such a pivot.

*Q*: So one can make a student into an ironist?

*RR*: The more history—especially history of ideas—that one reads, the more the sense of one's own contingency increases.

*Q*: What's the most important virtue of the ironist?

*RR*: Tolerance.

*Q*: Not flexibility? Because of his exposure to different vocabularies, your ironist might react more successfully to new situations.

*RR*: Okay, let's say that tolerance is the ironist's main social virtue, and flexibility her main private virtue. Tolerance has to do with people who are different. Flexibility has to do with the ability to redescribe oneself. Nietzsche and Proust were specialists in doing the latter.

*Q*: Do you think you can put the "ironist" next to the "sages" of ancient philosophy, especially the Pyrrhonist skeptics? For in their cases, it was also a matter of playing one position against another; in the end, there was no attempt to knock oneself out trying to attain truth. With them, there were also no privileged descriptions or foundational convictions.

*RR*: The difference between the ancients and us consists in the fact that we—except for those attracted by Zen Buddhism—no longer aspire to tranquility, or ataraxia. What's important for us is to be able to re-create ourselves. The ancients believed that the women and men of the future would not be essentially different from the women and men they knew. We, however, hope that our distant descendants will be very different from us. It seems to me that Hans Blumenberg is entirely right when he says that the moderns have adopted a posture toward the future that would have been impossible in ancient times.

We could, of course, think of the Pyrrhonist skeptics as protopragmatists: philosophers who thought of everything as a means to human happiness. If they are seen that way, then of course I find them sympathetic. But nowadays we know about kinds of happiness that they could never have envisaged.

*Q*: But you also maintain that the self-image of the ironist should only be recommended to intellectuals. Why?

*RR*: We call certain people "intellectuals" because they have the brains and the guts to keep their self-image flexible. This is not particularly easy to do, and not many people can accomplish it. The difference between intellectuals and the masses is the difference between those who can remember and use different vocabularies at the same time, and those who can remember only one.

*Q*: So the intellectuals are the vanguard and, little by little, some of their accomplishments trickle down to everyone else?

*RR*: Sometimes moral progress takes the form of a downward descent from the intellectuals to the masses. But sometimes the masses themselves are the vanguard.

I can think of two contrasting examples. After the abolition of slavery, white intellectuals in the U.S. think much about blacks. So, a hundred years later, guided by their religious leaders (who, for the most part, were not intellectuals), the blacks themselves rose up and initiated the civil rights movement, the single best thing that happened in the United States during the twentieth century. Although white intellectuals supported the civil rights movement, it mostly worked from the bottom up, as had the labor union movement a generation earlier. The black masses showed greater courage and initiative than the while intellectuals ever did.

The gay rights struggle, on the other hand, was mostly a top-down movement. Poor and uneducated gays couldn't affirm their homosexual identities—and couldn't speak out about being mistreated—without losing their jobs. For these reasons, virtually all the activism came from the top. The demand for the repeal of the antisodomy laws and for recognition of marriages between homosexuals, for example, came out of the universities, and worked its way down to the college-educated middle class.

*Q*: What is the relationship between the progress of democracy, on one hand, and the reduction of cruelty, on the other?

*RR*: What's important about a representative democratic government is that it gives the poor and weak a tool they can use against the rich and powerful, especially against the unconscious cruelty of the institutions that the powerful have imposed upon the weak. A democracy is distinguished not only by its form of government, but also by the presence of institutions such as a free press, free universities, and an independent judiciary. These institutions help the nation come to grasp the existence of previously unrecognized forms of cruelty and suffering: the cruelty of whites against blacks, for example, or the suffering of gays. In a fully democratic society, unnecessary suffering would not exist.

When you demur to claims about the rights and duties of "the" human being, you usually counter that we should only speak of species in a Darwinian, biological sense. This seems a good, pragmatic, deflationary strategy. In the fields of evolution and sociobiology, however, scientists tend to use a Darwinian vocabulary that is more normative and programmatic.

The sociobiologists seem to think that, thanks to their scientific expertise, they can predict the results of certain social experiments. But nothing so far indicates that they are really able to do so, or will ever be able to do so. Sociobiological theories have given us no reason to doubt that humans are as flexible as history and anthropology suggest they are. It seems to me that biology can tell us something about our hardware, but nothing about software. An infinite multiplicity of programs can run on the same hardware, and the same species can dream up an infinite diversity of cultures.

There is an intermediate region between human beings as creatures with one foot in a higher, immaterial, world and human beings as animals seeking to pass on their genes as efficiently as possible. This intermediate region is where culture dictates behavior. Culture is a "mere" human creation, but it can change human life in entirely unexpected and wonderful ways.

*Q*: The first chapter of all of those sociobiological tracts always offer a ritualistic dismissal of Descartes.

*RR*: The sociobiologists are proud of refuting Descartes, but after Hume, Wittgenstein, and Ryle there's no need for more refutations.

*Q*: This Descartes-bashing seems to have a different thrust. The Darwinian description of humanity is no longer the old "materialist" party line, but is instead recommended—in many popular-science books—as *the* basic "scientific" vocabulary, that is, the vocabulary best suited to the world and ourselves.

*RR*: If the kind of irony I'm talking about is good for anything, it is as a remedy against the idea that natural science, theology, or philosophy will one day be able to offer the only true and real description of the essence of humanity. It seems to me absurd to think that the biologists can tell us more about human beings than the anthropologists, historians, or poets. There are hundreds of useful descriptions of what a human being is, and none of them can or should be privileged as "the scientific image of the human being" or "the philosophical image of the human being." But the broader public tends to be deceived by people who present their favored images as rigorously "scientific."

Public opinion, unfortunately, has become receptive to the absurd idea that specific political measures have a "scientific" or "philosophical" basis. Some representatives of the political right, for example, employ sociobiology as an argument against the welfare state.

*Q*: The cognitive and neuroscientists, like the sociobiologists we've been discussing, encourage a similar, naturalistic vocabulary for our self-descriptive purposes. Faced with these situations, how does one act "therapeutically"?

*RR*: In my opinion, this is precisely the role that pragmatic philosophy should play: it should insist that neither reality nor humanity have a "nature" or "essence." In a pragmatic culture—in which everyone assumes that there are many descriptions of the same entity, and that different descriptions are useful for different ends, but none of them is the only true description—it would be implausible to bring in either the Bible or sociobiology when debating social policy.

The so-called postmodern critique of what Derrida refers to as the "metaphysics of presence" might be politically useful in this way. Western "common sense" continues to be infected by the Greek presumption that things have an essence, and that if we could know the essence of humanity—what men and women are in reality—we would finally know exactly what to do with ourselves. Pragmatists would like to get rid of this Greek idea.

In a pragmatist culture, one would no more use a scientific vocabulary in a moral or political discussion than one would a religious vocabulary.

*Q*: Do you think that this sort of pragmatic culture is possible?

*RR*: The idea that Western "common sense" can become pragmatic is no less plausible, right now, than was the proposal to secularize the education of schoolchildren two hundred years ago. That proposal caused a great deal of initial anger, but it was eventually put into practice. It brought about an enormous cultural displacement, but it was accomplished. If we can achieve a cultural displacement of this magnitude over the next two centuries, we may be able to replace essentialism with pragmatism.

*Q*: But wouldn't such a world stifle motivation? There wouldn't be the same impetus to theorize.

*RR*: Theories develop as solutions to problems; they are not the result of what Aristotle called "astonishment." We will never run out of problems, and thus we'll never run out of theories. The only theories that would cease to exist in a pragmatist culture would be beautiful but empty syntheses, syntheses without practical import, of the sort E. O. Wilson develops in his book *Consilience*.[2]

*Q*: Such theories might be too arrogant and sweeping, but can't they still be valuable? We can scrap the whole superstructure and mine the salvageable elements. Wouldn't it be some kind of loss if there were no more such theories?

*RR*: Wilfred Sellars once said that philosophy is "the attempt to explain 'things,' in the broadest sense possible of the word, in such a way that they 'hang together,' in the broadest sense of the word." There will always be "encompassing theories" of this type, because, to quote Hegel, there will always be new attempts to "capture one's own time in thought." But we need to distinguish between laudable attempts to draw the map of a culture during a specific time in a specific place (for instance, European culture in the twentieth century) and overambitious scientific and theological attempts to outguess history.

Attempts of the first type are often fruitful; for example, those by Weber, Heidegger, Dewey, Habermas, and Vattimo. But attempts of the second type will never get us anywhere. The promise that we might view the history of humanity from some higher, suprahistorical perspective will never be fulfilled.

Historicism and pragmatism go together. To capture one's own time in thought means to try to find a description of what is taking place here

2. E. O. Wilson, *Consilience: The Unity of Knowledge* (New York: Knopf, 1998).

and now, a description that might help us figure out how to make the future different from the past.

Q: Economists have gained considerable influence in recent years. You have spoken, in the past, of the marketplace of ideas. Does it bother you when such formulations are used out of context, especially to advance a neoliberal agenda?

RR: The free market of ideas and commodities is, all things being equal, a fine thing. But it does not provide a solution to all of our social problems, as the neoliberals pretend. These days, the political right in the United States is trying to claim that any redistribution of wealth represents a disruptive intervention in the freedom of the market, But the free market is not an end in itself. It is just one means among others to further the development of a utopian democratic society.

Q: What exactly do you mean when you call the university a "marketplace of ideas"?

RR: The university is a place where young people can discuss competing suggestions about how to capture our time in thought—thereby fostering debate about the changes that the rising generation ought to attempt to bring about. This social function is more important than the official task of the university: the pursuit of knowledge. That formulation is dubious, because it is frequently used to support the suggestion that the natural sciences should be the model for all academic disciplines.

Even if scientific research were taken out of the university and conducted in separate institutes, we would still need universities in order to form the moral consciousness of the new generation. The potential for moral progress is what is at stake in the study of sociology, history, literature, political science, and philosophy.

Q: In a lecture you recently gave in Vienna, you spoke of the gulf between European and analytic philosophy. Do you see any signs of reconciliation?

RR: Not many. The problem is that most nonanalytic philosophers work on the great dead philosophers, whereas contemporary analytic philosophy centers around discussion of the latest journal articles. Students in the two different traditions have very different images of themselves.

In Europe, a student of philosophy will also read a lot of history and literature. In the U.S. they may, but many of them do not. There it is still believed that symbolic logic is more important for students of philosophy than knowledge of a foreign language. The idea that philosophy forms part of humanistic culture is foreign to the majority of analytic philosophers.

In the United States, only a few professors in other disciplines have any sense of what is going on their university's philosophy department. In Europe, the other professors often take at least a polite interest in philosophical issues.

*Q*: But don't the professors of natural science have some idea about what's going on in philosophy departments?

*RR*: No. The typical physics or biology professor knows only that there are terrible people like Thomas Kuhn who have claimed that science will never find out the true and real essence of things. This thesis strikes them as shocking and repugnant, so they complain of what they call "postmodern relativism." But few of them bother to read Kuhn, or to follow the arguments going on in post-Kuhnian philosophy of science.

Analytic philosophy was, from the very beginning, conceived as a project that would make philosophy into a science. Philosophers, the founders of analytic philosophy thought, should be housed under the same roof with the physicists and the biologists, not the literature professors. But the natural scientists didn't particularly want to share their roof with anyone. They couldn't imagine that analytic philosophy had anything to contribute to their work. As a result, analytic philosophy has become a hermetic, self-enclosed institution, with few connections to the broader academic world. Analytic philosophers such as Davidson and Brandom do brilliant work, but no one outside their discipline has any idea of what they are up to.

The professors of literature, the historians, and the sociologists read Foucault, rather than Rawls or Davidson. For the most part, they know as little about analytic philosophy as do the professors of physics and biology.

*Q*: This theme also plays an important role in your recent book *Achieving Our Country: Leftist Thought in Twentieth-Century America.* Could you sketch a brief summary of that argument?

*RR*: *Achieving Our Country* argues that the United States once had a genuine social-democratic left, which existed between 1910 and 1965. Union organizers and intellectuals did a lot to shape the program of the Democratic Party in that period. This left was successful in many areas: they were responsible for Roosevelt's New Deal, and they had a lot to do with the social changes that Lyndon B. Johnson grouped under the watchword "the Great Society." By 1965, the United States had achieved something like a functioning welfare state. The rich could no longer do whatever they wanted.

This left collapsed during the late sixties under the burden of the conflagrations surrounding the Vietnam War. The generation of the so-called new left broke off from the older, reformist left and came to the cynical conclusion that the only thing that could possibly work would be a complete dismantling of the "system." All of a sudden, we had a revolutionary left, a left that took Marx seriously in a way that the older social democratic left rarely had.

After the failure of that revolution, and Nixon's subsequent victory over George McGovern in the election of 1972—a victory made possible by blue-collar voters who were disgusted by the antics of the new left—the belief spread throughout the student left that the country was a lost cause. Many people who belonged to this left went on to become university professors. They began to read Foucault, and created a cynical Foucauldian left—a left that profoundly distrusted bourgeois social-democratic politics but had nothing better to suggest.

Irving Howe, the editor of *Dissent*—our most useful and important leftist journal—once said of the Foucauldian left that "these people do not want to take charge of the government, only of the English department." They succeeded in accomplishing this latter goal, and an important and influential part of the university thus became a zone reserved for political activism. That activism, however, was more concerned with questions of race and gender than with questions of class.

Since the sixties, this left has done a lot for the rights of blacks, women, and gays. But it never attempted to develop a political position that might find the support of an electoral majority. It never attempted to practice a politics which could help elect a presidential candidate. It neglected economic questions when these were unrelated to racial issues or gender differences.

This left is not patriotic, and it distinguishes itself vehemently from the strongly patriotic left of the Progressive Era and of the New Deal. In my book, I argue that we should revive the older kind of leftist politics, the kind we had prior to the sixties. In my opinion, the academic left of the last few decades has exhausted its potential. The theme of growing economic insecurity (which everyone in the United States perceives, except the richest fourth of the population) has been left to be exploited by right-wing demagogues, people like Pat Buchanan. The time has come for the renaissance of an old social democratic politics, the one that produced the New Deal.

Q: So it's a book about the possibilities of civic engagement, and the future of the American left. To what extent does it take up philosophical themes?

RR: The book doesn't deal with philosophy at all. It's just a political polemic. The book's only connection to pragmatism is that John Dewey was one of the leaders of the older left.

*Translated by Eduardo Mendieta*
*and Gideon Lewis-Krauss*

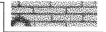

# 8

# On Philosophy and Politics

*Interview by Chronis Polychroniou*

*Question:* Professor Rorty, you have written an extraordinary amount of highly acclaimed and truly innovative material on philosophy, politics, and culture—and, quite frequently, all aimed at a wide audience. Yet many people, from both left and right, to use the traditional dichotomy, have been arguing for years that there is seemingly no easy way to define the essence of the view you hold. Do you take seriously such criticisms?

*Richard Rorty:* I do not think there is any need for one's views to have an essence. All that such an essence could amount to would be a set of propositions from which all his or her views on all subjects could be deduced. But the assumption that people think by deducing consequences from axioms has only to be stated to be rejected.

Philosophy professors are sometimes expected to have a system. But a philosophical system, like a scientific theory, is simply a bunch of propositions that reciprocally justify and buttress one another. I do indeed have a system when it comes to such topics as truth, knowledge, meaning, and the like. But just as scientists rarely try to integrate their theories about topics within their own specialized field with their political views or their cultural outlook, so there is no need for a philosopher to try to synthesize his views on topics falling within his professional competence with his views on other matters. My philosophical views are obviously compatible with any of a whole spectrum of political outlooks.

*Q*: Would it be a correct interpretation to say that what the right finds objectionable are your philosophical views while the left objects to your political views, or is this a simplification of the controversy your views have created among the philosophical and political community in the United States but also elsewhere?

*RR*: People on the political right often say that we must have "absolute moral values" or that "morality without religion is impossible." Such a philosophical or religious outlook is not necessitated by right-wing political positions, which can be defended quite nicely on merely utilitarian and pragmatic grounds (and often are). But those rightists who like to view themselves as the guardians of rationality and truth characterize pragmatists like Dewey, and followers of Dewey like myself, as undermining traditional values and frivolously corrupting the youth by teaching what they call "irrationalist relativism." We pragmatists are supposed to hold that "anybody's values are as good as anybody else's."

I have never met anyone who actually held this latter view. Indeed, it is hard to imagine how such a view could be put into practice—how it could ever be more than an empty form of words. For nobody can act without implicitly adopting some values rather than others.

What pragmatists do say is that our values—the values, for example, of social democrats like myself, or of right-wing opponents of the welfare state—are not capable of being "grounded" in something like the will of God or Plato's Idea of the Good. Pragmatists think that attempts to back up considered political judgments about what should be done with appeals to religious or philosophical facts are pointless gestures. This is because the appeals are at least as controversial as the original judgments. Everybody is able to concoct a religion or a metaphysics that suits his antecedent moral or political views. But why bother?

People on the political left (except for the few remaining orthodox Marxists) do not mind my philosophical views much. But they are often disappointed by my politics, since they see the lack of social justice in modern societies as something that can only be remedied by vast structural changes, on the scale of "the end of capitalism." I think that this lack can be remedied, if at all, by a series of incremental reforms. So I am what the Marxists used to call a "bourgeois liberal," of the same species as John Stuart Mill and John Dewey. My bourgeois liberalism does not rest on any

philosophical convictions, but simply on reflections on the relative suc-
cesses of revolutionary and reformist movements over the course of the
past century.

*Q*: Let's begin with your philosophical perspectives. I propose that I
list a philosopher's name or a philosophical phrase and then you respond.
Perhaps within the context of the analysis you provide to the epistemological essence and relevance of those philosophical names or traditions from
your standpoint of view, readers will find the "journey" into Rorty's world
of ideas a bit more flexible in comprehension. Doing it this way we might
also be able to do away with the criticism (which I think was launched
against you once) that Rorty does not lay all his cards on the table. Do you
agree with this procedure?

*RR*: I'd be glad to comment on individual philosophers. I agree that
this is a useful way of helping people to locate my views in philosophical
space.

### Plato—or, More Specifically, Platonic Dualisms

Plato is a many-sided figure. I have trouble putting the sides together.
I cannot figure out how the same man could have written the *Symposium*,
the *Laws*, and the *Timaeus*. But I agree with Nietzsche's and Heidegger's
account of the impact of Plato on the Western intellectual tradition. This
impact consists in his making certain dualisms—appearance versus reality,
contingent versus necessary, material versus immaterial, sensible versus in-
telligible, and the like—seem natural to countless generations of thinkers.

Dewey and Heidegger both hoped to make us suspicious of these dualisms, and to try to do our thinking without relying on them. One can appeal to both of these men in order to defend Socrates' interlocutors (such
as *Euthyphro* and *Meno*) against Socrates. Such a defense argues that there
is no reason to think that terms like *virtue* and *knowledge* are going to have
definitions, or that these words name entities that philosophers might find
out more about. Socratic criticism of received wisdom is of course a good
thing, because reflection on alternatives is always a good thing. But such
criticism does not require the Platonic assumption that abstract nouns sig-
nify essences which philosophical inquiry can enable us to represent more
accurately.

### The Enlightenment Project and "Reason"

There were at least two Enlightenment projects. One was to get the priests and the kings off the back of the people, and, more generally, to prevent the powerful and rich from stealing from the poor and weak. There was nothing new in this project. It was just the Christian message of brotherhood all over again.

The other project was to replace artifice and prejudice with more "natural" and "rational" social arrangements and shared convictions. Call this project "Enlightenment rationalism" as distinct from "Enlightenment egalitarianism." I don't see much point in saying that a more egalitarian and just society would be more natural or more rational than the ones we have now. It would simply be one in which there was less unnecessary human suffering. If we occupy ourselves with practical measures to decrease suffering, we can safely forget about whether we are bringing man back to his true nature, or whether the institutions we establish are "dictated by reason."

### Hegel

If Hegel is read not an a metaphysician who says that reality is spiritual in nature, but instead as a naturalistic historicist who says that the test of a knowledge claim or a cultural institution is its social utility rather than its correspondence to the intrinsic nature of reality, then his work can be seen as a turning point in the history of philosophy. There is a way of reading Hegel—coming into popularity thanks to the work of the late Klaus Hartman in Germany and of Terry Pinkard, Robert Pippin, and Robert Brandom in the United States—that emphasizes his similarities with Dewey rather than either his similarities with Berkeley or his relation to Marx. If we learn to read Hegel in his nonmetaphysical, quasi-pragmatic way, he may have a lot to teach us.

### Marx—Political Economy and Philosophy: Two for the Price of One?

I have often remarked that it was a pity that the leading political economist of the nineteenth century should have taken his degree in philosophy and become convinced that he could challenge Hegel on his own ground. Marx should have stuck to what he was good at. He was no match for Hegel, and Engels made things worse—helped make the socialist movement look a bit ridiculous—by inventing what he called dialectical materialism and scientific socialism.

Philosophy is as inessential to social concern as is religion. Just as it is a mistake to think that morality requires a religious basis, it is a mistake to think that politics requires a philosophical basis. You do not have to pretend to understand the movement of history in order to try to make life better for those around you. It is dubious that any reflections on the course of past history have had much predictive value.

### Nietzsche

I see Nietzsche and the American pragmatists as helping us to view art and politics as the growing points of human life, and as rightly insisting that philosophers from Plato on have paid too much attention to mathematics and science. Nietzsche and Dewey wanted to see the quest for knowledge as an attempt to satisfy human needs, not to find the true nature of reality. Plato, they rightly thought, was too interested in attaining certainty, and also too interested in making everything fit together in a coherent whole. Aristotle was more sensible in this respect.

I like Nietzsche's remark that the West is still suffering the consequences of Socrates' conviction that only the rational can be beautiful. Nietzsche's *Birth of Tragedy*, a book to which much of Heidegger's later work is a set of corollaries, seems to me a very valuable protest against the idea that the search for knowledge is or should be the center of human life.

I think that one can detach the good Nietzsche—the critic of Platonism—from the bad Nietzsche, the one who had no use for Christianity or democracy. The stuff about the Overman can safely be neglected, as can what Heidegger called "the metaphysics of the will to power." There is still a lot of valuable stuff left in his writings.

### Wittgenstein

The later Wittgenstein helped us stop thinking of language as a medium in which we attempt to represent reality and to begin thinking of it as a social practice. This way of viewing language ties in with the antirepresentationalist strain in Hegel, and has been fruitfully developed by such later philosophers of language as Davidson and Brandom. A Wittgensteinian social-practice account of language makes it possible to get rid of lot of pseudoproblems about the nature of meaning and the nature of reference which have long burdened this area of philosophy.

### Heidegger vs. Sartre

Heidegger's *Being and Time* is an interesting attempt to restate Kierkegaardian and Nietzschean ideas in rather pompously professional terms by treating them as parts of an "analytic of *Dasein*" carried out by a mysterious method called phenomenological ontology. There are a lot of good ideas in that book, but I find its pretensions to systematicity irritating. Fortunately, Heidegger deprofessionalized himself later on, when he began writing essays like "Building, Dwelling, Thinking" and "The Origin of the Art Work." I greatly admire the later work, even though I could do without all the stuff about "the question after the meaning of Being." At his best, Heidegger continues Nietzsche's attempt to make art central to culture, a centrality that Plato awarded to the quest for certainty.

Heidegger was of course a Nazi and a miserable human being, but he was also a man of great imaginative power, whose influence will endure. The narrative he left us of the movement of Western thought from Plato to Nietzsche is both powerful and original.

I think that Sartre was brilliant in certain passages of *Being and Nothingness*, particularly the discussions of *mauvaise foi* and of existential psychoanalysis. Some sections of that book say things Heidegger tried to say in *Being and Time* rather better than Heidegger managed to say them. Everything Sartre wrote, up to *Critique of Dialectical Reason*, is full of interesting ideas, even though the dogmatic tone is often irritating. I cannot find much interest in the work of his later years, however.

### Dewey and American Pragmatism

The claim common to Dewey and William James that the word *true* is a compliment we pay to beliefs that are serving to guide action better than their competitors, rather than a term signifying accurate representation of reality, seems to me to mark a great step forward in philosophy. It helped us get over the Platonic idea that there is an intellectual virtue called "the love of truth" (somehow distinct from the love of argument, the love of beautiful theories, the love of solving problems, and other more specialized desires). Plato made "Truth" into the name of a lovable object, and this suggested that there is a contrast between the love of truth and the love of happiness. That was a bad suggestion. On the pragmatist's view, we call beliefs true when the adoption of them makes us better able to achieve happiness.

### Postmodernism

I cannot find any good use for the term *postmodernism*. Lyotard's book *The Postmodern Condition* did not succeed in giving the term a useful sense, nor have later attempts. If one reads ten books with *postmodern* in the title one will emerge with at least five or six different meanings for that flexible term. I would prefer to talk about Foucault, Derrida, and the rest individually, rather than trying to lump them together as representatives of something called postmodern philosophy. I have no idea what is supposed to make a painting, or a novel, or a political attitude, "postmodern."

*Q*: Am I correct to say that the gist of all of the above is that there is very little to say about truth?

*RR*: It is certainly the case that "truth" is not a possible object of study, any more than is "knowledge." Neither has a nature to be understood. The kind of true beliefs that mathematicians acquire, the kind poets acquire, the kind engineers acquire, the kind politicians acquire, the kind mothers acquire, are not usefully viewed as species of a single genus. The idea that human beings are primarily knowers, that knowing and truth seeking are what makes them wonderfully different from animals, is a bad one, even though it goes back to Plato and Aristotle. It is high time we gave it up.

*Q*: Does this also mean that philosophy is not socially useful?

*RR*: All we philosophy professors think that many of the things done under the name *philosophy* by many of our colleagues are not socially useful. Descartes thought that scholastic philosophy was not socially useful. Dewey thought that discussion of the epistemological problems posed by Cartesian philosophers such as Locke and Kant was not socially useful. Heidegger thought that the neo-Kantianism pursued in the German universities when he was a student was not socially useful. I think that a lot of contemporary philosophy is socially useless, and is just academic hackwork. But, of course, the philosophers whom I admire (Donald Davidson, Jacques Derrida, for example) are also the ones for whom I should like to claim social utility—very long-run social utility, of the sort that can be attributed to changes in the intellectual atmosphere which eventually benefit society as a whole.

I do think that it would be a mistake for a young man or woman to become a philosophy professor in the hope of making life better for the poor and weak, or of making politics more rational. There are other areas of study which are more useful to those interested in promoting such ends.

*Q*: "Why should I be moral?"

*RR*: Every human being (even Nazis, even the mafiosi) have a moral identity. There are certain things the Nazi would rather die than do, just as there are certain things each of us bourgeois liberals would rather die than do. The question "Why should I do as my moral identity—my sense of what is most important in my life—dictates?" is pointless. What could be a *better* reason for acting?

So the question "Why should I be moral?" only makes sense if it means something like "Why should I have the moral identity I do?" There is no general answer to this question of the sort that people think philosophers might provide. The answer depends entirely on which alternative moral identities are under consideration. If I am considering abandoning Nazism for Quakerism, or the reverse, different considerations are relevant than if I am considering abandoning my honest business practices in favor of a criminal life of fraud and embezzlement, or the reverse. In all four cases, there will be much to be said on both sides, but little of it is of a sort that philosophers are peculiarly qualified to say.

*Q*: Can we rationally claim the superiority of certain works of literature, art, music, and so on, over others and, if so, on what basis? That is, does it make any sense to say that reading Shakespeare makes someone a better person or that classical music is not just a different but an aesthetically superior form of music?

*RR*: I don't have much use for the notion of "aesthetically superior." I would argue that Shakespeare and Mozart are "educationally superior" to a lot of lesser writers and composers because their works have endured—they keep being rediscovered with delight by new audiences. So it pays each new generation to give them a hearing in order to find out what so many have found so attractive, and in order to join in a conversation about Shakespeare and Mozart which has been going on for centuries. But I would admit that for a Chinese, whose countrymen have been having a different conversation, and who perhaps does not respond with any immediacy to either Shakespeare or Mozart, there may be no educational value in these men's works.

To reply more directly, I do not think that we can "rationally claim superiority" for the culture, or the cultural productions, we value most. The term *rationally* suggests a demonstration that can proceed from premises acceptable to all human beings, regardless of the cultural or historical location. There are no such demonstrations. But their absence does not matter. It is still rational to try to persuade our children to love what we have loved, admire what we admire.

*Q*: What specifically, in your view, is the role of philosophy in the age of DNA and biotechnology?

*RR*: If biotechnology raises unexpected problems for society, as perhaps it may, then the philosophy professors, the law professors, the politics professors, the history professors, the biology professors, the professors of medicine, and lots of other species of intellectuals will all doubtless find something to say about those problems. But there is no point in asking what "role" each discipline will play in dealing with them. The books these various kinds of scholars have read may or may not help them make a contribution to the solution of such problems. There is no way to tell in advance which sorts of books will be of help.

The whole idea that there is something august called "philosophy" which we can ask for help when problems arise is misguided. "Philosophy" is just a pigeonhole into which different things are stuffed in different centuries, and in different countries, and even in different universities in the same country at the same time.

*Q:* Does the history of philosophy differ from the history of the natural sciences?

*RR:* Sure. You do not have to study the history of a given natural science in order to be a skillful practitioner of that science. The problems facing your science at the present time can be described without reference to the problems that the discipline faced in earlier centuries. That is because the problems can be defined simply in terms of our inability to produce certain desired results (a vaccine against AIDS, a missile defense system, a way of teasing out the pattern of ionic exchange between neurons, etc.). Philosophical problems cannot be stated by reference to our inability to do certain things. One can only distinguish a genuine philosophical problem from a pseudoproblem by acquaintance with the history of philosophy. Simply taking one's teachers' word for what counts as a philosophical problem is a recipe for parochialism and early obsolescence.

*Q:* What is going to be the role of higher education in the twenty-first century?

*RR:* Its role is the same as in all previous centuries: to make people more aware, through the study of alternatives to present institutions and ways of thinking, of the possibility that the future might be made better than the present. If we put vocational training—the sort of training that makes you a good plumber or a good physicist or a good physician—and stick to the sort of training that every citizen of a democracy ought to have, then we can say that the point of such training is to free up the imagination. Getting acquainted with the imaginative power of men like Shakespeare, Mozart, St. Paul, Jefferson, Pericles, Plato, Napoleon, and the like is probably the best way to get people to use their imaginations.

*Q:* Let's move on to the political spectrum of your ideas. I think it is a well-known fact that you grew up in a household where both of your parents were at one point members of the American Communist Party, and the ideas of socialism in general were the building blocks of your formative years. I understand that the name of Trotsky was an especially powerful presence in your family surroundings.

*RR:* Yes, not because of anything specific Trotsky said or did, but simply because he had become the symbol of Stalin's betrayal of the Bolshevik revolution.

*Q*: I read somewhere that as a child, in addition to being attracted to Trotsky, you had a fascination with wild orchids and you pursued with single-mindedness the ideas of reconciling Trotsky and the orchids. Tell me more about this—I think it is fascinating.

*RR*: In an autobiographical essay called "Trotsky and the Wild Orchids," published in my recent collection of essays *Philosophy and Social Hope*, I said that I felt torn, as a boy, between the private thrills of finding the secret places in the woods where the wild orchids grew—thrills of the sort that Wordsworth describes well in his poems about the child's relation to nature—and the public duty to further the cause of social justice. In my childish way, I had the feeling that I was betraying Trotsky, and the class struggle, by spending time on, and delighting in, socially useless flowers.

*Q*: But eventually you moved away from Trotsky and Marxism in general.

*RR*: I still thought of socialism as a desirable political goal in my thirties, but by 1970 or so I had begun to conclude that market economies were probably with us forever, and that therefore we would have to use other ways of preventing social injustice than getting rid of private capital. I think this is a change of opinion that has come over most intellectuals in the West by now, resulting largely from the apparent inability of any country in which the state makes all the economic decisions to allow the existence of democratic freedoms. I am not sure why this inability exists, but I have decided that Hayek had a point, even if he carried it too far, when he resisted almost all forms of state interference with the economy.

*Q*: Was your rejection of Marxian socialism in any way related with the critique you begun to develop rather early on of the Cartesian tradition?

*RR*: No, the two had nothing to do with each other. The critique of Cartesianism is a very parochial affair, of interest only to philosophy professors. The critique of Marxism has nothing to do with philosophy, but is simply an empirical judgment about which socioeconomic institutions are likely to promote human happiness.

*Q*: What were the sources of your stimulation and the circumstances that led you to embrace the tradition of social democracy?

*RR*: Social democracy is the fallback position for anyone concerned about justice but unwilling to undertake a commitment to revolutionary change. Such a commitment makes sense in places like Burma and North Korea, but I am not sure it makes sense in places like the United States and Greece.

*Q*: You went on to study at Chicago and later on at Yale. What was the political climate of the time like in those elite institutions, and did they reflect the political mood of the country as a whole?

*RR*: Chicago was filled with leftists and indeed with Stalinists. In the mid-forties the editor of the student newspaper at Chicago was a paid flunkey of the Communist Party, assigned to do agitprop at the university. I found myself one of only two students at a student government meeting to favor a resolution condemning Stalin's invasion of Czechoslovakia in 1948. At Chicago I was, so to speak, on the right. At Yale, which was still a bastion of the WASP establishment (a place where most of the undergraduates were like Bush—affable people who never seriously questioned their own privileges), I found myself on the left.

The two universities were very different indeed. Chicago was a place for intellectuals, and Yale is still a place for gentlemen. Fortunately, Yale nowadays is much more like Chicago. That is why President Bush thinks that his alma mater has gone to the dogs.

*Q*: You have used extensively the term *social hope* in your works in the context of keeping alive alternative scenarios that will culminate in an egalitarian, classless society. What are those alternative scenarios that you think are viable today?

*RR*: There is a scenario which seemed plausible at the end of the Second World War, in which the rich democracies would unite in a world federation which would gradually bring democracy and prosperity to the rest of the world. That scenario now sounds much less plausible. But it is the only one I can envisage that might actually have good results. There is no reason except selfishness and greed why, for example, the rest of Latin America could not imitate the example of Costa Rica, or the rest of India could not imitate the example of Kerala. If public opinion in the rich democracies could be persuaded to see such developments as a way of assuring peace in the world, maybe social hope could be revived.

*Q*: There are voices of "pessimism" expressed from several influential quarters today stating that there are basically no alternatives, which also implies that social democracy can no longer be practiced in the age of global capital. How do you respond to such grim outlooks?

*RR*: I can't see why the globalization of the market makes social democracy less desirable than it always was. Has anyone come up with a better idea? There is, to be sure, plenty of reason for pessimism, but it would be better to do what one can to get people to follow an improbable scenario than to simply throw up one's hands.

*Q*: You do agree, however, that the globalization process has altered substantially the way politics is exercised?

*RR*: Sure. Now that states have very little control over their own economies, the options open to statesmen are more limited than they were in the days of Jaures or of Roosevelt. To bring the multinational corporations under control would require something like a world government, with authority to, for example, close tax refuges like the Swiss banks. Such a world government might be able to do to global corporate power what Roosevelt did to corporate power in the U.S.

*Q*: What are your views on the return of the Republicans to the White House?

*RR*: It is a true disaster, for the U.S. and for the world. The new administration will spend money that should be spent on the poor on absurd and dangerous projects such as the missile defense system, and the religious right, which is a truly dangerous, potentially fascist movement, will be greatly strengthened. I can see no bright side to the next four years.

*Q*: Eight years of the Clinton-Gore team in power did not produce any tangible rewards for the working-class people in the United States. Economic prosperity or not, the nineties were a decade that increased substantially the gap between haves and have-nots. In the most recent poll I saw, the majority of the American people no longer believe in the American dream. How do you explain all these trends?

*RR*: Clinton and Gore did prevent the rich from stealing as much from the poor as the Bush administration will encourage them to steal. But it is true that no important measures were taken during the last eight years to make things better for the poor in the U.S. As an admirer of Clinton's, I should like to think that this was because he had to deal with a Republican Congress for the last six years. But perhaps historians will decide that he could have done more than he did. I cannot explain the failure of the American electorate to rise above selfishness and greed. I wish I could. My country has enjoyed unparalleled power and wealth for a decade, and has not used either its power or its wealth to decrease human suffering. It seems to me to be a great tragedy.

*Q*: Is the Democratic Party the only viable means for progressive politics in the United States?

*RR*: Yes. Efforts to form a new party have either fizzled or resulted, as did Nader's candidacy, in the left stabbing itself in the back. If there is a second great depression, a populist party like the one Huey Long might have led is possible. But it is more likely to be a right-wing than a left-wing party.

*Q*: Immigration has emerged in the last several years among the most controversial issues in American public discourse. Further, the newly elected president of Mexico stated a few days after his victory that he can see the day (though it may be ten to fifteen years from now) when the borders between the U.S. and Mexico will be open. What are your own views on this matter? Are there substantial differences between the two parties on immigration? Has NAFTA had any major impact so far on the loss of American jobs?

*RR*: On the one hand, there is an obvious desire on the part of the public that America's wealth be used for the benefit of those who are presently American citizens. This is reflected in slogans like "American jobs for American citizens." On the other hand, the entire economy of certain sections of the country (most notably California) would be destroyed if there were no immigrant labor—no illegal residents from Mexico, Nicaragua, and the like to do the dirty work of serving the food and cleaning the toilets and trimming the hedges, no temporary and legally imported engineers from India to write the codes for the software programs produced here in Silicon Valley. The white middle class of California would not know what to do if all the brown-skinned waiters and janitors and ditch diggers and gardeners suddenly disappeared, nor would Silicon Valley know what to do if they had to hire only American citizens.

It is in the interest of the rich in the U.S. to keep the borders permeable in order to keep the cost of labor down. It is in the interest of African Americans, the descendants of the slaves, to keep the Mexicans and Central Americans and Asians out so that they can get the minimum-wage jobs which immigrants are presently taking away from them. The Republican Party has no interest in the welfare of the poor (many of whom are African American). The Democratic Party tries to capture the vote of the poor, but they also want campaign contributions from the people who employ immigrant labor. By and large the poor in America do not vote; only the middle class does. Since both parties get most of their money from the middle class, we can expect the status quo to continue.

I doubt that the border with Mexico will ever be open. NAFTA has not changed matters much, and probably will not. If there is a depression in the U.S., the Immigration and Naturalization Service (one of the most backward and cruel agencies of the U.S. government) will simply start shipping lots of brown-skinned people back across the Mexican border. They will also cancel the visas of all the software engineers from India. They will clean out all the immigrants they can in order to prevent popular unrest due to unemployment. At the moment, with full employment, there is no need to do so.

*Q*: Do you think the twenty-first century will also be an American century? In which ways could the U.S. help to make the world a more humane place?

*RR*: The U.S. could do what it did under President Carter—say that human rights around the world were the chief priority of American foreign policy—and then actually act on this conviction. The U.S. can't bring peace and democracy to the world all by itself, but it could do a lot by setting a good example. I do not think there is any hope of this happening, so I see no reason to think that the twenty-first will be an American century. The century will probably see the U.S. displaced by China as the most powerful nation, and this will probably mean that world leadership will switch from a democracy to a dictatorship. We shall go from a leading nation that provides a not very good example to one that supplies a really awful example.

# 9

# The Best Can Be an Enemy
# of the Better

*Interview by Eduardo Mendieta*

*Question:* You, along with many feminists, have talked about solidarity as being central to our quest for justice and civility. I wonder, however, if your understanding of solidarity would also include the ideas of solidarity with and responsibility for the past?

*Richard Rorty:* No. I can't make much sense of the idea of "solidarity with the past." Pity for past suffering, maybe, and a determination that it will not be repeated in the future but "solidarity" seems the wrong term for our relation with the dead. It is best used, I think, to express our relation to those contemporaries whom we think of as "us" comrades in struggles for good causes.

I am also not sure about "responsibility for the past." This term does not seem appropriate for our sense that justice requires that children be repaid for what was unjustly done to their parents. Our sense of justice in such cases is independent of the question of whether the injustice was done by our own parents. The Germans should learn something from the Holocaust and the white Americans something from the history of segregation and slavery, but it is one thing to say that they should learn something and another thing that they should feel responsibility for the past. Collective hereditary guilt does not strike me as a useful concept.

*Q*: Do you think that contemporary U.S. citizens have a special duty to pay reparations for two hundred years of slavery? In other words, do you think that the advocates of black reparations have valid and serious arguments?

*RR*: There are valid and serious arguments, but there are also valid and serious arguments for taxing the citizens of the First World down to the standard of living of the average inhabitant of the Third World, and distributing the proceeds of this taxation to the latter. But since neither set of arguments will lead to any such action being taken, I am not sure how much time we should spend thinking about them, as opposed to thinking about measures that have some chance of actually being carried out. It would be better to think about what might actually be done than to think about what an absolutely perfect world would be like. The best can be an enemy of the better.

*Q*: Do you think that the demographic transformations that the United States has been undergoing over the last fifty years, by which I mean more specifically the growth of Asian Americans and Latinos, will have an impact on the project of "achieving our country"? Or do you think that ethnicity is irrelevant to the idea of "America" as a project?

*RR*: I think that it is irrelevant, except when it comes to black people. Latinos and Vietnamese will be thought of as "white," and as appropriate for intermarriage, by the middle of the century, just as the Irish and the Italians (initially viewed as too foreign to be assimilated and intermarried with) came to be thought of as fellow citizens after a few generations. But the idea that "one drop of black blood pollutes" will linger on as the heritage of slavery and the Achilles' heel of American democracy.

*Q*: Did you know that the U.S. is certainly the fourth largest Spanish-speaking nation in the world, and will very soon become the third largest after Mexico, and Spain? Do you think that the United States might one day become a bilingual nation?

*RR*: No. Nor would it be a good idea. It would not have been a good idea to have the schools of New York and Boston provide instruction in Italian and in Gaelic in the year 1900, nor for ballots to be have been printed in those languages. The pressure for bilingualism in the U.S. Latino community is extremely shortsighted. It is one thing to make things easier for recent immigrants, but another thing to suggest that their children use the parents' language rather than the language of the employers and the universities.

Q: Why do you think bilingualism is a bad idea? Europeans tend to be at the very least bilinguals, most are polyglots. In fact, the American condition seems to be the exception. Further, at the dawn of the twentieth century, the US became a "cemetery of languages" for racist, ideological, and political reasons. Today, I have a sense that we have become more cosmopolitan about language, partly because of the kind of work you champion. In California, where you live and hope to retire, and where your grandchildren are growing, Spanish is becoming the dominant language. Don't you think that your grandchildren would be better off if they grew up bilingual and with a sense of respect for others and a cosmopolitanism that talking in other languages grants people?

*RR*: I think it's great for people to know as many languages as possible, but I see no reason why Californian kids should learn Spanish, rather than German or Chinese, simply because many recent immigrants to California speak Spanish.

The political discourse of the country is conducted in English, so it behooves the immigrants to get in on English in order to become citizens who can organize pressure groups, take over municipal and state governments, and so on. It behooves the nonimmigrants (that is, the descendants of older generations of immigrants) to stop treating recent immigrants badly. But learning Spanish is not going to help much with that. Lots of Anglos on the northern side of the US-Mexico border speak Spanish, but they use this linguistic ability to keep the Latinos down. They use it as a tool in their business dealings, not as a way of being cosmopolitan. I don't see that mutual respect between the older and the newer citizens of the country would be much affected by more of the former learning Spanish, but it will be affected by more of the latter learning English. Bilingualism and all the talk about "appreciation of diverse cultures" seems to me a distraction from the problem that new waves of immigrants have always faced—being stuck in the dirtiest and lowest-paying jobs. Forgetting about your parents' culture in the process of getting Americanized, and getting better jobs, is something that happened with the Irish, the Italians, the Poles, and so on. I don't see that it's a bad thing. It would be nice for people to inhabit several cultures at once, but only us professors have the leisure to attempt such a project.

*Q:* Do you think language matters to philosophy, or to thinking in general? And here by language I do not just mean language as a philosopheme, in the sense Gadamer and Heidegger might have meant language. Rather, I mean language in a more pedestrian sense, in the sense of natural languages, the vernaculars of quotidian existence.

*RR:* No, no more than it matters to physics. The translations of Ortega and Heidegger into English make it possible for us to talk reasonably about them, just as the translations of Austin and Dewey into Spanish make it possible for Spanish-speaking philosophers to talk reasonably about them. Something is lost in translation in both cases, but not enough to matter. Philosophy is, and should be, rootlessly cosmopolitan.

*Q:* Languages, like empires, rise, shine, become despotic, decay, and then fade and become museum pieces. Is the history of philosophy related to the fates of languages? And do you think one day you will be read like we read Plato, Augustine, Aquinas, Descartes, and Derrida, that is, in translation from a former imperial language, in the language of the subaltern?

*RR:* I doubt that I'll be read, but maybe Dewey will. Sure, someday all our contemporaries will only be read, if at all, in some language that few of us now know. But if Aristotle can be read now, Dewey can be read then. The history of philosophy is no more related to the fates of language than the history of physics. Heidegger's sentimentality about the special virtues of the Greek and German languages is silly.

*Q:* In a review-essay on Gadamer in the *New Republic*, Richard Wolin levels a series of important criticisms against you. These accusations are related to the prior question about language, historicity, and cultural memory. But let me quote Wolin: "That Rorty allows himself to be duped by the pieties of hermeneutics suggests two things: the perils of decontextualized, purely immanent, and somewhat self-interested readings of philosophical texts, from which the actual historical careers of ideas have been eliminated; and the conceptual weakness of Rorty's own position. His fear of metaphysics has become a fear of reason and a fear of truth."[1] Have you been duped by hermeneutics, are your readings self-serving, and are you afraid of reason and truth?

*RR*: Richard Wolin seems to think that the first thing you should do with a philosopher whom you find interesting is to figure out whether he or she has been "complicit" with some bad political views. I don't care about such complicity. I just pick out the ideas I want to use from the philosopher's texts and ignore the rest of their life and work. (For a defense of such decontextualization and of self-interested reading, see the piece called "On Heidegger's Nazism," in my *Philosophy and Social Hope*.) I have no idea why Wolin thinks that doing things my way demonstrates fear of reason and truth. Attempts to link up a thinker's ideas with his or her politics or personal life are not irrational, and they may produce truths. But they are optional. Wolin seems to want to make them compulsory.

*Q*: Some people who conflate politics and philosophy like to think of Rorty having a relationship to American imperialism like the one that Heidegger had with National Socialism. In other words, what do you say to the accusation that your postmodern liberalism with a human face is the philosophical justification of a Pax Americana?

*RR*: This charge seems as implausible as the similar charges that were leveled at Dewey by the Marxists of his day—by George Novack, for example.[2] These Marxists share Wolin's view that the first thing you should do with a philosopher is figure out whether he is good or bad for the political movements in which you are interested. I do not share this view.

*Q*: Some figures like Martin Albrow, Ronald Robertson, Niklas Luhmann, even Giddens to a certain extent think that globalization is a qualitatively different order of society. Do you think that we should take seriously all this talk about globalization? Is globalization any different than accelerated modernity?

*RR*: It seems to me just more accelerated modernity. Its principal effect is to give still more power to the rich. It is easy to imagine a dystopic

1. Richard Wolin, "Untruth and Method," *New Republic* (May 15, 2000), 45.
2. George Edward Novack, *Pragmatism Versus Marxism: An Appraisal of John Dewey's Philosophy* (New York: Pathfinder Press, 1975).

future in which all the world's governments are simply tools in the hands of a few multinational corporations, corporations which function as conspiracies of the rich against the poor. But I am not sure why this should be thought of as a "qualitatively different order of society." The rich have always been good at putting the latest technological developments to use in ripping off the poor.

*Q*: Do you think that postcolonial criticism and postcolonial theory have anything to teach us citizens of the U.S.? What would you say to the suggestion that in fact the U.S. also has its own postcolonial subjects: Puerto Ricans, Chicanos, Filipinos, Koreans, Vietnamese, Nicaraguans, and so on.

*RR*: That suggestion seems plausible. But I am not sure that there is anything important called "postcolonial criticism and postcolonial theory." These strike me as academic fads rather than forces for social change— ways of keeping the intellectuals focused on the past instead of thinking about what is to be done. My postcolonial cousins in Ireland are divided into people still thinking about what the English did to the Irish and people thinking about how to strengthen Ireland's role in the European Community. The latter sort of thinking seems preferable.

*Q*: I was always very puzzled by the following contrast. On the one side we have Derrida's demystification and questioning of the disciplinary boundaries between philosophy and literature, and Habermas's critique of such a leveling of the disciplines; on the other side, we have Rorty's similar strategy of dismantling philosophy's sovereign solitude and independence, and Habermas's rather positive reaction to your work, or if not positive, at least not so severely critical. What makes a difference here?

*RR*: Habermas thinks that philosophy should make universal validity claims, but that perhaps literature need not do so. As I say in my exchanges with Habermas in *Rorty and His Critics*, I have no use for the notion of "universal validity claims." So I think of the difference between philosophy and literature historically rather than epistemologically. Habermas and Derrida both think of philosophy as more clearly demarcated from the rest of culture than I do. I do not think tracing a border is a useful exercise. The interesting border is between scholastic philosophy and academic poetry on the one hand and original philosophy and poetry on the other.

*Q*: Do you think that philosophy is different from literature? Or perhaps more clearly, what is the difference between Sartre's *Nausea* and Heidegger's *Being and Time*? Can we distinguish a philosophical work from an allegedly nonphilosophical work? Or is this all a fiction produced by a canon?

*RR*: If you have to be reasonably familiar with Plato, Kant, and so on, to get much out of the book, then it's probably a philosophy book. The difference between *Nausea* and *Remembrance of Things Past* is that you can read the latter knowing nothing about philosophy, whereas to get much out of the former you have to have read *Being and Nothingness*, *Being and Time*, and the rest, and to get much out of them you have to have read Plato, Kant, and others. In that sense, *Nausea* is a philosophy book as well as a novel. Santayana's *The Last Puritan*, by contrast, is a novel that happens to have been written by a philosopher, something you need not know to read the book with profit.

*Q*: In an essay entitled "Philosophy and the Future," you note: "We have to agree with Marx that our job is to help make the future different from the past, rather than claiming to know what the future must necessarily have in common with that past." I take this to be a recontextualizing of Marx's eleventh thesis on Feuerbach. In my view, this turns philosophy into a utopian project, or rather, philosophy becomes the art of figuring the future. Yet, in the same paragraph in which you seem to be suggesting this, you affirm that philosophers have to be more like engineers and lawyers, that we must find what our clients need. This latter injunction suggests that philosophy should become social engineering, a sophisticated type of public relations. How can philosophy be about the future, when it should serve the "needs" of its clients?

*RR*: Our clients, like Marx's, are the poor and wretched. Marx was practicing a sophisticated type of public relations. So was Dewey. What we need is more and better public relations agencies working for otherwise underrepresented clients. We do not need attempts to predict the future. Marx made himself look silly when he claimed to know what was going to happen next, as opposed to making suggestions about what ought to happen next. A good public relations agency helps make the future different from the past.

*Q*: The Internet, and in general the information revolution, has already revolutionized our world, and it will continue to do so in even more radical ways, as Jeremy Rifkin, Manuel Castells, and Vandana Shiva suggest. Do you think that philosophy, or let us say, critical thinking, will have a whole new spectrum of questions to deal with, and that we might have to begin a new subdiscipline named something like cyber-philosophy?

*RR*: Maybe, but I see no special reason to think so. The telephone and the telegraph didn't create a tele-philosophy, so I am not sure that the Internet need produce a cyber-philosophy. I think a lot of the stuff about the information revolution is media hype.

*Q*: Many people were extremely disappointed that the National Bioethics Advisory Committee did not issue an unequivocal condemnation of cloning. Can and should philosophers say anything important and enlightening about cloning? In fact, I suspect that a Rortyan might be opposed to both a categorical rejection of cloning and some sort of moral censure of it. For, as you note in many places, we have to give up the notion that humans are animals with "an extra-added ingredient." Clones would be just other types of living entities, neither inferior nor superior to humans, just differently grown and conceived.

*RR*: I think that the desirability of cloning is a pragmatic matter, to be discussed by working out alternatives and scenarios, scenarios that can only be written by people who know a lot more about current lines of biological and medical research than I do. Metaphysical questions about the nature of human beings are irrelevant here, as elsewhere. I have no expertise that would let me have a reasoned opinion about cloning.

*Q*: What do you think of Habermas's arguments against cloning, which reproduce Hans Jonas's arguments against it on the grounds that it would be a violation of an individual's right to an open future, which allegedly cloning preempts or forecloses?

*RR*: I haven't read Habermas's writings on this topic. Maybe when I do I will revise what I say in answer to the last question.

*Q*: You noted in another interview that "if we took care of freedom, truth would take care of itself." I find this statement very appealing, but also disconcerting: can we take care of freedom without appealing to truth, in the way, for instance, that to talk about the evils of sexism, racism, and poverty we must couch our talk in terms of the "truth" of the deleterious, adverse, devastating, debilitating, and demoralizing effects of these forms of discrimination, exclusion, privation, and so on.

*RR*: My idea was this: if we can take care of freedom by creating a free press, a free judiciary, free universities, and so on, then those who have suffered, or are otherwise aware of, the effects of sexism, racism, and poverty will be able to make these effects known to more people. I tried to make this point by saying that "truth" is a name for what is most likely to come to be believed under Habermasian ideal conditions of communication, the sorts of conditions promoted by a free press, a free judiciary, and free universities. I do not see that we do anything called "appealing to truth." We appeal to the statements of the tortured, the records in the archives, the monuments of the past, the slides under the microscope, the images in the lens of the telescope, and so on, but not to "truth." Insistence on the existence or the importance of truth seems to me empty, at least by comparison to insistence on the need for freedom.

*Q*: The 2000 election has been seen by many as national debacle. Some speculate that the way in which the Supreme Court intervened has irreparably tarnished not just the image of that holiest of holy branches of the government, but also that it dealt a severe blow to the popular thrust in the legitimacy of our electoral system. In light of your defense of the primacy of politics to philosophy vis-à-vis Rawls's clarification of his theory of justice, I wonder if many might not see in the events of the last election a regrettable confirmation of your perspective. Yet, you also wrote somewhere, "As our presidents, political parties, and legislators become ever more corrupt and frivolous, we turn to the judiciary as the only political institution for which we can still feel something like awe. This awe is not reverence for the Euclid-like immutability of the Law. It is respect for the ability of decent men and women to sit down around tables, argue things out and arrive at a reasonable consensus."

*RR*: I quite agree that the Supreme Court tarnished its own image and dealt a severe blow to the legitimacy of the system. I think that Justice Scalia will be seen as having done more damage to the court, and to American democracy, than any of his predecessors since Taney, the author of the Dred Scott decision. The sentence you quote from me about the awe felt for the judiciary is now obsolete.

*Q*: Paraphrasing something you said about Wittgenstein and Heidegger in the same sentence, you seemed to have read everything, although you come to what you read with very definite opinions. When I read you, I do not feel like I am reading an "American philosopher." You read and sound like a European, a renaissance man or woman. How did you develop such reading practices? If you were advising a young, prospective philosopher, what practical advice would you give them about their reading practices and habits?

*RR*: I haven't read very much, but I probably have read more than the average U.S. analytic philosopher. I think that the contrast with a philosophical profession that does not ask its students to read many old books creates the illusion that I am especially learned. I would not advise a young person who wants to read widely, and to be able to place his work in philosophy in a larger cultural context, to enter one of the standard-model U.S. graduate programs in philosophy. I usually advise students of this sort to go instead to such interdisciplinary programs as the Committee on Social Thought at the University of Chicago.

*Q*: Is there something you are sorry you wrote, or that you wish you had written?

*RR*: I wish I had written Robert Brandom's and Michael Williams's books such as *Making It Explicit* and *Unnatural Doubts*. They combine my own views on philosophical issues with an argumentative skill and a precision of thought that I have never been able to manage. I just don't have a brain of the right sort.

*April 24, 2001*
*San Francisco–Stanford*

# 10

# On September 11, 2001

*Interview by Eduardo Mendieta*

*Question*: September 11 has already become a unique date in the time line of the United States. Personally, I feel as though that I have aged a hundred years in the life of a citizen. Many people have asked why did this happen? Or, how could this happen? But I would like to ask you, what does 9/11 mean, or should it mean, for us as Americans?

*Richard Rorty*: It means that there is enough money in the hands of international criminal bands to pay for complex and ambitious terrorist schemes. This is something we have known for a long time, but September 11 brought the point home. September 11 should not be taken to show that there is something wrong with the U.S. (though there is). It does not represent a revolt of the Third World poor against the First World rich (though there may well be such a revolt at some point). The success of Bin Laden's people does not teach us any large general moral. It tells us that even the richest and most complacent countries are now within reach of attack by international gangsters, but that is all.

Q: Do you think that the character of this terrorist attack on the United States warranted the kind of military action that has been unleashed in Afghanistan?

*RR*: Yes. Our government of course lies to us all the time, so we shall never know whether the campaign in Afghanistan was justified by intelligence reports. But assuming that we have been more or less told the truth about the terrorist camps outside Kandahar, then the military action the U.S. took seems justified. Indeed, if it had not been taken, our government would not have been doing what we pay it to do—lessening the chances of Americans being killed by criminals.

Q: In an editorial that you wrote very soon after 9/11, and which has appeared in *Die Zeit,* you appealed to the friends of the United States to be on the lookout for attacks on civil rights by a further militarized U.S.[1] Do you think that the fears you expressed in this editorial have been ratified by recent executive orders and actions on the part of Ashcroft, the State Department, and the White House?

*RR*: Yes. Attorney-General Ashcroft embodies one of my worst nightmares—a minister of justice who has no interest in constitutional protections and every interest in expanding the power of the police. The nonsense about restrictions on broadcasting Bin Laden's videotapes, setting up military tribunals, and the like increases my sense that the current administration just wants to concentrate more and more power in the hands of the executive branch. The inaction of the congressional Democrats in the last few months seems to me inexcusable.

Q: In this same editorial you end with the words, "I hope that these friends will not be disappointed in the decisions that my government will shortly be taking—not only those concerning immediate retaliatory measures, but those which will affect the future of American democracy." I wondered if you think that the friends of America as republic are disappointed or should be disappointed?

*RR*: It is too soon to tell. There may be a reaction against the new restrictions on civil rights once the campaign in Afghanistan is over.

Q: Do you think that the administration could, or should, have handled the response to this terrorist attack on the United States differently?

*RR*: Not much differently, no. I suspect any president would have done pretty much what Bush did. I probably would have myself, if I'd been president.

   1. "Die militarisierung Amerikas," *Die Zeit* (September 17, 2001).

*Q*: It is all too evident that the Bush administration began on a unilateralist, isolationist, and imperialistic tone, with a heavy dose of macho posturing. Do you think that this attitude has been changed at all?

*RR*: No, it hasn't changed much. The repudiation of the ABM treaty, without the consent of Congress, shows how arrogantly anti-internationalist Bush is still capable of being. Bush has been forced to take more of an interest than before in bribing and cajoling other governments to do what the U.S. wants done, but that is the only change.

*Q*: This is a hard question, but let me see if I can articulate it. It is hard because it could give the impression that what it presupposes is actually an acceptable and defensible position, namely that in some way Rorty the philosopher and public intellectual could be thought of as both provincial and jingoistic. But of course, this is farthest from the truth. There are very few U.S. philosophers who have been as cosmopolitan and hermeneutically charitable as you have been. Nonetheless, here is the question. The events of 9/11 have been blamed partly on our blindness, self-involvement, and lack of awareness of the world, on our self-imposed ignorance and naivety. Succinctly, 9/11 has been blamed on our jingoism and chauvinism. Many took your avowed "ethnocentrism" as a form of that jingoism and chauvinism. I imagine that somewhere, someone is already weaving a narrative in which Rorty's "us" and "self-confessed ethnocentrism" are to blame for our "having deserved" this wake-up call of 9/11. In what way would you say that your defense of a self-confessed ethnocentrism is unrelated to the type of jingoism and chauvinism that many are fingering as justification and rationale for 9/11?

*RR*: Blaming our (perfectly real) jingoism and chauvinism for the terrorist attack is like blaming the capitalist system for the U.S. and Russian mafias. It's pointless. People like Bin Laden have an agenda which is not greatly affected by any particular thing the U.S. does or will do.

*Q*: Do you think that there is an anti-Americanism that is healthy that should not be confused with an anti-Americanism that derides "America" as a republic, or "America" as the *patria de la justicia*, the fatherland of justice, to use the expression of Pedro Henriquez Ureña?

*RR*: There is of course the normal critique of the government of a democratic country by the citizens of that country, and by world public opinion. I would, God knows, heartily join in many such criticisms—criticisms of what our government is doing, and not doing, both at home and abroad. But such criticism is not a matter of "anti-Americanism."

The people who get called anti-American are, typically, intellectuals who insist that America should never use military force outside its borders. But that insistence is absurd. As long as we do not have an international police force in place, the world will, inevitably and reasonably, expect the U.S. to play the role of global policeman. Getting such an international force in place is a very desirable goal. If the other nations would get together to create such a force (perhaps using the E.U. as nucleus) then the U.S. would gradually become less of a bully. But as long as there is only one nation with the money and the power to serve a police function, American military intervention in hot spots and accusations of "bullying" will be inevitable. The anti-Americanism of the intellectuals is like their anticapitalism: they do not have any clear idea of an alternative to reliance on America when Bosnia or Rwanda or Kosovo or international terrorism makes intervention necessary, nor do they have any alternative to propose to the growth of market economies. They just pretend to have alternatives for rhetorical purposes. The energy that non-American intellectuals put into being anti-American should be put into forwarding policies which will increase their countries' independence from the U.S. Though America often is, as they rightly say, an arrogant bully, pointing out this obvious fact yet again is not a helpful contribution to political discussion.

*Q:* I would like to turn our conversation in the direction of some of your most recent work, namely on the role of religion in contemporary life. Do you think that we should consider 9/11 as an event that could not have been possible, even thinkable, without the explosive convergence of fanaticism, wealth, and high tech, as they were synergized and catalyzed through religion?

*RR:* That's much too fancy and theoretical a way of describing the ability of a discontented spoiled-brat Saudi playboy to get together enough money and enough naive young idealists to do what he did on September 11. Religion was of course a big help to Bin Laden's self-centered and murderous schemes, but "synergized and catalyzed" is overstating and overdramatizing its role.

*Q*: Do you think it makes sense at all to talk as Samuel Huntington does of the "clash of civilizations," where civilization is understood in terms of religious worldviews?

*RR*: No. Falwell and Robertson—the televangelists who have been referred to as "the American Taliban"—are not representatives of Christianity any more than Bin Laden is a representative of Islam. Like the Renaissance popes, both of these figures seem to me to be people who use religion for their own selfish purposes.

*Q*: In your recent Meister Eckhart Book Prize acceptance speech, in my opinion a beautiful text, you speak about how the debate between atheists versus theists has become obsolete, mostly because science and common sense have won what was really a cultural struggle, a struggle about how we would define our public lives. At the same time, you wished that instead of using the term *atheism* to describe your views, you had used the term *anticlericalism*, which in your view is more appropriate to describe your position, one which sees "organized" religion as a political threat. As you wrote, "religion is entirely unobjectionable as long as it is privatized—as long as religious belief is regarded as entirely irrelevant to public policy." But is it possible to think of our American culture without the way in which religious language and belief underwrites our deepest beliefs about justice, fairness, and distributive justice? Is it not the case that Americans' commitment to a republic of law is entwined with a civil religion that provides it with its vitality and durability, in such a way that we would never have had a Martin Luther King, Malcolm X, the Berrigan brothers, the many religious workers who went to Central America to stand, and die, as witnesses for peace, and so many "prophets" who have made the U.S. a land of religious freedom but also of civil rights?

*RR*: Whether the possibility of rearing new Martin Luther Kings is worth the risk of rearing new Jerry Falwells is a matter of risk management. To my mind, the advantage of getting rid of the Falwells is worth the risk of getting rid of the Kings. But I have no knock-down argument to bring to bear. I just suspect that the continued existence of the churches is, by and large, more of a danger than a help to the rise of a global democratic society.

*Q*: At a more general level, however, can we dissociate the West, the Occident, from its onto-metaphysical roots, to use Heideggerian language, in which both the past and the future harbor unique promises? Don't you think that even your own views, as evidenced by the following quotes, are secularizations of the Judeo-Christian promise of a divine justice that is worked out historically? "Holiness resides in an ideal future"; and the "holy . . . is bound up with the hope that someday, any millennium now, my remote descendants will live in a global civilization in which love is pretty much the only law. In such a society, communication would be domination-free, class and caste would be unknown, hierarchy would be a matter of temporary pragmatic convenience, and power would be entirely at the disposal of the free agreement of a literate and well-educated electorate."

*RR*: I don't much care whether they are secularizations of the idea of divine justice or replacements for that idea. How could one tell which they were? How could it matter? It's certainly true that Christianity softened Europe up for the idea of egalitarian democracy. But I suspect the idea would have emerged eventually even if we had all worshipped Baal.

# 11

Worlds or Words Apart?
The Consequences of Pragmatism
for Literary Studies

*Interview by Edward Ragg*

*Question*: I wanted to ask you first about holism. Clearly holism doesn't just mean being interdisciplinary. Nor, as you argue in *Philosophy and the Mirror of Nature*, is it merely a question of antifoundationalist polemic. Rather, you say it marks "a distrust of the whole epistemological enterprise."[1] Could you explain what you mean by that?

*Richard Rorty*: If you weren't some kind of foundationalist you wouldn't bother to get into epistemology. Epistemology only looks attractive if you think that there is a topic called knowledge whose nature can be studied. The idea is that once you have learned its nature, you might get more of it than you had before. Only someone who thinks that knowledge has foundations located in sense perception, or pure reason, or divine revelation, or something, would take the idea of studying knowledge, its nature and limits, seriously. I think of holism as just the view that people change their beliefs in such a way as to achieve coherence with their other beliefs, to bring their beliefs and desires into some sort of equilibrium—

1. Richard Rorty, *Philosophy and the Mirror of Nature* (Oxford: Blackwell, 1980), 181.

and that that is about all there is to be said about the quest for knowledge. There are no rules for which beliefs you sacrifice in order to accommodate other beliefs, or which desires you change to accommodate changed beliefs. Because there aren't any rules, there aren't any methods you can study in order to improve the way you achieve equilibrium. The whole idea of studying how belief is changed is pretty hopeless. It's just too holistic a process to be an appropriate topic of study.

Q: Holism is obviously a natural corollary of pragmatism because pragmatists urge bringing as many different useful vocabularies to discussion as we can. This reminds me of your definition of "literariness." In *Contingency, Irony, and Solidarity* you describe literary skill as the ability to effect "surprising gestalt switches by making smooth rapid transitions from one terminology to another."[2] Would it be fair to say, then, that thinking holistically is, to some degree, literary?

*RR*: No, I don't think so. It would be more appropriate to say thinking holistically, in the sense of not being limited to a given context or disciplinary framework, is a matter of thinking imaginatively. Politicians and theologians and engineers think imaginatively just as much as literary people do. To call it literary would be unduly to privilege literature.

Q: Would you say that, as a writer, your own work has been treated holistically: first in the sense that your texts are seen as a growing body of thought—that is, that there is a difference between the writer of *Philosophy and the Mirror of Nature* and the author of *Contingency, Irony, and Solidarity*—and, second, in the sense that people have thought holistically about your ideas, have brought them to bear on literature, philosophy, social science, the very demarcations you want to transcend?

*RR*: I think that the stuff I do is more interesting to people outside of philosophy than to those inside it. This is an example of the same phenomenon that led Kuhn to be much more read by people outside the hard sciences than by people within them. My stuff, like Kuhn's, debunks certain views that various earlier philosophers, especially the positivists, had tried to impose on the culture. My readers are people who are looking for a way out from the view they absorbed, without much liking it, when they

2. Richard Rorty, *Contingency, Irony, and Solidarity* (Cambridge: Cambridge University Press, 1989), 78.

were young. People inside of philosophy, however, often regard all this debunking as endangering the problems they have devoted their lives to solving. They do not want the problems dissolved, because that would dissolve their solutions as well. So they welcome it less than do outsiders.

*Q*: One of the markers of your holistic desire to conceive of philosophy as a form of literary criticism is your tendency to refer to major philosophers as strong poets. And yet the authors you discuss are predominantly novelists, for example, Nabokov and Orwell.[3] Admittedly, it is not uncommon to use novelists rather than poets to talk about narratives. I am thinking of Walter Benn Michaels and *Our America*.[4] But why have you refrained, generally speaking, from discussing poetry in greater detail? Is the Bloomian notion of strong poets just a convenient metaphor?

*RR*: Yes, it's just a term I picked up from Harold Bloom and extended a bit. It seemed a handy piece of terminology to use when emphasizing the fact that people like Plato and Galileo and Marx, people with great imaginations, people who altered the vocabularies with which we think about various matters, were no more offering conclusive arguments, or indeed anything much in the way of argument at all, for their views than poets. They just put their new visions on the table and made it possible for us to occupy a different perspective. So I adopted the term *strong poet* to denote anyone with a lot of imagination who has the courage to try to make everything in his or her field new, to change the way we look at things.

*Q*: But would you say that poetry is not generally quite as accessible as prose and the narratives that novels suggest? Do you find poetry less obviously useful as a medium?

*RR*: No, that's just an idiosyncrasy. I'm not a very good reader of poetry. Bloom has read just about every poem published in English and remembers each of them. Poetry is what comes first to his mind. It just doesn't happen to be the first thing that comes to my mind.

*Q*: One of the arguments in *Contingency, Irony, and Solidarity* is that reading books encourages empathy: that we can empathize through the

3. See, for example, Richard Rorty, *Contingency, Irony, and Solidarity*, part 3.
4. Walter Benn Michaels, *Our America: Nativism, Modernism, and Pluralism* (Durham, N.C.: Duke University Press, 1995).

solidarity of imagining other people's pain. Books are supposed to do this. But isn't that position rather idealistic? Wouldn't a pragmatist happily concede that literary, or any linguistic communication, depends upon the intersection of vocabularies, on reaching "intersubjective agreement," and that, as ironists, we can't be sure whether or not vocabularies will fulfill such useful purposes as being able to empathize? After all, the ironist you describe in *Contingency* needs to read as many books as possible to optimize the possibility of consensus, but knows that we cannot answer the Nazis by getting them to read Anne Frank.

*RR*: We can't be sure, but we know that it's happened in the past. We know of the effect that Dickens, Harriet Beecher Stowe, Orwell, and others, have had on the way we think about politics and contemporary social issues. I think that the fact you need intersubjective agreement is perfectly compatible with the fact that a whole lot of people can suddenly undergo a gestalt switch as a result of reading a novel.

*Q*: You've often accused thinkers such as Derrida and Heidegger— particularly Heidegger—of thinking in quasi-metaphysical terms about the properties of language. I am thinking of your cautionary conclusion to "Wittgenstein, Heidegger, and the Reification of Language," where you say: "Heideggerese is only Heidegger's gift to us, not Being's gift to Heidegger."[5] Obviously your preferred way of thinking about language use is more Davidsonian and Darwinian. But wouldn't you say that one of the things literature can do is to question the ability of language to perform useful communication? Doesn't literature point up the limitations of the marks and scratches human beings transact? Or does that sound too de Manian? I am thinking of what Richard Poirier calls the "illusion of literature's resourcefulness," and the misguided notion in humanities teaching that, again, reading books will make us better people.[6]

*RR*: I think they often have made us better people. I can't see why Poirier thinks it's an illusion. It doesn't always work, but it isn't that we have many better tools. So we might as well use the tools we have.

5. Richard Rorty, "Wittgenstein, Heidegger, and the Reification of Language," in *Essays on Heidegger and Others: Philosophical Papers II* (Cambridge: Cambridge University Press, 1991), 65.

6. Richard Poirier, *The Renewal of Literature: Emersonian Reflections* (London: Faber and Faber, 1988), 4.

*Q*: You say: "Criteria . . . are never more than the platitudes which contextually define the terms of the final vocabulary currently in use."[7] So, what criteria would you say a pragmatist brings to a literary text?

*RR*: I don't think texts are best approached with criteria in mind; unless you know exactly what you want to get out of the text in advance. If you're reading a training manual that is explicitly written to enable you to perform a certain task, then of course you have criteria to bring to the text: you have tests to apply which will tell you whether it was what you wanted. But when we read literary texts, typically we don't know in advance what we want. So we're not in a good position to bring criteria to bear on the text. We read in order to enlarge ourselves by enlarging our sensitivity and our imaginations. For that purpose applying criteria isn't really a relevant technique.

But is it possible to step outside the criteria that are already presupposed by the language we use to describe texts? I agree that one of the reasons people read literature is to discover more resourceful ways for describing themselves or altering their vocabularies for a variety of purposes. But I'm not sure that you could avoid coming to a literary text without a set of criteria, however much you might want to avoid it.

You certainly can't avoid approaching it without a certain set of expectations. But a lot of the time what you're hoping for, if only subconsciously, is to have those expectations upset. You would like to be swept off your feet. You would like to be plunged into doubt about a lot of things which you hadn't previously doubted. So I would prefer to say that although any reader comes to a text out of a background, the good readers are those who try to let the text dominate the background rather than vice versa.

*Q*: This brings us back to Poirier's comment, because I think what he was accentuating—in attacking the idea of literature being resourceful in a conventional, didactic sense—is that some of his preferred texts are ones that aren't going to declare a moral message, not going to have the kind of narrative that, say, *Uncle Tom's Cabin* has (you mentioned Stowe). His preferred writers—and I know you've criticized Foucault for this—are those who want to write without a human face, or at least with a kind of disappearing act. I think he just wants to get away from the idea that literature might have some kind of moral foundation. But are you resistant to

7. *Contingency, Irony, and Solidarity*, 75.

the idea of pragmatists having criteria because you abhor the idea of there being a pragmatist literary theory? And even if such a theory were untenable, don't you think that pragmatism still has certain things to recommend to people studying literature?

*RR*: No, I guess I don't. I think of pragmatism as primarily therapeutic philosophy—therapy conducted on certain mind-sets created by previous philosophers. Insofar as reading pragmatism frees you up from various old habits and convictions, it does it in the same way that a startling new literary text does. It makes you think, "Gee, I never knew you could look at it that way before!" But therapy isn't the same as providing criteria, or a theory.

*Q*: But, to turn that around, isn't that precisely why pragmatism is useful for studying literature, because it guards against the fads of theory, those that have quasi-foundationalist appearances, or those that attempt master vocabularies, even antifoundationalist ones?

*RR*: Yes, but on the other hand, there are lots of hymns of praise for the unfettered imagination sung by nonphilosophers. These are at least as effective as pragmatist philosophy for encouraging the desired therapy.

*Q*: I suppose, though, one of the most immediate ways in which pragmatism might be therapeutic is that it provides us with quite a handy vocabulary for talking about vocabularies.

*RR*: Does it really? I would have thought it took away vocabularies rather than supplying new ones. It's supposed to be a medicine which dissolves the old medicines but doesn't in fact leave its own trace in the bloodstream. I think there's a certain danger in trying to turn pragmatism into something stronger than it really wants to be.

*Q*: Well, hopefully we can return to that; and I'd like specifically to ask you about the much-used phrase "the banality of pragmatism." But I'd like to turn first to the charge of relativism. Davidson famously pointed out that thinkers who inhabit different paradigms or different "thought worlds" may not be "worlds, [but] only words apart."[8] He does this to puncture the question-begging conceptual relativist claim that the speak-

8. Donald Davidson, "On the Very Idea of a Conceptual Scheme," in *Inquiries into Truth and Interpretation*, by Donald Davidson (Oxford: Clarendon Press, 1984), 189.

ers of different languages have mutually exclusive understandings of their environments, even though those understandings stem from the "same" world. For him relativism is a question of scheme-content distinctions and the dubious notion of the "failure of intertranslatability."[9] But isn't the attack on relativism something of a straw-target affair? Pragmatists are obviously accused of relativism, which is something you've written on. But wouldn't it be best for pragmatists simply to avoid talking about relativism? After all, pragmatism itself urges against the use of our critics' terminologies, or any language which gives credibility to whatever we want to dismiss. In any case, as far as I can see, and as far as pragmatism argues, it's not possible to be a relativist anyway.

*RR*: Well, I think what Davidson is talking about is incommensurability and denying that it's a real phenomenon, something we have to worry about. Unlike a lot of followers of Derrida and de Man who make a big deal out of the failure to commensurate, I agree with Davidson about that. But I think that relativism is something different. If you think of relativism not as the claim that there are incommensurable discourses—and that you can't get outside of your own—but rather as the claim that no discourse has any epistemological or ontological privilege, discussion of relativism is still of interest. For the claim that you should stop asking whether your views are those of the universe, or whether they correspond to the intrinsic nature of reality, or whether they are epistemologically sound, is a claim about the form that intellectual life should take. To say it should become relativistic is obviously the wrong way. To say it should become anti-absolutist makes a certain amount of sense—at least if you take absolutism to mean the view that the right beliefs are made right not by social agreement but by something large and nonhuman such as God or the Real.

*Q*: So you think it is important to debate relativism and defend pragmatism from the charge of relativism?

*RR*: I think it's important for pragmatists to say that the fact that there aren't any absolutes of the kind Plato and Kant and orthodox theism have dreamed doesn't mean that every view is as good as every other. It doesn't mean that everything now is arbitrary, or a matter of the will to power, or something like that. That, I think, has to be said over and over again.

9. Donald Davidson, "On the Very Idea of a Conceptual Scheme," 190.

*Q*: Let's turn to the specific reception of your ideas in literary studies. I am curious as to why pragmatism has not traditionally held, at least since the formation of literary studies as a discipline in its own right, the kind of popular place in literary theory that other discourses—deconstruction, psychoanalysis, queer theory, structuralism, historicism and so on—have come to possess. Is it because pragmatism is too holistic? That is, if we view literary criticism holistically we will not think of such criticism as a privileged discourse? Or, less generously, do you think it is because literary critics, generally speaking, are simply unfamiliar with the consequences of pragmatism for literary studies? The literary theory I was taught never breathed a word of pragmatism.

*RR*: I think that literary theory was fashionable only for a rather brief period. It seems now to be on its way out. It became fashionable because it looked like an easy way to write literary criticism. You mastered the theory and then you applied it. New Criticism was the obvious example in America when I was young. You read Eliot and Cleanth Brooks and Allen Tate and imitated them, and thereby produced a publishable work of academic criticism. When people got bored with New Criticism, they turned to other things. But the idea was always to, first, master a set of principles and then to apply them. This is a terrible way to be a critic, as people are now, perhaps, beginning to realize. This idea of "applying a theory" would never have arisen if it weren't for the need to give credentials to thousands of members of departments of English literature. But I think that now everybody is so sick of formulaic criticism that we don't need to worry about literary theories anymore. In particular we don't need to worry about whether pragmatism counts as one of them.

*Q*: But doesn't that suggest that people have become more pragmatic about reading texts, that they realize the potential for theory to be a totalizing rather than an enabling or therapeutic affair? So, although, for obvious reasons, a pragmatist wouldn't privilege something called a pragmatist literary theory—that, in your sense, would be oxymoronic—you could see that we might be in a more pragmatic period in terms of how people approach texts?

*RR*: I think pragmatism may have done its little bit. But I think it was mostly that no one could stand reading any more of these machine-processed literary critical essays. They were so easily parodied that the whole enterprise began to fall of its own weight.

*Q*: I can understand why you wouldn't want to overestimate pragmatism's part in contributing to a weariness with theory. But I still can't get away from the notion that if you think as a pragmatist thinks, you are likely to be more sensitive than other kinds of readers are to the prospect of falling into reductive reading or additional theoretical problems.

*RR*: Well, yes, in the following sense: if you had somehow been convinced that there was something called a firm philosophical basis for a certain kind of criticism, as the New Critics sometimes were, the Marxists usually were, and the deconstructionists fervently were, then you might stumble upon pragmatism and read it as a kind of antiphilosophical philosophy. Reading pragmatism might encourage you not to take philosophy as being foundational with respect to other disciplines. That might be a useful, therapeutic agent.

*Q*: Certainly the critical schools you mention propped themselves up with particular philosophical views. Just thinking of the critics who have written on, say, Wallace Stevens bears this out. There are scholars who fall foul of reading texts reductively because of the presumptions they have about texts. For example, John Crowe Ransom wrote a book called *The World's Body*.[10] He thought that poetic form somehow derived from the world and that poetry was a means of putting us back in touch with reality. To a pragmatist that makes very little sense indeed. Or, to take another example, R. P. Blackmur reacted very badly to Stevens's later work, because he found that late Stevens didn't possess the unity or cohesion, or the particular criteria Blackmur privileged when he came to read that verse. In fact the absence of what attracted Blackmur was exactly what attracted the deconstructionists to Stevens's later work, in particular the notion of decreation. So, I'm wondering if you agree that whatever worldview you have, or whatever philosophical presumptions you might have, does effect how you look at texts.

*RR*: I'm a little wary of calling them philosophical presumptions. I think that philosophical presuppositions are just clothes that you drape over your initial attitude. You get into literary criticism because you have certain favorite poets, and certain poets you can't see the point of—ditto for certain novelists, essayists, and so on. But if you're sufficiently gull-

10. John Crowe Ransom, *The World's Body* (New York: Scribner's Sons, 1938).

ible you will look around for philosophical reasons for saying that these are good poets and others aren't. But I think that the better critics don't bother with this attempt to put a philosophical frosting on their elective affinities.

*Q*: Yes, it's not that they need those criteria. But you could see how a more engaged critic might have the holistic intention of considering how the poets he or she studies, that he or she happens to like, chime in certain ways with other areas of discourse?

*RR*: Well, I think that the way they should do it is to say, "If you like this poet, you might like this philosopher." Maybe even to say that certain philosophers go with certain texts, or go with other philosophers or poets. But you can say that without ever thinking that it's the philosophy that makes the difference.

*Q*: In "Philosophy as a Kind of Writing" you observe that the "tradition of onto-theology" is kept going by the tendency for radical critiques of past philosophy, even antifoundationalist ones, to become dangerously dominant master vocabularies in their own right. In particular you suggest that Derrida and Derridean philosophy might be dubiously deified because, "We may find ourselves thinking that what Heidegger thought could not be effed really can be, if only *grammatologically.*"[11] Do you think pragmatism is ever in a similar danger of being divinized? Or is it too self-aware of its own linguistic inscription?

*RR*: Well, something like the divinization of pragmatism did happen in the U.S. in the thirties and forties, when American intellectuals typically thought of themselves as Deweyan pragmatists, without ever having read much Dewey (and in particular not having read the philosophers Dewey was arguing against). This is analogous to the way that a lot of people thought of themselves as Derrideans without having read much Derrida, or, even if they had read a lot of Derrida, not really knowing what Derrida was going on about because they did not have enough background reading in the history of philosophy. With both Dewey and Derrida there was a certain amount of jumping on the bandwagon, in Dewey's case by intellectuals primarily concerned with social and political affairs rather than with

11. Richard Rorty, "Philosophy as a Kind of Writing," in *Consequences of Pragmatism* (Minneapolis: University of Minnesota Press, 1982), 101.

literature. In Derrida's case it was more the literary types. But it was the same kind of half-baked appropriation of a philosopher's views without really taking part in the conversation between philosophers.

*Q*: I was thinking, rather, of that later stage of pragmatism, after Dewey and James, about those later neopragmatist thinkers who are specifically interested in language (including Davidson, even though he denies being a pragmatist). I was thinking more about Quine and Sellars and the stage you have also criticized, where it was thought that all problems in philosophy might be solved or dissolved by restatement as problems of language—a position which had a certain vogue when you were editing *The Linguistic Turn*. What I meant by pragmatism's being aware of its own linguistic inscription was referring to this later phase of pragmatism, not its earlier manifestation. So, could neopragmatism avoid being divinized because of its concern with language?

*RR*: Not for that reason. There are two ways in which philosophers are concerned with language. There is the Wittgensteinian way, which I think is continued in Davidson and Brandom and, to some extent, Putnam—the people I like to lump together as neopragmatists. That way of thinking about language doesn't treat it as anything special, or as a new topic for philosophical inquiry. The other kind of philosophy of language takes it with the same utter seriousness with which we used to take experience or knowledge or consciousness. My favorite example is Michael Dummett, who once wrote incautiously that since a theory of meaning is first philosophy, Wittgenstein must be wrong. For if we didn't have a theory of meaning of the sort that Wittgenstein told us we couldn't have, we wouldn't have the foundation of all other philosophy. We'd have to go out of business altogether. That is something Brandom or Davidson would never say.

*Q*: In another essay, "Idealism and Textualism," you argue that the twentieth-century obsession with texts is continuous with the nineteenth-century idealism that began to question the foundational status of empirical science. You do this to contextualize the position of the then Yale school and the American version of deconstructionist theory. However, when you turn to other kinds of critics such as M. H. Abrams and Gerald Graff you state, "Epistemology still looks classy to weak textualists."[12] Obviously that comment was written twenty years ago. But how would you describe the current practices of weak and strong textualists? Do weak readers still want to endow writers with significant epistemological statuses?

*RR*: I just don't know. My feeling is that epistemology isn't in vogue among literary critics anymore because cultural studies, at least in this country, has taken over. You don't need epistemology to do cultural studies, you just need resentment. So I think for the time being, at least in the literature departments of American universities, epistemology just isn't very visible.

*Q*: This brings us back to dialogues between literature and philosophy, and the extent to which they may or may not be useful. One of the things you have been criticized for is your distinction between public and private spheres.[13] Derrida, for example, doesn't accept your point that his philosophy is only indirectly relevant to conventional politics and that Derridean discourse is useful only on the level of cultivating private self-images or advocating antifoundationalist thinking.[14] I suspect people have missed the subtlety of the distinction. As a holistic thinker, you would never recommend separating off wholeheartedly the public and the private (even if one could do so). On the other hand, your criticisms of the academic left have led you to side with Irving Howe's remark that the problem with literary critics is that they "don't want to take over the government; they just want to take over the English Department."[15] That would seem to suggest that you think studying literature might go some way to operating more powerfully in engaging with things outside the English department, wouldn't it? How would you tally those two positions?

12. Richard Rorty, "Idealism and Textualism," in *Consequences of Pragmatism*, 156.

13. See, for example, Simon Critchley, "Derrida: Private Ironist or Public Liberal?" in *Deconstruction and Pragmatism*, ed. Chantal Mouffe (London: Routledge, 1996), 22 ff.

14. See Jacques Derrida, "Remarks on Deconstruction and Pragmatism," trans. Simon Critchley, in *Deconstruction and Pragmatism*, ed. Mouffe, 78 ff.; and Rorty's critique, also titled "Remarks on Deconstruction and Pragmatism," in *Deconstruction and Pragmatism*, 13–18.

15. See Rorty, "Remarks on Deconstruction and Pragmatism," 15.

*RR*: Well, I don't think that which academic discipline you are in has any particular relation to your interest in public affairs, or your activities as a citizen.

*Q*: Well, maybe I've missed Howe's point. What kind of criticism do you think he's making?

*RR*: What I think he's saying is that in the old days an American professor would have thought of himself as a leftist if he were marching on picket lines, or doing something recognizable such as attempting to influence national public opinion, trying to get his fellow citizens to prefer one candidate or policy over another. At a later period, you got the impression that some English professors thought that if you could replace followers of Cleanth Brooks with followers of Paul de Man you had somehow struck a blow for human freedom—as though that replacement itself should count as leftist political activity. There's an essay by the American intellectual historian David Hollinger, called "I Gave at the Office," which is about this. He says that in the old days you could get the professoriate to turn out for demonstrations, but now when you try to do that they say, "I've just finished my latest book on cultural studies—I gave at the office."

*Q*: As we've already discussed, you want to keep politics in one sphere and philosophy in another, and state that people should understand when to employ different vocabularies. Does this mean that pragmatism can be holistic only up to its point of use? Does utility demarcate the extent to which we join various vocabularies with one another?

*RR*: Yes, the way it dictates everything else. But works of imagination, or exercises of imagination, can extend our notion of what might be useful. So sometimes you don't know in advance what's going to be useful. As Dewey said, the discovery of the failure of old means to old ends changes your ends as well as changing the means. It isn't as though you can appeal to utility as a criterion. *Utility* is just a blanket label for whatever rationale you have for doing what you're currently doing.

*Q*: So what do you make of those literary critics who have made particular efforts to become more acquainted with philosophy? Do you notice something ominous in a forced connection between literature and philosophy designed to prop up in some way both disciplines?

*RR*: Well, I think that neither of them should ever have been disciplines. There is an intellectual tradition running from Plato to Derrida that you can study in order to contribute to it. But I think there are other intellectual traditions, running from Sophocles to Stevens, that you can also study and to which you can contribute. The idea of either of them as a *discipline* seems to me misleading. It's more like a conversation you are joining than like a set of practices to which you are conforming.

*Q*: So do you think academics find themselves in a slightly curious position, particularly pragmatists (and maybe those literary critics who have embraced pragmatism), in the sense that they find themselves within particular departments and institutional structures that are—what's the evolutionary word, vestigial? Structures that overhang as old historical constructs. In other words, do the very institutions academics work in inscribe the things they want to critique or do away with?

*RR*: Sure. But another way to look at it is: by pretending to do something called research, by pretending to have quasi-scientific methods, by pretending to have disciplinary standards, we can get ourselves a place at the public trough. We can be supported in doing what we want to do. This pretence that philosophy and literary criticism are "disciplines" with "methods," "research techniques," "results," and the like is one that not many people really take seriously. But it's a pretence that keeps the money coming into the humanities. I have no better method of financing to suggest.

*Q*: Do you think, then, that the language people use to describe their own practices is often at odds with those practices?
*RR*: Sure.

*Q*: For example, the fact that I was talking about disciplines a few moments ago?
*RR*: Sure. In the so-called hard sciences it's very clear that there is what Kuhn called a disciplinary matrix, and you have to learn how to fit into it; and if you don't, you're just a bad scientist. Generally, that matrix stays pretty much the same from the days you were a student to the days when you are a teacher, and so on, to the end of your career, with occasional modifications. In the humanities, you're in graduate school and, as

an untenured academic, forced to do the kind of thing for which people will give you degrees and promotion. But the nice thing is that once you get tenure you can simply turn your back on the matrix that shaped you and do whatever you damn well feel like. The strength of the humanities is proportional to the willingness of people to use academic security to do that. Of course, the second- and third-rate people never use the freedom that this kind of security gives them. They just keep trying to please the ghosts of their old graduate school teachers, or old mentors, rather than trying to do something new.

*Q*: This reminds me of a study Bourdieu did called *Academic Discourse*, which looked at how French students in French universities either learned to speak "the speak" the teaching body was replicating in the name of academic standards, or failed to do so—failing equally to make the necessary grades, pass their degrees, and so on.[16] But I wonder how you would describe pragmatism's place in this? Or is pragmatism too good at not leaving its mark, its own trace? I mentioned earlier this phrase "the banality of pragmatism," which maybe I don't understand fully. Does it mean that pragmatism looks dull simply because it refuses to ask certain kinds of nominally interesting questions, questions at least of interest to traditional philosophy?

*RR*: On the one hand, it means that pragmatism doesn't have the grandeur of the kind of universalist attempt to win through to the final truth, or win through to the way things really are. On the other hand, neither does pragmatism offer the sort of romantic ardor that leads you to say, "We will break all the sacred vessels, we must overthrow the system, all things must become new." So pragmatism misses out on these two ways of being nonbanal.

*Q*: But does it necessarily do that? I don't think speaking of pragmatism in terms of banality does it any favors. When I say that I'm not colluding with the notion that we should put pragmatism on the map as *the* philosophical mode of inquiry. But I'm thinking of the way you describe the Romantics in *Contingency, Irony, and Solidarity*, that their excitement comes from the fact they were very good at redefining ideas of what it was

16. Pierre Bourdieu et al., *Academic Discourse: Linguistic Misunderstanding and Professorial Power*, trans. Richard Teese (Cambridge: Polity Press, 1994).

to be human, and that meant coming up with very new vocabularies for things. Pragmatism may not be metaphysical, but doesn't it do something similar? Doesn't it do something more exciting than the "banality of pragmatism" suggests?

*RR*: I don't know. I think that pragmatism should pride itself on being a form of low cunning rather than being exciting. Insofar as pragmatism privileges the imagination over argumentation, it's on the side of the Romantics. Insofar as it prizes intersubjective agreement, it's on the side of plain ordinary democratic politics. I don't see how to make it exciting to the general public. Within philosophy, within this particular little disciplinary matrix, it can sometimes seem exciting because if you've been hypnotized by Descartes, and pragmatism makes you free from Descartes, that's obviously a big thrill. But most people have never read Descartes and couldn't care less.

*Q*: So you think pragmatism only seems exciting to people wanting to topple towers within academe?

*RR*: Exactly, yes.

*Q*: If someone were to come to you as a graduate student and say that he or she wanted to research pragmatism, would that fill you with a certain horror?

*RR*: Not horror, but I would try to suggest that they think again, and figure out which of the so-called pragmatists interests them, and not try to study pragmatism in general. I think all these attempts to find what Peirce, Dewey, and James have in common are pretty pointless. Books that say what Putnam, Davidson, Brandom, and I have in common are probably also pretty pointless.

*Q*: So what work would you want to engage in as a philosopher now?

*RR*: Well, it's not a field that's worth being in unless you're excited by toppling some tower or other. You can't tell a student, "Get an interest in toppling this tower." Either they're interested or they aren't.

*Q*: But how do you feel about the trajectory of your own career? Is there a feeling that once you've toppled various towers you can only go on saying the same things, because there's little left to topple?

*RR*: Yes, I think so. I think I've been discouraged by the fact that every time I think I've had a new idea I turn out to have published it twenty years ago. Most philosophers typically have one set of ideas which they repeat over and over again. There are occasional exceptions. Heidegger and Wittgenstein both actually had two sets of ideas in the course of their lives.

*Q*: But hasn't the style of your writing changed as a result of that? I'm not trained in philosophy at all and found sections of *Philosophy and the Mirror of Nature* quite difficult to read—not being sure how various pieces of terminology are being used—whereas *Contingency, Irony, and Solidarity* or *Philosophy and Social Hope* are clearly far easier to follow.

*RR*: There wasn't a change in ideas. I was trying to please an audience of analytic philosophers when I wrote *Mirror*, and I wasn't trying to please that audience when I wrote *Contingency*. I realized, after reading the reviews of *Mirror*, that I'd never make any headway with the analytic philosophers, so I stopped having a particular audience in mind.

*Q*: We've touched on this already, but I'd like to ask you more about universalism versus nominalism. Your criticism that people like Norris and Derrida are wrong to think that philosophy is something we are all implicated in is fundamentally anti-universalist and nominalist. You state categorically, in "Two Meanings of 'Logocentrism,'" that though Heidegger and Derrida are important, you "doubt very much that they speak to a universal human, or even a universal Western, condition."[17] This reminds me of your references elsewhere to Dewey's warning that philosophical answers tend to be totalizing, to have "a universal meaning that covers and dominates all particulars." For Dewey such answers "do not assist inquiry. They close it."[18] Pragmatism says, by contrast, "if it ain't broke don't fix it." Does pragmatism, therefore, guard us against totalizing, against universalizing and generally getting into problematic thinking?

*RR*: In the sense that pragmatism is equivalent to satire or tower

17. Richard Rorty, "Two Meanings of 'Logocentrism': A Reply to Norris," in *Redrawing the Lines: Analytic Philosophy, Deconstruction, and Literary Theory*, ed. Reed Way Dasenbrock (Minneapolis: University of Minnesota Press, 1989), 205.

18. See Richard Rorty, "Response to Ernesto Laclau," in *Deconstruction and Pragmatism*, ed. Mouffe, 72.

toppling, yes; it encourages the sense that there is something dragging us down that we need to cut free of. But that sense of needing to be free of the past is so ubiquitous in intellectual life that you can't really identify it with pragmatism. To do so would give pragmatism more of an importance than it should claim.

*Q*: Turning back to literary criticism, then, I understand the extent to which you want not to overprivilege pragmatism's relevance to literature. But would you agree that pragmatism does instruct us to guard against universalizing forms of reading? I'm thinking of your criticisms of Paul de Man, in particular his insistence that all close reading comes down to the "impossibility of reading."[19] De Man seems to need a universal principle, as you put it, "the dead, but luminous, God of Presence," in order to demonstrate his "living but invisible God of Absence."[20] That's totalizing, isn't it?

*RR*: Yes. But I have nothing against being obsessively narrow. Dostoevsky was obsessively narrow, but we're grateful for his obsessiveness. I can imagine being grateful for de Man's obsessiveness, that is, his habit of reducing to nothingness any given texts he reads. When de Man does it it's interesting, but when you get thousands of Dostoevsky clones and thousands of de Man clones, it's merely formulaic. I don't think anyone would have objected to de Man if he had been a kind of Kenneth Burke figure, not training up generations of students. But he happened to hit the American academy at a moment when all the students desperately wanted a new gimmick. So you got these thousands and thousands of little de Mans finding the nothingness at the heart of everything. It just became a joke. (Bloom is a far more interesting and important critic than de Man, but it is far from easy to imitate Bloom. There are no little Bloomians.) So I don't want to criticize de Man, I only want to criticize de Manianism. We owe everything to individual obsessions on the part of new, creative, imaginative people. You don't want to criticize them as totalizing because if you are obsessive you see everything through a very small window, a narrow set of blinkers. I think it becomes criticizable only when it becomes received doctrine.

19. See Rorty, "Two Meanings of 'Logocentrism,'" 209.
20. Ibid., 212.

*Q*: I suppose the distinction would be that what one would criticize in de Man as being totalist or universalizing would be where the obsession starts to be absolutist, where it starts to admit that there are not other viable and alternative ways of reading.

*RR*: Well, I think Dostoevsky is not about to admit that there are any exceptions to Christianity, or that de Man is about to admit that there are useful alternative ways of reading. That's too much to expect of an original mind. So I think of totalization not as something you yourself can individually guard against, but as a social phenomenon which requires a constant supply of satire and debunking if it is to be overcome.

*Q*: My own research involves the work of Wallace Stevens. You rarely mention Stevens in your work, and this is not surprising given his own dubious philosophizing and the plethora of conflicting quasi-philosophical positions in his writing.[21] You have, though, approved of Thomas Grey's claim that Stevens is a poet capable of making us feel what it is to be a pragmatist.[22] My own view is that pragmatism can tell us a lot about how to *approach* Stevens's poetry, but that the poetry only rarely speaks as a pragmatist might feel. How would you qualify Grey's thesis?

*RR*: I don't know enough to really comment on Grey. A lot of Stevens I find too hard to understand. A lot of it I like a great deal. Grey's book seemed to me to make sense of a lot of Stevens that I hadn't made sense of before. I don't know Stevens well enough to give Grey's book a critical reading. I wouldn't trust my own judgment.

*Q*: I'm just wondering what your reading experience of Stevens is though? My own view is that Stevens criticism over at least the past fifty years has been pretty much speaking the language of the poet's own verse and prose without recourse to more useful, non-Stevensian vocabularies. And this is why pragmatism becomes useful: not so much to say this is how

21. One interesting reading of Stevens can be found in Rorty's introduction to *Truth and Progress: Philosophical Papers III* (Cambridge: Cambridge University Press, 1998), 1.

22. See Richard Rorty, "The Banality of Pragmatism and the Poetry of Justice," in *Philosophy and Social Hope* (New York: Penguin, 2000), 97. See also Thomas C. Grey, *The Wallace Stevens Case: Law and the Practice of Poetry* (Cambridge, Mass.: Harvard University Press, 1991).

you should read Stevens, but paradigmatically to suggest that maybe there are more interesting bits of language in Stevens, or elsewhere, with which to read the poet than those habitually cropping up in the criticism. For Stevens was extremely adept in creating his own master vocabulary: I'm thinking of poetry as the supreme fiction, major man, the first idea, and so on. Is that something you've found in reading him?

*RR*: Well, I was reading his prose pieces a while back and I guess what impressed me was that I found it very hard to take any language away from them. I didn't pick up the jargon. It seemed to me that there wasn't enough obsessiveness, so to speak, to give you a line that would enable you to talk the talk. But maybe I just didn't read enough.

*Q*: I don't want to dwell on Stevens, but that's a very interesting response. There is something oddly unmemorable about his work, not in the sense that the writing is uninteresting, but that it is, particularly with the poetry, hard to remember or memorize, despite all the obvious pyrotechnics of Stevens's style. Was it your feeling, then, that this fantastic display of language provides you with few critical hooks for approaching his writing, despite the wealth of figures and tropes?

*RR*: Yes, that's what I suspect. But I'm not sure I really know enough about it.

*Q*: Interestingly, someone who I think taught you, Paul Weiss, took issue with Stevens's philosophizing in "The Figure of the Youth as Virile Poet," when that essay first appeared.[23] Weiss is also mentioned on more friendly terms in Stevens's highly problematic essay "A Collect of Philosophy." Stevens quotes Weiss in that essay as saying, "If by a poetic view we mean one which probes beneath those used in daily living, or one which cuts across the divisions which are normative to ordinary discourse, then all philosophy must be said to be poetic in conception and doctrine."[24] First, would you agree with Weiss in his view of the poetic nature of philosophy? And, second, to ask a different question, what do you think would

23. For Stevens's recollection of Weiss's criticism, see *Letters of Wallace Stevens*, ed. Holly Stevens (1966; reprint, Berkeley: University of California Press, 1996), 476.

24. Wallace Stevens, "A Collect of Philosophy," in *Opus Posthumous*, ed. Milton J. Bates (London: Faber and Faber, 1990), 271.

have infuriated Weiss about Stevens?

*RR*: That sentence from Weiss is perfectly true, but it's also something of a platitude. It would be hard to find people disagreeing with it. But I doubt Weiss and Stevens really made any intellectual contact. Weiss tended to slot everyone he talked to into a ready-made pigeonhole. I would doubt if he ever really absorbed much of Stevens.

*Q*: It's a whole problematic area though—and maybe one pragmatists would simply refuse to talk about—namely, the relations between philosophy and poetry. It seems to me just to cause language problems, in the sense that discourse on poetry and philosophy too often tells us very little about either thing in the attempt to establish some kind of relationship. We've talked about your tendency to use Bloomian metaphors for talking about original thinkers. But don't you think poetry is just such an amorphous term that philosophers should avoid talking about whether or not, say, Heidegger is poetic?

*RR*: Yes. I think as soon as you try to re-create the Platonic contrast between poetry and philosophy you're in danger of reifying your favorite philosopher and calling that philosophy and reifying your favorite poet and calling that poetry. Heidegger makes a distinction between poets and thinkers that I have never been able to make sense of. I don't know how you're supposed to tell which are which. I think the topic "What is the relation between poetry and philosophy?" something of a nonstarter. You can get something interesting if you do what Nietzsche did in *The Birth of Tragedy* and talk about the relation between Socrates and Aeschylus. That makes sense. Or, about the relation between Wordsworth and Schelling. But at the abstract level of poetry versus philosophy it doesn't work.

*Q*: So do you think someone like Stevens talked in that way because it was oddly edifying, that it allowed him to write poetry even if it was a nonstarter of sorts?

*RR*: Yes, I think he had some kind of image of Platonic enlightenment, or Platonic transcendence of self, or something like that, which he labeled philosophy, and then used that as something to bounce off when he was writing his poems.

*Q*: But I'm wondering just how valuable you find intersections between literature and philosophy to be. I'm thinking of Reed Way Dasenbrock's attempts to rehabilitate elements of analytic philosophy in the minds of literary critics.[25] What is your general view of the work that has been done?

*RR*: I think what Dasenbrock has done is to make Davidson a figure of interest to people in literature. But that isn't exactly bringing philosophy and literary criticism together. It's just saying, "Here's this particular philosophical view that might relieve your critical cramps," or perform some other kind of Wittgensteinian, therapeutic function. People in many disciplines sometimes pick up a book by a philosopher and say, "Hey, this is just what I needed! It breaks the chains of my training," or something like that. But the book in question is a therapy which works only for certain people trained in certain ways. I don't think it makes sense to advise people in a different discipline to go learn some philosophy. It does make sense to say, "You might want to read so and so"—some particular philosopher whom they might find intriguing.

*Q*: Not so long ago I interviewed the Shakespeare scholar Stanley Wells and was struck by his holistic intentions in editing, particularly editing Shakespeare. He said, "One of my objects in life is to raise awareness of the textual issues in people's lives."[26] Given your adherence to Wilfrid Sellars's view that all meaningful awareness is a linguistic affair, how significant would you say pragmatism is in highlighting how our lives are always linguistically, if not textually, inscribed?[27] Or do you think pragmatism is something discussed by philosophy professors, without use to anyone else?

*RR*: I think the turn away from the empiricist question "What is

25. See, for example, the following, all edited by Reed Way Dasenbrock: *Redrawing the Lines; Literary Theory After Davidson* (University Park: Pennsylvania State University Press, 1993); and *Truth and Consequences: Intentions, Conventions, and the New Thematics* (University Park: Pennsylvania State University Press, 2001).

26. Edward Ragg, "The Oxford Shakespeare Re-Visited: An Interview with Professor Stanley Wells," *Analytical and Enumerative Bibliography*, new ser. 12:2 (Illinois: Bibliographical Society of Northern Illinois, 2001), 86.

27. For Rorty's discussion of Sellars's "psychological nominalism," see *Philosophy and the Mirror of Nature*, 182 ff.

given in experience?" or "What is experience really like?" (which was it-self an heir to the question "What is reality really like?"), to the question "Which of all the available languages would be the best for describing this particular thing?" is going to be very important for the future of culture. The linguistic turn, construed in those terms, seems to me to be a big deal because it suggests a kind of polytheism. It suggests that there are lots of ways for describing things; and that we choose among languages on the basis of utility, not on the basis of correspondence to the true nature of ex-perience. So if the notion of multiple descriptions chosen on the basis of utility took hold it would change the tone of cultural life. But I don't think you can give the pragmatists the credit for the linguistic turn. It happened all over the place at the same time. Frege and Peirce, as Ian Hacking has said, were both taking the turn at roughly the same time. Heidegger and Carnap were taking the turn at the same time. Philosophers who didn't have anything in common with one another were suddenly beginning to whoop it up for language. That's much more important than pragmatism versus something else. Pragmatists got in on the act, but so did a lot of other philosophers.

Q: But I suppose what the pragmatists were seeking to critique was how language was being used by the logical positivists: the whole idea that language would be the preserve where you would be able to find incorri-gible truth.

RR: Well, what the logical positivists did was to change the subject to language and then be just as metaphysical about language as previous philosophers had been about reality, experience, and so on. They kept say-ing things like, "Now, thanks to the new symbolic logic, we will discover the real structure of language." The nice thing about the later Wittgenstein was the debunking of the notion of the real structure of language, and of language as having a nature to be understood. When the later Wittgenstein is described as a sort of pragmatist what is meant is that he is anti-absolut-ist, antimonotheist. He reminds us of our ability to use many languages to describe the same things.

Q: But even if pragmatism's place in the linguistic turn could be overexaggerated, wouldn't you agree that pragmatism does have certain things to recommend for literary study: for example, pointing out that ideas are not separate things to language, that ideas about texts are linguistically informed? So that, if pragmatism cannot spawn something called a "pragmatist literary theory," it can nevertheless debunk various metaphysical notions and the tendency to think about texts in an essentialist way: for example, the dubious idea that human beings have a special essence and that their texts have essences that it is the duty of every critic to get to the heart of? Maybe I'm coming out with another banality or platitude, but I would say pragmatism is useful because it is antifoundationalist, anti-essentialist, and recommends this holistic interest in multiple vocabularies. Are there any other ways in which you might conceive pragmatism being useful to literary study?

*RR*: No, I think that's it. I think anti-essentialism is the heart of the matter.[28] In a culture, either religious or scientistic, that says "Yes, but this is appearance, what we want is reality," or "This is accident, what we want is essence," you get a kind of authoritarian sadomasochism: the wish to subordinate oneself to something larger. I think of pragmatism, either when applied to democratic practice in politics, or when applied to literary criticism, as precisely debunking the appearance-reality, essence-accident distinctions. Pragmatists say, "Look, there isn't any authority that we can appeal to settle the quarrels between us. We're going to have to deal with them ourselves." That's the kind of change in self-description which could in the end make a difference.

*Q*: Maybe I find pragmatism more exciting than you do simply be-

28. Rorty has written from a specifically anti-essentialist position against Umberto Eco's distinction between the use and interpretation of texts: "[In] 'Intentio lectoris' . . . written at roughly the same time as *Foucault's Pendulum*, [Eco] insists upon a distinction between *interpreting* and *using* texts. This, of course, is a distinction we pragmatists do not wish to make. On our view, all anybody ever does with anything is use it. . . . I was dismayed to find him [Eco] insisting on a distinction similar to E. D. Hirsch's distinction between meaning and significance—a distinction between getting inside the text itself and relating the text to something else. This is exactly the sort of distinction anti-essentialists like me deplore—a distinction between inside and outside, between the non-relational and the relational features of something. For, on our view, there is no such thing as an intrinsic, non-relational property." Richard Rorty, "The Pragmatist's Progress," in *Interpretation and Overinterpretation*, ed. Stefan Collini (Cambridge: Cambridge University Press, 1992), 93–94.

cause I've spent less time with it. But I'm reminded of a point in *Contingency* where you say that the majority of people are metaphysicians. It's less true in the U.S., but it's certainly the case in Britain that people have moved generally away from God. Stevens was atypical in trying to find something to replace God; though I don't think he ever got to the stage of suggesting that we didn't in fact need to replace God with anything. Obviously you can be metaphysical without being religious. But this is why I've asked you about a pragmatist attitude to literary texts: because if most people are metaphysicians in some form, surely this must inform the work they will do on texts? For example, asking questions like: "What is the relation of this poem to ideas of truth?" or reality, or morality, or something larger than themselves?

*RR*: I'd be inclined to say not so much "inform" or "change the way" they work on texts, but rather that a pragmatist view of themselves changes their attitudes toward themselves as readers and as other people as readers. It isn't that they're going to do anything very different; it's that they're going to think differently about what they're doing.

*Q*: I'd like to turn back to your own position in all this. Why do you think figures such as Hilary Putnam and Donald Davidson have been at such pains to distance themselves from you?[29] Have these thinkers failed in your view to take the corollaries of Darwinism to their logical ends? Have they failed, in other words, to be as naturalistic as you would urge?

*RR*: I think Davidson is as naturalistic as you can get, though I'm not so sure about Putnam. Their distancing themselves from me, insofar as they have done so, has to do with the fact that I got known after the publication of *Mirror* as someone who was an enemy of analytic philosophy as an institution. Putnam and Davidson don't want to think of themselves as enemies of that institution. They don't want to be thought of as joining me in making wholesale criticisms of the institution of American academic philosophy. I think that the actual substantive differences in philosophical doctrine between either me and Davidson, or me and Putnam, are pretty hard to detect. Whenever I try to write about these differences I find them disappearing under my eyes.

29. For Rorty's response to Putnam see "Hilary Putnam and the Relativist Menace," in *Truth and Progress*, 43–62. For his response to Davidson see "Pragmatism, Davidson, and Truth," in *Objectivity, Relativism, and Truth: Philosophical Papers I* (Cambridge: Cambridge University Press, 1991), 126–50.

*Q*: So do you feel in one sense oddly out on a limb as the foremost exponent of American pragmatist thought? Or would you prefer not to be characterized in that way?

*RR*: I think I'd prefer not to be characterized in that way. I wouldn't mind being characterized as someone who tried to retrieve some stuff in Dewey that I thought was in danger of being forgotten. But that's about as far as I go.

*Q*: Do you think that the fact you have been caricatured as an enemy of analytic philosophy has to do with what we were talking about earlier, that people feel their self-definition is linked to particular disciplines and to particular departments? And do you think that these are the same people who are challenged by the nature of your writing?

*RR*: Yes, I do think so. I wish philosophers were more willing to give up on this model of quasi-scientific inquiry. If you think of yourself as participating in that kind of inquiry then you'll think of yourself as part of an ongoing research program. You won't realize that you are completely dependent on the occasional emergence of geniuses like Kant, Hegel, Heidegger, and Wittgenstein. I insist that we're all at the mercy of people of genius. They can, and should, kick over the chessboard. A lot of people really hate the idea that the next genius to come down the pike is going to kick over the chessboard at which they have been sitting all their lives. That's the main animus people have against my stuff. It isn't exactly that I'm a relativist, it's rather that I cast doubt on their self-images as quasi scientists who are dealing with the same problems dealt with by Plato and Aristotle, but using more refined methods.

*Q*: So what does you own work currently involve? Would you define it in negative terms?

*RR*: I would define it in negative terms. I spend all my time just replying to critics. It saves having any new ideas. I haven't had any of the latter lately.

*Q*: So would I be right in thinking that in your view there couldn't be a research program looking into pragmatism and literature that could be particularly useful?

*RR*: Well, it's the wrong size of things to have a dialogue between. I think people who read both James and Stevens are in a better position to write about either. Just as people who read both Maritain and Eliot are in a better position to write about them. But that's not the same thing as a dialogue between two great big things called literature and pragmatism, or literature and theology.

Q: Because they're too amorphous to talk about?
*RR*: Yes.

Q: I suppose this is one of the arguments that comes out in *Contingency*, that rather than working on particular disciplines, or privileging particular areas as foundational, we should be working on particular authors, or particular writers.
*RR*: Yes, exactly. Just pick up authors and see if they can be of any use, and see if they can be brought into dialogue with authors you've already read. I like the way Harold Bloom handles philosophers. He's never written extensively about a philosopher, but every once in a while he picks up a book by Derrida, or whoever, and says something really acute about it. The same goes for Frank Kermode. Nobody would think of either of them of as bringing philosophy and literary criticism together. They just read philosophers when they feel like reading philosophers. That seems to me just the right way to go about it. It's not a question of mastering a discipline. It's just being able occasionally to read an author who works in an unfamiliar genre.

Q: So without wanting to fall foul of typifying Bloom in a particular way, you could say that he is practicing a pragmatist form of reading?
*RR*: Yes, he and Kermode are not buffaloed by philosophy. Consider Kermode's essay on Heidegger and Stevens. Kermode isn't buffaloed by Heidegger. Kermode doesn't ask himself, "Do I have a proper grasp of Heidegger?" or of philosophy, or whatever it might be.

Q: Do you think there's a danger, then, particularly among students—among those who haven't had years and years of experience of reading books—that there is the feeling of not having the authority to talk about big names such as Heidegger, or Derrida, or Stevens, until one's totally read a corpus? Do you think because of the power academic disciplines wield, the way in which universities are organized, the rhetoric university professors transact, and so on, that this inculcates a sense of unnecessary inferiority?

*RR*: Yes, there is. But there's also something special about Anglo-Saxon academic culture. In France and Germany all intellectuals have read a certain amount of philosophy. You get it in the last year of high school. You're expected, as an educated person, to have some sense of what's going on in philosophy. If you are an academic, you cannot survive in the *Geisteswissenschaften* without some acquaintance with Plato, Kant, and some of their successors. This simply isn't the case in America or Britain. You can get on perfectly well, anywhere in the university, without having read any of those people. So when Americans or Brits pick up Derrida they have to take what he says about Plato and Kant on face value; this makes things more awkward for them, because they know perfectly well they're on thin ice. European intellectuals can read people like Derrida slightly more critically than most Anglophones.

# 12

# Biography and Philosophy

*Interview by Andrzej Szahaj*

*Question*: You were born in a leftist family. Many years ago you mentioned to me that some Polish trade-union activists were sometimes guests at the home of your parents. Do you remember them? What did the political activity of your parents consist of?

*Richard Rorty*: Many of my parents' friends were connected with the U.S. trade union movement, particularly the Amalgamated Clothing Workers. Most of them were Polish Jews, who kept up connections with Poland insofar as they could, and particularly with the trade union movement there. These friends, and their Polish visitors, were around a lot in my childhood, but I cannot remember any particular names or dates. I do remember that my parents and I were informed about the Katyn Forest massacre shortly after it occurred, and that my father tried to publicize the fact that it was done by the Russians rather than the Germans. I also remember that my parents (and I, on their recommendation) read Milosz's book *The Captive Mind* when it first appeared (in, I think, 1948—simultaneously with Orwell's *1984*).

My father had edited one of the American Communist Party's magazines in the mid-twenties. By the early thirties, my parents had become what the Stalinists called "Trotskyites"—nominally believers in revolution, but drifting toward more conventional social democratic views. By the forties and fifties they had become militant anticommunists—warning the U.S. against putting any faith in Stalin. They were, simultaneously, active in movements in support of relieving the condition of poor un-unionized agricultural workers, and of blacks. For a time during the forties they were employed as publicists and lobbyists by one of the black unions—the Brotherhood of Pullman Car Porters.

*Q*: Did you have any personal contact with Dewey during your youth? Was it connected with your family, with the work of your parents? You mentioned to me once that there were some Polish accents in Dewey's life? What was it?

*RR*: My mother told me that I passed sandwiches around at a party which Dewey attended when I was seven years old. That was the only time I was in his presence.

Dewey spent a year in Philadelphia gathering information about the Polish immigrant community there. There are accounts of what he did during that year in the various biographies. He was also very active in the discussions concerning the post–First World War government of Poland, and intervened, unsuccessfully, with Woodrow Wilson on behalf of one of the groups that claimed to represent Poland. I don't know the details, but you can find them in the various biographies of Dewey.

*Q*: You studied at the University of Chicago. Who was the most influential teacher during the time of your studies, in terms of your personal development? Did Carnap or Sellars exert an influence on you? What was Sellars like as a teacher and as a man? Who was the most important person you ever met in terms of your own philosophical and political development, and why?

*RR*: I was impressed by several teachers at Chicago—Leo Strauss, Charles Hartshorne (a student of Whitehead's), Richard McKeon, and Carnap.

I learned my first lessons in analytic philosophy from Carnap (who assigned Ayer's *Language, Truth, and Logic,* which I initially found very persuasive). Eventually, however, I was persuaded by Quine and Sellars to reject some of Carnap's best-known views. Sellars was never my teacher; I just read his writings with admiration.

*Q*: I know that Allan Bloom was one of your colleagues during your studies at Chicago. I know also that you were in touch with him later as well. Could you tell me something about the University of Chicago at the time of your and Bloom's studies, about the Leo Strauss circle, and about Bloom himself? In one of your interviews you said that the University of Chicago had been very leftist during the time of your studies. I was a bit surprised, because the University of Chicago has been seen mostly as a den of conservatism, so to speak.

*RR*: Chicago was still leftist when I was there (1946–52). The conservatives only came along later. Strauss was a mysterious, charismatic figure. Bloom believed what Strauss said about the need to go back to Plato and Aristotle when thinking about political matters, but I was never convinced. Strauss's students were the brightest people in the university, so I was glad to be part of his circle, even though I never really grasped his point of view.

*Q*: What was your relation to the so-called counterculture movement?

*RR*: I smoked a little pot and let my hair grow long, but that was about all. I soon decided that the radical students who wanted to trash the university were people with whom I would never have much sympathy. I never took seriously the idea that American culture was "sick" and needed to be replaced by an alternative culture.

*Q*: You worked for many years at Princeton. Why did you leave Princeton? What was the reason for your dissident attitude toward analytic philosophy, visible in your essays written while still at Princeton? For the past twenty years you always wanted to work outside any philosophical department. Why?

*RR*: After I began to think that analytic philosophy, of the sort practiced by my Princeton colleagues, was not as wonderful as I had first imagined, I began to teach Nietzsche and Heidegger. But I felt that graduate students in philosophy who wanted to work with me on authors such as these, and who shared my doubts about analytic philosophy, were in danger of not having proper academic careers. So I thought it best to find a job outside of a philosophy department, one in which I did not have to worry about advising doctoral candidates, and therefore stood in no danger of wrecking their careers by luring them into areas of interest which would make them unpopular with departmental colleagues.

Q: You are one of the Great Four of American philosophy: Davidson, Putnam, Quine, Rorty (in alphabetical order). All of you can be situated (maybe except Davidson) somewhere between analytic philosophy and some other traditions, mostly pragmatism, and it seems to me that that is why they are so interesting and inspiring. It seems to me that philosophical heterodoxy is always more interesting than any kind of orthodoxy. What do you think of that? What is your opinion about the role of Quine, Davidson, and Putnam in the process of changing American philosophy, analytic philosophy and philosophy as such? Have they been successful in doing that? Have you been successful in doing that? It seems to me that most American philosophy departments are still fortresses of a very traditional version of analytic philosophy. Stanford seems to be a good example of that. Why is that?

*RR*: I agree about heterodoxy. But I think that the Big Four in postwar analytic philosophy are Quine, Sellars, Davidson, and Brandom. Putnam's and my own contributions are less important. Davidson radicalized Quine, and Brandom radicalized Sellars, and both of them ended up with quite similar views. The conjunction of their views seems to me pragmatist treatment of mind and language that is more perspicuous than that offered by the classical pragmatists.

Davidson and Brandom are, alas, marginal to contemporary American analytic philosophy. They are respected, and have many admirers, but they are not "mainstream." This is because they offer no research programs of the sort that other analytic philosophers of mind and language do: they dissolve a lot of old problems without putting forward new ones for the graduate students to work on.

Q: Why is it that only you among those Great Four have reached out so openly to the so-called Continental tradition in philosophy? Even Putnam, who de facto repeats some elements of neo-Kantianism in his philosophy, does not seem to be fully aware of the presence and richness of this tradition. Why this separateness of analytic philosophy? What was the impulse to overcome it in your case?

*RR*: I do not think there are any very deep reasons why Putnam and

I took divergent paths in this respect. I just happened to get on a certain course of reading while he got on another. I had the advantage, however, of having had a better training in the history of philosophy than Putnam had had, for such training was one of Chicago's specialties. Putnam has never, as far as I know, shown much interest in Hegel, whereas I had already read some Hegel when I was in my teens. Putnam swerved briefly in the direction of Hegelian historicism in his book *Reason, Truth, and History*, but historicism has never attracted him as much as it attracts me. (By *historicism* I do not mean claims about historical inevitability, of the sort Popper rightly criticized in *The Poverty of Historicism*, but rather the idea that our philosophical vocabularies and problematics are attempts to deal with contingent historical circumstances rather than "perennial" or "basic" ones.)

*Q*: What is really new and interesting in American philosophy today?

*RR*: The figure from whom I have learned most is Brandom. I think that his oeuvre may prove to be the upshot of the last fifty years of work in analytic philosophy of mind and language. Nobody else combines an ability to expound a full-fledged systematic account of mind and language with the ability to spin a dramatic narrative of the history of philosophy. He seems to me in a different class from practically every other American philosopher of his generation. Nobody else would even have dreamed of synthesizing Frege and Hegel, but Brandom has managed to do so, brilliantly.

Politics

*Q*: As far as I know you have always been leftist and anticommunist at the same time (I know for example that as a student you were an author of resolution of sympathy with the students of Charles University in Prague who did not want to accept communism in 1948). Was it easy in the U.S.? You are often treated as a neoliberal thinker. Is there any difference between being leftist and being liberal?

*RR*: In the U.S., *liberal* means what *social democrat* means in Europe. In the early years of the Cold War there were still American leftists who were apologists for Stalin, but they disappeared fairly quickly in the fifties, as did Marxism. There was a revival of interest in Marxism in the U.S. in the mid-sixties, but it was short-lived. The students who read Marx in the sixties, and who wanted to "overthrow the system," called themselves radicals as opposed to liberals. They tried to deny the title of "leftist" to people who favored working within the system. Some of these people are still around, working as professors in American universities, and they still use "mere liberal" as a term of contempt.

*Q*: The great Polish poet Czeslaw Milosz wrote that people of good will became spokesmen of communism because of "Hegel bite," the conviction that history must necessarily head in a good direction and that communists need only realize its plan. This "Hegel bite" was typical not only for Polish intellectuals but, for example, for French ones too. I think that the scale of this phenomenon in the U.S. was much less than in Europe. What was the reason for that?

*RR*: The idea of "the inevitable movement of history" was never very popular among American intellectuals, except in the rather short period between the beginning of the Great Depression in 1929 (when it did indeed seem that capitalism might collapse) and the revelations of Stalin's crimes in the middle and late thirties. Dewey, who was then the most influential American philosopher, had no patience with the idea of historical inevitability. Philosophy has never had the interest or the prestige among American intellectuals that it has had among European ones, and very few American intellectuals in the twentieth century ever read a word of Hegel.

*Q*: You are known for your friendly attitude toward Eastern Europe. You have visited probably all East European countries, and some, like Poland, several times. What has been the meaning of the Eastern Europe experience for leftist political thought, in your opinion?

*RR*: I think the main impact of the liberation of Eastern Europe is to permit American intellectuals to look back on the Cold War and think of it as a good, successful war. If one adopts the point of view of people in Guatemala, Vietnam, or Chile, by contrast, it is very difficult to see the long struggle against the Soviet Union as a good, much less an heroic one. But people in Eastern Europe do seem grateful to the U.S. for having kept up the pressure on the Soviet Union for all those decades, and this makes

Americans feel that what their country was doing between 1949 and 1989 had some redeeming features, despite the tragedy of Vietnam and the guilt they feel over replacing Allende with Pinochet.

*Q*: In *Achieving Our Country* you try to show the importance and value of the so-called old left, interested mostly in economical issues, as compared with so-called new left or cultural left, interested mostly in problems of multiculturalism, politics of difference, and politics of recognition. You are very much in favor of the old left. Don't you think that interests of the new left in cultural issues result from the silent conviction that nothing can be changed in the area of the economy? It can be treated as an expression of helplessness in the face of a new stage of evolution of world economy; I mean the transition from regulated, national markets to a deregulated global market. It seems that this kind of politics, typical for the old left, was efficient when the economy was mainly a national one, simply because one could easily find the possible target of political intervention: the state. Today it is much harder because the fight with global capital is in a sense a fight with a shadow: one never knows for sure where the enemy is (some people are not convinced that a global capital and its operations are any threat at all, by the way). Global capital would have to be taken under control, but nobody knows how to do it. Sometimes it is also said that the old left is over because a classical working class is over. What do you think about that?

It seems to me that it lacks any plausible alternative for today's economical system. We are witnessing something like Fukuyama's prophecy being fulfilled, not at the level of politics (global triumph of liberal democracy) but at the level of economy (global triumph of neoliberal economics of the Chicago boys' style). Nobody knows what an alternative economic system could be. Perhaps this is the most visible triumph of the right: success in persuading people that there is no alternative for the status quo. By the way, is there any?

*RR*: I entirely agree. I have no idea how to arrange the global economy so as to produce global social justice. I don't want the Chicago school economists to run the world, and yet the people who demonstrate against the IMF and the World Bank also, it seems to me, have no positive proposals to offer. The old left has no proposals to make other than to recommend the usual social-democratic welfare-state measures that worked in the rich democracies, but may never be feasible in really poor countries. Neither does the new left. Nobody does. That may indeed be why leftists are turning away from economics to culture. But I do not think that this turn will do anybody much good.

*Q*: Are the classical analyses by C. W. Mills still valid in the case of the U.S.? I mean his analyses of elites of power, oligarchies, and so on.

*RR*: I read Mills so long ago that I have, I'm afraid, forgotten what his analyses were. I was not greatly impressed by his work, which did not strike me as particularly original.

*Q*: You said in your discussion with Angela Davis held at Stanford several months ago that Europe was ahead of America. What did you mean by that?

*RR*: I meant that the welfare state was better developed in Europe than in America, and that secularism was more advanced in Western Europe than in the U.S. I think that the development of a secularist culture is very important for social progress, and I very much regret the recent rise of evangelical Protestantism, particularly of the fundamentalist variety, in the U.S.

*Q*: During the same debate you recalled the notion of the West as something very precious, which should be defended or even spread. This is an attitude rather rare among leftist or liberal scholars, in an epoch of the influential ideology of multiculturalism. Reading a lot about these issues lately, I was astonished by the verve and popularity of anti-Western attitudes among scholars in America. Sometimes they are very anti-American too. Frankly, it seems to me to be a little funny, because while reading them one can have impression that Western culture is the most oppressive culture of all and the U.S. is the most oppressive state of all. Coming from such a country as Poland and remembering quite well the communist times, I am a little bit irritated by such announcements, frankly. To tell the truth, I am under the impression that some of those radical critics do not know what real oppression is. What is your opinion about these issues?

*RR*: I agree that they have little sense of what real oppression is, and they seem unable to appreciate the immense strides toward freedom and justice that have been made in the West in the course of the last two hundred years. There is a line in one of the Gilbert and Sullivan operettas that comes to mind: "The idiot who praises, in enthusiastic tone / Every century but this, and every country but his own."

*Q*: Don't you think that recent interest in group consciousness, community, and so on can be connected with the sense of uncertainty and fear so typical of what Ulrich Beck has called the "risk society"? In one interview you emphasized the need to put communities behind us in the process of self-creation. Don't you think that this is a good scenario only for strong people, for Nietzschean *Übermensch*? People try to find safety and support for themselves as human beings in a world of sharp competition and fight for survival so typical for deregulated capitalism. As individuals they feel helpless and powerless. Group solidarity, especially ethnic or racial solidarity, is probably the easiest and cheapest medicine for lack of certainty and safety. So it seems to me that multiculturalism is a typical Western way of inventing cultures and communities in order to fight the fear present in today's society (in Europe it is probably nationalism instead of multiculturalism). Apart from that, it also seems to be a tool used in a political fight for power. What do you think of that?

*RR*: We all need communities to belong to, but the best communities are the ones that are flexible enough to allow their members a lot of room for self-creation. I see what you mean about the need for solidarity in risky situations, but I don't think that the multiculturalist movement is to be explained in those terms. I think it is a very parochial phenomenon of contemporary Western (especially U.S.) academic life, and has little resonance or appeal outside the academy.

*Q*: What is your opinion about political correctness? Is this really a new type of McCarthyism, as is sometimes said?

*RR*: Most of the things the right calls "politically correct" and makes fun of are very good things—for example, ceasing to tell women humiliating sexist jokes, ceasing to discriminate against gays and lesbians, and so on. Occasionally there are people who carry their watchfulness against sexism and homophobia and racism to absurd extremes, and they sometimes behave in ways for which the term "McCarthyism" is appropriate. But they remain rare exceptions.

*Q*: You live in a very religious society, and so do I. Can religion still play a significant role in changing society for the better, in pragmatist progress?

*RR*: Sometimes it has been useful. "Liberation theology" was useful in Latin America until the present pope decided to stamp it out. The black churches in the U.S. were indispensable in the civil rights movement of the fifties and sixties. But on the whole I think religion still does more political harm than good. Certainly in the U.S. the "born-again Christians" who support Bush make up a reactionary, and very dangerous, movement.

*Q*: You are very much in favor of patriotism (I remember well your article "The Unpatriotic Academy") and individualism at the same time. You do not like all this talk about group consciousness, multiculturalism, community, and so on. But how can one be patriotic without being communal? To put it another way: what should be an object of patriotism in the case of a country like the U.S.? Nation? Political system? Democracy? Constitution? In Europe, we don't have trouble identifying the object: the nation is always seen mostly in terms of ethnicity, like in Germany, or in terms of a common culture, like in France. But it seems that in the U.S. such an idea of nation has no appeal.

*RR*: French culture is a different thing for French rightists than for French leftists, and a different thing for American rightists than for American leftists. For the latter, it is a matter of taking pride in the heritage of figures like Jefferson, Lincoln, Wilson, Roosevelt, Martin Luther King, and so on. I think it is important for political movements within a country to identify the events and figures in whom citizens of that country can take pride, to use this pride as a means of generating sympathy for its political aims. My article "The Unpatriotic Academy" was a rebuke to the American "cultural left" for not being willing to try to build an electoral majority. One cannot build such a majority if one proclaims that one's country is no good.

*Q*: In your works (*Achieving Our Country* and others) you postulate a world democratic government as an element of the future political order. How can one be patriotic and a partisan of a democratic world government at the same time? Doesn't one need to be cosmopolitan in order to postulate the government in question?

*RR*: One can be an American patriot and a cosmopolitan at the same time by taking pride in America's role, since the time of Woodrow Wilson, in constructing an international order, and especially in giving some credibility to the United Nations. This order is the one that President Bush is in the process of destroying, but U.S. presidents from FDR to Clinton did much to build it up. Should the internationalist momentum that American presidents have given to world affairs be resumed after Bush leaves office, it may become possible for Americans to view the gradual turnover of national sovereignty to international authority as the natural outcome of pride in their country's history. Surrender of American sovereignty can be viewed as the ideological Americanization of the world—as having persuaded the nations to come together in the way that the thirteen original American colonies came together in the eighteenth century.

*Q*: Such a government would demand a certain kind of surrender of the dominant position of the U.S. in today's world. Do you think that it would be possible? If so, what would have to be changed in the U.S. in order to be ready to accept such a government? Is America still an unfinished project? If so, what should be done to finish it?

*RR*: It is very unlikely to happen, but such a surrender seems the only way to avoid nuclear war between the U.S. and China at some point in the present century. Unless the U.S., Russia, China, and the European Union agree on international peace-keeping measures, and unless they cooperate in setting up a world police force, we are probably doomed. To accomplish what is necessary to avoid an eventual nuclear war, an American president would have to persuade the country that there was more safety in multilateralism than in U.S. unilateralism. This would be a hard, but not impossible, sell. Gore might well have attempted it.

*Q*: What is the future of the U.S.? What kind of concrete social reforms should be implemented in the U.S. in order to improve this country economically and socially? Some people are very afraid of the balkanization of America, which is supposed to take place as a result of uncontrolled immigration; changes in demographics (white people are already the minority in California and in many huge cities like New York, Los Angeles, Detroit, and Chicago, and they will be the minority in the entire country in about 2050); and the potential resistance of some groups against assimilation (Cubans in Florida are probably the best example of successful refusal of assimilation, successful in terms of economical and cultural independence from the majority). Do you think that all of this is a real threat for this country?

*RR*: The Cubans are indeed setting a very bad example. But the U.S. has been successful in incorporating immigrants so far, and I don't think that there is any reason why we should suddenly become much worse. The alarm about nonwhite majorities is no more realistic than the worry, a hundred years ago, that the newly arrived immigrants from Europe would somehow submerge the "real" Americans whose ancestors had arrived earlier. A lot, of course, depends on the willingness of children of previous immigrants to marry children of recent immigrants. Such intermarriage has been essential in the past, and remains essential in the future. Mexican Americans and Vietnamese Americans, for example, are now viewed by people who would call themselves "white" as "marriageable," even though black Americans are not.

*Q*: I remember that you told me once the history of your own family as an example of successful assimilation. How was that done?

*RR*: My grandfather came over from Ireland around 1850, at a time when Irish immigrants were treated like dirt by most Americans—as badly as Polish and Italian and Jewish immigrants were treated somewhat later in the nineteenth century. He married above his station, into a family that had emigrated from England in the eighteenth century. It took another couple of generations for Irish immigrants as a group to win complete social acceptance, but it was complete by 1950. By that date, it was almost, if not quite, complete for the Poles and Italians. By now, Americans don't usually ask questions about the ancestry of the people their children marry, except in the case of black-white intermarriage, which is still very rare. (Marriage between Jews and non-Jews, by contrast, is very common. My mother, for example, was the daughter of a German-American Protestant clergyman, but two of her brothers, as well as her son, married Jewish women.)

*Q*: To tell the truth I was shocked when I read that separation between black and white people is now nearly the same as it was at the beginning of the civil rights movement (this was the conclusion of research done at Harvard University, published several months ago). I do not want to believe it, but it seems as though this problem has not been solved so far. Why is this? It seems to me that it might be the expression of failed expectations on the part of blacks: because you white people do not accept them fully, they separate themselves from you to demonstrate that they do not need you.

*RR*: I would not blame the blacks for the continuing separation. It is not their choice, it is still being forced upon them. The problem is that the heritage of slavery has produced the so-called black underclass—millions of uneducated, unemployed, and almost unemployable black people living in the big American cities. This underclass contains, naturally, a lot of criminals. So whites are scared of poor black men, and try to stay as far away from them as possible. The problem of the black underclass could be gradually solved by the government, but only by means of a huge increase in public spending. The whites remain too selfish to pay the taxes that would be necessary to rescue black children from misery.

It would also help, of course, if the whites would stop thinking that one drop of black blood (unlike one drop of Irish or Polish or Jewish blood) "pollutes." That belief is why black-white marriage is so rare. It is not a belief shared by the blacks.

*Q*: Are you optimistic or pessimistic about the future of your own country and the world as such?

*RR*: Very pessimistic indeed, for the reasons given above. I do not see how nuclear war is to be avoided or how the poor nations are to be raised to the level of the rich ones.

*Stanford, April 2003*

# Bibliography of Richard Rorty's Writings

This bibliography was compiled by Gideon Lewis-Krauss, and updated and emended by Chad Kautzer.

BOOKS

Book entries are followed by the publication information for foreign translations.

"Whitehead's Use of the Concept of Potentiality." Master's thesis, University of Chicago, 1952.

"The Concept of Potentiality." Ph.D. diss., Yale University, 1956.

[Ed.] *The Linguistic Turn: Recent Essays in Philosophical Method.* Chicago: University of Chicago Press, 1967. 2nd enlarged ed., Chicago: University of Chicago Press, 1992.

―――. Spanish translation: *El giro lingüístico: Dificultades metafilosóficas de la filosofía lingüística.* Trans. Gabriel Bello. Barcelona: Paidós, UAB, Instituto de Ciencias de la Educación, 1990.

[Ed., with Edward Lee and Alexander Mourelatos.] *Exegesis and Argument: Essays in Greek Philosophy Presented to Gregory Vlastos.* Amsterdam: Van Gorcum, 1973.

*Philosophy and the Mirror of Nature.* Princeton, N.J.: Princeton University Press, 1979.

―――. German translation: *Der Spiegel der Natur: Eine Kritik der Philosophie.* Trans. Michael Gebauer. Frankfurt am Main: Suhrkamp, 1981.

―――. Italian translation: *La filosofia e lo specchio della natura.* Trans. Gianni Millone and Roberto Sallizone. Milan: Bompiani, 1986.

―――. Portuguese translation [Portugal]: *A filosofia e o espelho da natureza.* Trans. Jorge Pires. Lisbon: Publiçaoes Dom Quixote, 1988.

―――. Chinese translation: *Che hsüeh ho tzu jan chih ching.* Trans. Youzhen Li.

Taipei Shih: Chiu ta wen hua ku fen yu hsien kung ssu: kuei kuan t'u shu yu hsien kung ssu, 1990.

―――. French translation: *L'Homme spéculaire*. Trans. Thierry Marchaisse. Paris: Seuil, 1990.

―――. Serbo-Croatian translation: *Filozofija i ogledalo prirode*. Trans. Zoran Mutic, Amela Simic, and Nebojsa Kujundzic. Sarajevo: Veselin Maslesa, 1990.

―――. Japanese translation: *Tetsugaku to shizen no kagami*. Trans. Keiichi Noe. Tokyo: Sangyo Tosho, 1993.

―――. Polish translation: *Filozofia a zwierciadlo natury*. Trans. Michal Szczubi-alka. Warsaw: Fundacja Aletheia–Wydawnictwo Spacja, 1994.

―――. Portuguese translation [Brazil]: *A filosofia e o espehlo da natureza*. Trans. Antônio Trânsito. Rio de Janeiro: Relumé-Dumara, 1994.

―――. Spanish translation: *La filosofia y el espejo de la naturaleza*. Trans. Jesús Fernández Zulaica. Madrid: Cátedra, 1995.

―――. Russian translation: *Filosofiia i zerkalo prirody*. Trans. V. V. Tselicheva. Novosibirsk: Izd-vo Novosibirskogo Universiteta, 1997.

―――. Bulgarian translation: *Filosofiiata i ogledaloto na prirodata*. Trans. Nevena Tosheva. Sofia: Nauka i iskustvo, 1998.

―――. Korean translation: *Chorhak kurigo chayon ui koul*. Trans. Chi-su Pak. Seoul: Kkach'i, 1998.

―――. Slovak translation: *Filozofia a zrkadlo prírody*. Trans. Egon Gál. Bratisla-va: Kalligram, 2000.

*Consequences of Pragmatism: Essays, 1972–1980*. Minneapolis: University of Min-nesota Press, 1982. [Contains the following essays, flagged below with (CP): 1982e, 1972d, 1976b, 1976d, 1976a, 1977d, 1978a, 1981d, 1981a, 1980a, 1981c, 1981b, 1982a.]

―――. Japanese translation: *Tetsugaku no datsukochiku: puragumatizum no kik-etsu*. Trans. Shugeru Cho, Hideo Hama, Tetsuhiro Kato, Hisashi Muroi, and Hiroshi Yoshioka. Tokyo: Ochanomizu Shobo, 1985.

―――. Italian translation: *Conseguenze del pragmatismo*. Trans. Fabrizio Elefante. Milan: Feltrinelli, 1986.

―――. Serbo-Croatian translation: *Konsekvence pragmatizma*. Trans. Dusan Kuzmanovic. Belgrade: Nolit, 1992.

―――. French translation: *Conséquences du pragmatisme*. Trans. Jean-Pierre Cometti. Paris: Seuil, 1993.

―――. Korean translation: *Siryongjuui ui kyolgwa*. Trans. Tong-Sik Kim. Seoul: Minumsa, 1996.

―――. Spanish translation: *Consecuencias del pragmatismo*. Trans. José Miquel Esteban Cloquell. Madrid: Tecnos, 1996.

―――. Polish translation: *Konsekwencje pragmatyzmu.* Trans. Czeslaw Karkowski. Warsaw: Wydawn, IFIS PAN, 1998.

[Ed., with J. B. Schneewind and Quentin Skinner.] *Philosophy in History: Essays on the Historiography of Philosophy.* Cambridge: Cambridge University Press, 1984.
―――. Spanish translation: *La filosofía en la historia.* Trans. Eduardo Sinnot. Barcelona: Paidós, 1990.

*Contingency, Irony, and Solidarity.* Cambridge: Cambridge University Press, 1989.
―――. German translation: *Kontingenz, Ironie, und Solidarität.* Trans. Christa Krüger. Frankfurt am Main: Suhrkamp, 1989.
―――. Italian translation: *La filosofia dopo la filosofia: Contingenza, ironia, e solidarietà.* Trans. Giulia Boringhieri. Rome: Laterza, 1989.
―――. Danish translation: *Kontingens, ironi, og solidaritet.* Trans. Morten Haugaard Jeppesen and Søren Christensen. Aarhus: Modtryk, 1991.
―――. Spanish translation: *Contingencia, ironía, y solidaridad.* Trans. Alfredo Eduardo Sinnot and Jorge Vigil. Barcelona: Paidós, 1991.
―――. Dutch translation: *Contingentie, ironie, en solidariteit.* Trans. Kees Vuyk. Kamper: Kok Agora, 1992.
―――. Portuguese translation [Portugal]: *Contingência, ironia, e solidareadade.* Trans. Nuno de Ferreira da Fonseca. Lisbon: Editorial Presença, 1992.
―――. French translation: *Contingence, ironie, et solidatité.* Trans. Pierre-Emanuel Dauzat. Paris: Armand Colin, 1993.
―――. Serbo-Croatian translation: *Kontingencija, ironija, i solidarnost.* Trans. Karmen Basic. Zagreb: Naprijed, 1995.
―――. Turkish translation: *Olumsallik, ironi, ve dayanisma.* Trans. Mehmet Küçük and Alev Türker. Istanbul: Ayrinti, 1995.
―――. Czech translation: *Nahodilost, ironie, solidarita.* Trans. Pavel Toman. Prague: Pedagogická Fakulta Univerzity Karlovy, 1996.
―――. Korean translation: *Uyonsong aironi yondaesong.* Trans. Tong-Sik Kim and Yu-son Yi. Seoul: Minumsa, 1996.
―――. Polish translation: *Przygodnosc, ironia, i solidarnosc.* Trans. Waclaw Jan Popowski. Warsaw: Wydawnictwo Spacja, 1996.
―――. Russian translation: *Sluchainost, ironia, i solidarnost.* Trans. I. Khestanova and R. Khestanova. Moscow: Russkoe Fenomenologicheskoe Obshchestvo, 1996.
―――. Hungarian translation: *Esetlegesség, irónia, és szolidaritás.* Trans. János Boros and Gábor Csordás. Budapest: Jelenkor Kiadó, 1997.

————. Swedish translation: *Kontingens, ironi, och solidaritet.* Trans. Joachim Retzlaff. Lund: Studentlitteratur, 1997.

————. Chinese translation: *Ou-jan fan feng yü t'uan chieh.* Trans. Wen-rwei Hsu. Hong Kong: Ch'eng-pang, 1998.

————. Romanian translation: *Contingenta, ironie. si solidaritate.* Trans. Corina Sorana Stefanov. Bucharest: Editura All, 1998.

————. Bulgarian translation: *Sluchainost, ironiia, i solidarnost.* Trans. Ina Merdzhanova. Sofia: Izdatelska kushta "Kritika i Khumanizum," 1999.

————. Estonian translation: *Sattumuslikkus, iroonia, ja solidaarsus.* Trans. Märt Väljataga. Tallinn: Vagabund, 1999.

————. Latvian translation: *Nejausiba, ironija, un solidaritate.* Trans. Vevere Velga. Riga: Petergailis, 1999.

————. Japanese translation: *Guzensei aironi rentai.* Trans. Junichi Saito, Ryuichi Yamaoka, and Masahiko Okawa. Tokyo: Iwanami Shoten, 2000.

————. Greek translation: *Tikheotita, ironia, allilengye.* Trans. Kostas Kouremos. Athens: Alexandria, 2002.

*Essays on Heidegger and Others: Philosophical Papers II.* Cambridge: Cambridge University Press, 1991. [Contains the following essays, flagged below with (EHO): 1986m/1989i, 1984d/1992h, 1989e/1993h, 1991g, 1984c, 1989h, 1989c, combination of 1990a and 1995i, 1986j, 1984a, 1988a, 1989g/1990c. Two labels separated by a slash indicates an initial publication in foreign translation followed by the publication of the English original.]

————. Italian translation: *Scritti filosofici II.* Trans. Barbara Agnese. Rome: Laterza, 1993.

————. Spanish translation: *Ensayos sobre Heidegger y otros pensadores contemporaneos.* Trans. Jorge Vigil Rubio. Barcelona: Paidós, 1993.

————. French translation: *Essais sur Heidegger.* Trans. Jean-Pierre Cometti. Paris: Presses Universitaires de France, 1995.

————. Hungarian translation: *Heideggerol és Másokról.* Trans. András Barabás, András Beck, István Bujalos, István Kelemen, and Zsófia Vitézy. Budapest: Jelenkor Kiadó, 1997.

————. Portuguese translation [Brazil]: *Ensaios sobre Heidegger e outros.* Trans. Marco Antônio Casanova. Rio de Janeiro: Relume-Dumará, 1999.

————. Portuguese translation: [Portugal]: *Ensaios sobre Heidegger e outros.* Trans. Eugenia Antunes. Lisbon: Instituto Piaget, 2000.

————. Romanian translation: *Pragmatism si filosofie post-Nietzscheana.* Trans. Mihaela Cabulea. Bucharest: Editura Univers, 2000.

*Objectivity, Relativism, and Truth: Philosophical Papers I.* Cambridge: Cambridge University Press, 1991. [Contains the following essays, flagged below with (ORT): 1984i, 1987d, 1988d, 1983c, 1985d, 1991f, 1987c, 1986n, 1988b, 1987e, 1988e, 1983b, 1986h, 1985c.]

————. French translation: *Objectivisme, relativisme, et vérité.* Trans. Jean-Pierre Cometti. Paris: Presses Universitaires de France, 1994.

————. Italian translation: *Scritti filosofici I.* Trans. Massimo Marraffa. Rome: Laterza, 1994.

————. Spanish translation: *Objetividad, relativismo, y verdad: Escritos filosóficos I.* Trans. Jorge Vigil Rubio. Barcelona: Paidós, 1996.

————. Portuguese translation [Brazil]: *Objetivismo, relativismo, e verdade: Escritos filosóficos I.* Trans. Marco Antônio Casanova. Rio de Janeiro: Relume-Dumará, 1997.

————. Polish translation: *Obiektywnosc, relatywizmi, i prawda.* Trans. Janusz Marganski. Warsaw: Fundacja Aletheia, 1999.

————. Romanian translation: *Obiectivitate, relativism, si adevar.* Trans. Mihaela Cabulea. Bucharest: Editura Univers, 2000.

*Hoffnung statt Erkenntnis: Einleitung in die pragmatische Philosophie.* Vienna: Passagen, 1994. [This volume contains three lectures delivered in Vienna and Paris in 1993, subsequently published in English as chapters 2–4 of *Philosophy and Social Hope.*]

————. French translation: *L'Espoir au lieu de savoir: Introduction au pragmatisme.* Trans. Claudine Cowan and Jacques Poulain. Paris: Albin Michel, 1995.

————. Hungarian translation: *Megismerés helyett remény.* Trans. János Boros. Budapest: Jelenkor Kiadó, 1997. [Also includes "Relativism: Finding and Making" and "Philosophy and the Future."]

————. Spanish translation: *Esperanza o conocimiento? Una introducción al pragmatismo.* Trans. Eduardo Rabossi. Buenos Aires: Fondo de Cultura Economica, 1997.

————. Polish translation of chapter 3, "Ethics Without Universal Obligations": "Etyka baz powszechnych powinnosci." *Etyka* 31 (1999).

————. Portuguese translation [Brazil]: *Pragmatismo: A filosofia da criacao e da mudanca.* Trans. Cristina Magro and Antonio Marcos Pereira. Belo Horizonte: Editora UMFG, 2000. [Also includes translations of "Trotsky and the Wild Orchids" and "Philosophy and the Future."]

*Truth, Politics, and "Post-Modernism."* Assen: Van Gorcum, 1997. [Contains the Spinoza lectures, delivered at the University of Amsterdam in May 1997: "Is It Desirable to Love Truth?" and "Is 'Post-Modernism' Relevant to Politics?"]

*Achieving Our Country: Leftist Thought in Twentieth-Century America.* Cambridge, Mass.: Harvard University Press, 1998. [Contains 1995b and 1996e as an appendix.]

———. Dutch translation: *De voltooing van Amerika.* Trans. Henk Moerdijk and Kitty Jonk. Amsterdam: Boom, 1998.

———. Russian translation: *Obretaia nashu stranu: Politika levylch v Amerike XX veka.* Trans. I. Khlestanova and R. Khlestanov. Moscow: Dom intellekt. kn., 1998.

———. German translation: *Stolz auf unser Land.* Trans. Hermann Vetter. Frankfurt am Main: Suhrkamp, 1999.

———. Italian translation: *Una sinistra per il prossimo secolo.* Trans. Luca Bagetto. Garzanti, 1999.

———. Portuguese translation [Brazil]: *Para realizar a América.* Trans. Paulo Ghiraldelli, Jr., Leoni Henning, Alberto Tosi Rodrigues. Rio de Janeiro: DP e A, 1999.

———. Spanish translation: *Forjar nuestro país: El pensamiento de izquierdas en los Estados Unidos del siglo XX.* Trans. Ramón José del Castillo. Barcelona: Paidós, 1999.

———. Greek translation: *I aristeri skepsistin ameriki tou 20-ou aiona.* Trans. Thanos Hatzopoulos. Athens: Polis, 2000.

———. Hebrew translation [partial]: Trans. Michal Rosenthal. In *Mikarov* 4 (2000).

———. Japanese translation: *Amerika mikan no purojekuto.* Trans. Teruhiko Ozawa. Kyoto: Koyo Shobo, 2000.

———. French translation: *L'Amerique: Un projet inacheve.* Trans. Didier Machu. Pau: Publications de l'Université de Pau, 2001. [With a new introduction.]

*Truth and Progress: Philosophical Papers III.* Cambridge: Cambridge University Press, 1998. [Contains the following essays, flagged below with (TP): 1995f, 1993c, 1994f, 1994m, 1993f, 1993d, 1992k, 1991a, 1995j, 1984e, 1992g/1994i, 1995k, 1995d.]

———. German translation: *Wahrheit und Fortschritt.* Trans. Joachim Schulte. Frankfurt am Main: Suhrkamp, 2000.

———. Spanish translation: *Verdad y progreso.* Trans. Angel Manuel Faerna. Barcelona: Paidós, 2000.

*Philosophy and Social Hope.* New York: Penguin, 2000. [Contains the following essays, flagged below with (PSH): selection from 1996h, 1992o, *Hoffnung statt Erkenntnis,* in English, 1990e, 1996i, 1989b, 1989f, 1992j, 1996k, 1994c, 1997c,

1990b, 1998b/1999k, 1995g, 1992b, 1997i, 1996g, 1994a, 1997a.]
————. Japanese translation [partial]: *Riberaru-Yutopia to iu kibo.* Trans. Nori-
hide Suto and Hiromasa Watanabe. Tokyo: Iwanami Shoten, 2002.

[Ed., with Gianni Vattimo.] *The Future of Religion.* New York: Columbia University Press, 2005.

COLLECTIONS OF ARTICLES IN FOREIGN TRANSLATION

*Rentai to jiyu no tetsugaku: Nigenronno gensoo koete* [Philosophy of/for Solidarity
and Freedom: Beyond the Illusions of Dualisms]. Trans. Yasuhiko Tomida. To-
kyo: Iwanami Shoten, 1988. [Contains Japanese translations of: 1984i, 1985d,
1983c, 1984e, 1988e, 1986n.] (RJT)
*Solidarität oder Objectivität?* Trans. Joachim Schulte. Ditzingen: Reclam, 1988.
[Contains German translations of: 1984i, 1988e, 1986j.] (SO)
*Science et solidarité: La Verité sans le pouvoir, la philosophie sans authorité.* Trans.
Jean-Pierre Cometti. Paris: L'Eclat, 1990. [Contains French translations of:
1986n, 1987d, 1988d, 1984c.] (SS)
*Solidariteit of objectiviteit: Drie filosofische essays.* Trans. H. J. Pott, L. van der Sluis,
and R. de Wilde. Meppel: Uitgeverij Boom, 1990. [Dutch translation of the
three essays included in *Solidarität oder Objectivität?*] (SO)
*Heidegger, Wittgenstein, en pragmatisme.* Trans. Liesbeth van der Sluis. Amsterdam:
Uitgeverij Kok Agora, 1992. [Contains Dutch translations of: 1983c, 1985d,
1991f, 1986m/1989i, 1984d/1992h, 1989e/1993h.] (HWP)
*Hou zhe xue wen hua* [Toward a Postphilosophical Culture]. Shanghai: Shang
Hai Yi Wen Chu Ban She, 1992. [Contains Chinese translations of: 1982e,
1986m/1989i, 1988d, 1995i, 1990a, 1988e, 1983b, 1986n, 1980a, 1987d.] (HZX)
*Chung Wei Literary Monthly* 22:7 (December 1993). [A Rorty issue containing Chi-
nese translations of: 1992o, 1992k, 1991a, 1995i, 1992j.] (CW)
*Eine Kultur ohne Zentrum: Vier philosophische Essays.* Trans. Joachim Schul-
te. Stuttgart: Reclam, 1993. [Contains German translations of: 1988d, 1987c,
1991g, 1984c.] (EKZ)
*La svolta linguistica.* Trans. Stefan Velotti. Milan: Garzanti, 1994. [Contains Italian
translations of: 1967b, 1977b, 1990i.] (SL)
*Scritti sull'educazione.* Trans. Flavia Santoianni. Florence: Nuova Italia, 1996.
[Contains a new preface as well as Italian translations of: 1982d, 1989b.] (SE)
*Cadernos de tradução da F.F.C.: Textos de Richard Rorty.* Trans. Paolo Ghiraldelli,
M. C. P. Martins, and Alberto Tosi Rodrigues. Marilia: Unesp Marilia Publica-
ções, 1998. [Contains Portuguese translations of: 1992l, 1997c, 1997a.] (CT)
*El pragmatismo, una version: Antiautoristarismo en epistemología y ética.* Trans. Joan

Verges Gifra. Barcelona: Ariel, 2000. [Contains Spanish translations of: a lecture entitled "Pragmatismo y Religion," 1998l, 1994l, "Panrelacionismo," "Contra la profundidad," part 3 of *Hoffnung Statt Erkenntnis*, 1997k, "Queda nada
valioso por salvar en el empirismo?" and "El empirismo de McDowell."] (PV)
*Philosophie und die Zukunft.* Trans. Matthias Graesslin, Reinhard Kaiser, Chris-
tiane Mayer, Joachim Schulte. Frankfurt am Main: Fischer Taschenbuch,
2000. [Contains German translations of 1994j, 1995k, "Analytic Philosophy
and Transformative Philosophy," 1997k, "Spinoza, Pragmatism, and the Love
of Wisdom," 2000e, 1992o, "Interview: Ueberreden ist Gut."] (PZ)
*Filosofía y futuro.* Trans. Javier Calvo and Angela Pilari. Barcelona: Gedisa, 2002.
[Spanish translation of this volume.]

ARTICLES

Initials of book titles in parentheses indicate that the piece was reprinted in
*Consequences of Pragmatism* (CP), *Objectivity, Relativism, and Truth* (ORT), *Essays
on Heidegger and Others* (EHO), *Truth and Progress* (TP), *Philosophy and Social
Hope* (PSH), or one of the collections of articles in foreign translation noted above
(SO, RJT, SS, HWP, EKZ, CW, HZX, SL, SE, CT, PV, PZ).

*1955*

1955a. Contribution to a colloquium, *Theses on Presuppositions by David Harrah*.
*Review of Metaphysics* 9:117.

*1961*

1961a. "Pragmatism, Categories, and Language." *Philosophical Review* 70:2 (April):
197–223.
1961b. "Recent Metaphilosophy." *Review of Metaphysics* 15:2 (December): 299–
318.
1961c. "The Limits of Reductionism." In *Experience, Existence, and the Good,* ed.
I. C. Lieb, 100–116. Carbondale: Southern Illinois University Press.

*1962*

1962a. "Second Thoughts on Teaching Communism." *Teacher's College Record* 63
(April): 562–63.
1962b. "Realism, Categories, and the 'Linguistic Turn.'" *International Philosophical Quarterly* 2:2 (May): 307–22.

*1963*

1963a. "Empiricism, Extensionalism, and Reductionism." *Mind* 72 (April): 176–86.

1963b. "Comments on Prof. Hartshorne's Paper [Charles Hartshorne's 'Real Possibility']." *Journal of Philosophy* 60:21 (October 10): 606–8.

1963c. "Matter and Event." In *The Concept of Matter*, ed. Ernan McMullin, 497–524. Notre Dame: Notre Dame University Press. [A revised version appears in *Explorations in Whitehead's Philosophy*, ed. Lewis S. Ford and George L. Kline, 68–103 (New York: Fordham University Press, 1983).]

1963d. "The Subjectivist Principle and the Linguistic Turn." In *Alfred North Whitehead: Essays on His Philosophy*, ed. George L. Kline, 134–57. Englewood Cliffs, N.J.: Prentice-Hall.

*1964*

1964a. "Questions to Weiss and Tillich." In *Philosophical Interrogations*, ed. Beatrice and Sidney Rome, 266–67, 369–70, 392–93. New York: Holt, Rinehart, and Winston.

*1965*

1965a. "Mind-Body Identity, Privacy, and Categories." *Review of Metaphysics* 19:1 (September): 24–54.

———. Reprinted in *Philosophy of Mind*, ed. Stuart Hampshire, 30–62. New York: Harper and Row, 1966.

———. Also reprinted in *Modern Materialism: Readings on Mind-Body Identity*, ed. John O'Connor, 145–74. New York: Harcourt, Brace, 1969.

———. Also reprinted in *Materialism and the Mind-Body Problem*, ed. David M. Rosenthal, 174–99. Englewood Cliffs, N.J.: Prentice-Hall, 1971.

———. Also reprinted in *Folk Psychology and the Philosophy of Mind*, ed. Scott Christensen and Dale Turner, 17–41. Hillsdale, N.J.: L. Erlbaum, 1993.

*1966*

1966a. "Aristotle." *The American Peoples' Encyclopedia*. Vol. 2. Ed. Walter D. Scott. Chicago: Spencer Press.

*1967*

1967a. "Do Analysts and Metaphysicians Disagree?" *Proceedings of the Catholic Philosophical Association* 41:39–53.

1967b. Introduction to *The Linguistic Turn: Recent Essays in Philosophical Method,* ed. Richard Rorty, 1–39. Chicago: University of Chicago Press. (SL)

1967c. "Intuition." *The Encyclopedia of Philosophy.* Vol. 4. Ed. Paul Edwards. New York: Macmillan and Free Press.

1967d. "Relations, Internal and External." *The Encyclopedia of Philosophy.* Vol. 7. Ed. Paul Edwards. New York: Macmillan and Free Press.

*[1968]*

*[1969]*

*1970*

1970a. "Incorrigibility as the Mark of the Mental." *Journal of Philosophy* 67:12 (June 25): 399–429.

1970b. "Wittgenstein, Privileged Access, and Incommunicability." *American Philosophical Quarterly* 7:3 (July): 192–205.

1970c. "In Defense of Eliminative Materialism." *Review of Metaphysics* 24:1 (September): 112–21.

———. Reprinted in *Materialism and the Mind-Body Problem.* Ed. David M. Rosenthal, 223–31. Englewood Cliffs, N.J.: Prentice-Hall: 1971.

1970d. "Strawson's Objectivity Argument." *Review of Metaphysics* 24:2 (December): 207–44.

1970e. "Cartesian Epistemology and Changes in Ontology." In *Contemporary American Philosophy,* ed. John E. Smith, 273–92. New York: Humanities Press.

*1971*

1971a. "Verificationism and Transcendental Arguments." *Noûs* 5:1 (February): 3–14.

*1972*

1972a. "Indeterminacy of Translation and of Truth." *Synthese* 23:4 (March): 443–62.

———. Polish translation: "Niezdeterminowanie Przekladu i Prawdy." In *Filozofia jezyka,* ed. B. Stanosz. Warsaw: Spacja, 1993.

1972b. "Dennett on Awareness." *Philosophical Studies* 23:3 (April): 153–62.

1972c. "Functionalism, Machines, and Incorrigibility." *Journal of Philosophy* 69:8 (April 20): 203–20.

1972d. "The World Well Lost." *Journal of Philosophy* 69:19 (October 26): 649–65. (CP)

———. German translation: "Die glücklich abhandengekommene Welt." In *Moderne Sprachphilosophie*, ed. Michael Sukale, 175–89. Hamburg: Hoffman und Campe, 1976.

## 1973

1973a. "Criteria and Necessity." *Noûs* 7:4 (November): 313–29.

1973b. "Genus as Matter: A Reading of Metaphysics Z-H." In *Exegesis and Argument: Essays in Greek Philosophy Presented to Gregory Vlastos*, ed. E. N. Lee, A. P. D. Mourelatos, R. M. Rorty, 393–420. Assen: Van Gorcum.

## 1974

1974a. "Matter as Goo: Comments on Marjorie Grene's Paper." *Synthese* 28:1 (September): 71–77.

1974b. "More on Incorrigibility." *Canadian Journal of Philosophy* 4 (September): 195–97.

1974c. "Minds and Machines." *Empire State Study Modules Series.* Saratoga Springs, N.Y.: Empire State College.

## [1975]

## 1976

1976a. "Professionalized Philosophy and Transcendentalist Culture." *Georgia Review* 30:4 (Winter): 757–69. (CP)

———. Reprinted as "Genteel Syntheses, Professional Analyses, Transcendentalist Culture." In *Two Centuries of Philosophy in America*, ed. Peter Caws, 228–39. (Oxford: Blackwell, 1980).

1976b. "Keeping Philosophy Pure." *Yale Review* 65:3 (March): 336–56. (CP)

1976c. "Realism and Reference." *The Monist* 59:3 (July): 321–40.

1976d. "Overcoming the Tradition: Heidegger and Dewey." *Review of Metaphysics* 30:2 (December): 280–305. (CP)

## 1977

1977a. "Wittgensteinian Philosophy and Empirical Psychology." *Philosophical Studies* 31:3 (March): 151–72. [Reprinted as portions of chapter 5 of *Philosophy and the Mirror of Nature.*]

1977b. Review of *Why Does Language Matter to Philosophy?* by Ian Hacking. *Journal of Philosophy* 74:7 (July): 416–32. [Reprinted in *The Linguistic Turn*, 2nd ed.] (SL)

————. Spanish translation in *El giro lingüístico*. Trans. Gabriel Bello. Barcelona: Paidós, UAB, Instituto de Ciencias de la Educación, 1990.

1977c. "Derrida on Language, Being, and Abnormal Philosophy." *Journal of Philosophy* 74:11 (November): 673–81.

1977d. "Dewey's Metaphysics." In *New Studies in the Philosophy of John Dewey*, ed. Steven Cahn, 45–74. Hanover, N.H.: University of New England Press. (CP)

*1978*

1978a. "Philosophy as a Kind of Writing: An Essay on Derrida." *New Literary History* 10:1 (Autumn): 141–60. (CP)

————. French translation: "La Philosophie comme forme d'écriture." *Chemin de Ronde* 5:1 (1984).

————. Polish translation: "Filozofia jako rodzaj pisarstwa: Esej o Derridzie." In *Postmodernizm i filozofia*, ed. S. Czerniak and A. Szahaj. Warsaw: IFIS PAN, 1996.

1978b. "Epistemological Behaviorism and the De-Transcendentalization of Analytic Philosophy." *Neue Hefte Fur Philosophie* 14:117–42. [Reprinted as portions of chapter 4 of *Philosophy and the Mirror of Nature*.]

————. Reprinted in *Hermeneutics and Praxis*, ed. Robert Hollinger, 89–121. Notre Dame: University of Notre Dame Press, 1985.

1978c. "A Middle Ground Between Neurons and Holograms?" *Behavioural and Brain Sciences* 1:2:248.

*1979*

1979a. "From Epistemology to Hermeneutics." *Acta Philosophica Fennica* 30:11–30. [Reprinted as portions of chapter 7 of *Philosophy and the Mirror of Nature*.]

————. French translation: "De l'epistemologie a l'hermeneutique." *Dialectica* 33 (1979): 165–88.

1979b. "Transcendental Argument, Self-Reference, and Pragmatism." In *Transcendental Arguments and Science*, ed. Peter Bieri, Rolf-P. Hortsman, Lorenz Kruger, 77–103. Dordrecht: D. Reidel.

1979c. "The Unnaturalness of Epistemology." In *Body, Mind, and Method: Essays in Honor of Virgil C. Aldrich*, ed. Donald Gustafson and Bangs Tapscott, 77–92. Dordrecht: D. Reidel. [Reprinted as portions of chapter 5 of *Philosophy and the Mirror of Nature*.]

*1980*

1980a. "Pragmatism, Relativism, and Irrationalism." *Proceedings of the American Philosophical Association* 53:6 (August): 719–38. (CP, HZX)

1980b. "Freud, Morality, and Hermeneutics." *New Literary History* 12:1 (Autumn): 177–85.

1980c. "Reply to Dreyfus and Taylor." *Review of Metaphysics* 34:1 (September): 39–46.

1980d. [With Hubert Dreyfus and Charles Taylor.] "A Discussion." *Review of Metaphysics* 34:1 (September): 47–55.

1980e. "Idealism, Holism, and the 'Paradox of Knowledge.'" In *The Philosophy of Brand Blanshard*, ed. P. A. Schilpp, 719–38. La Salle, Ill.: Open Court.

1980f. "Searle and the Special Powers of the Brain." *Behavioral and Brain Sciences* 3:3:445–46.

*1981*

1981a. "Nineteenth-Century Idealism and Twentieth-Century Textualism." *The Monist* 64:2 (April): 155–74. (CP)

1981b. "From Epistemology to Romance: Cavell on Scepticism." *Review of Metaphysics* 34:4 (June): 759–74. (CP)

1981c. "Method, Social Science, and Social Hope." *Canadian Journal of Philosophy* 11 (December): 569–88. (CP)

———. Earlier version: "Method and Morality." In *Social Science as Moral Inquiry*, ed. Norman Hahn, Robert Bellah, W. M. Sullivan, and Paul Rabinow, 155–76. New York: Columbia University Press, 1983.

———. Reprinted in *Interpreting Politics*, ed. Michael Gibbons, 241–59. New York: New York University Press, 1987.

———. Also reprinted in *The Postmodern Turn: New Perspectives on Social Theory*, ed. Steven Seidman, 46–64. Cambridge: Cambridge University Press, 1994.

———. French translation: "Methode, Science Sociale, et Espoir Social." *Critique* 42:471–72 (1986): 873–97.

1981d. "Is There a Problem About Fictional Discourse?" *Funktionen Des Fictiven: Poetic und Hermeneutik* 10. Munich: Fink. (CP)

———. Journal later reprinted as book of the same title, ed. Dieter Henrich and Wolfgang Iser, 67–93. Munich: Fink, 1983.

1981e. "Zur Lage der Gegenwartsphilosophie in den USA." *Analyse und Kritik* 3:1:3. [English original appeared later as 1982a.]

1981f. "Reply to Professor Yolton." *Philosophical Books* 22:3:134–35.

*1982*

1982a. "Philosophy in America Today." *American Scholar* 51:2 (Spring): 183–200. (CP) [English original of 1981e.]

————. Hungarian translation in *Magyar filozofiai szemle* 3–4 (1985): 583–99.

1982b. "Comments on Dennett's 'How to Study Human Consciousness Empirically.'" *Synthese* 53:2 (November): 181–87.

1982c. "Contemporary Philosophy of Mind." *Synthese* 53:2 (November): 323–48.

————. Reprinted as "Mind as Ineffable." In *Mind in Nature*, ed. Richard Elvee, 60–95. Nobel Conference 17. San Francisco: Harper and Row, 1982.

1982d. "Hermeneutics, General Studies, and Teaching." *Synergos* 2:1–15. (SE)

————. Also published as *Richard Rorty on Hermeneutics, General Studies, and Teaching: With Replies and Applications.* Fairfax, Va.: George Mason University, 1982.

————. Reprinted in *Why Literature Matters: Theories and Functions of Literature*, ed. Rüdiger Ahrens and Laurenz Volkmann, 23–36. Heidelberg: Winter, 1996.

1982e. Introduction to *Consequences of Pragmatism*, xiii–xlvii. Minneapolis: University of Minnesota Press. (CP)

————. Reprinted as "Pragmatism and Philosophy." In *After Philosophy: End or Transformation?* ed. Kenneth Baynes, James Bohman, Thomas McCarthy, 26–66. Cambridge, Mass.: MIT Press, 1987.

————. Abridged version: "The Fate of Philosophy." *New Republic* (October 18, 1982), 28–34.


*1983*

1983a. "What Are Philosophers For?" *Center Magazine* 16:5 (September–October): 40–51.

1983b. "Postmodernist Bourgeois Liberalism." *Journal of Philosophy* 80:10 (October): 583–89. (ORT, HZX)

————. Reprinted in *Hermeneutics and Praxis*, ed. Robert Hollinger, 214–21. Notre Dame: University of Notre Dame Press, 1985.

————. Also reprinted in *Postmodernism: A Reader*, ed. Thomas Docherty, 323–28. New York: Columbia University Press, 1993.

————. Czech translation: in *Filosoficky Casopis* 45:4 (1997): 609–16.

————. Polish translation: "Postmodernistyczny liberalizm mieszczanski." In *Postmodernizm: Antologia przekladow*, ed. R. Nycz. Kraków: Baran i Suszylski, 1997.

1983c. "Pragmatism Without Method." In *Sidney Hook: Philosopher of Democracy and Humanism*, ed. Paul Kurtz, 259–73. Buffalo: Prometheus Books. (ORT, RJT, HWP)

*1984*

1984a. "Habermas and Lyotard on Post-Modernity." *Praxis International* 4:1 (April): 32–44. (EHO)

———. Reprinted in *Habermas and Post-Modernity*, ed. R. J. Bernstein, 161–76. Cambridge: Polity Press, 1985.

———. French translation: "Habermas, Lyotard, et la postmodernité." *Critique* 40:442 (March 1984): 181–97.

———. Polish translation: "Habermas i Lyotard o postmodernizmie." Trans. J. Holzmana. *Colloquia Communia* 4–5 (1986): 147–56. [Reprinted in *Postmodernizm—kultura wyczerpania?* ed. M. Gizycki, 67–85 (Warsaw: Akademia Ruchu, 1988).]

———. Spanish translation: "Habermas y Lyotard sobre la postmodernidad." *Revista de Occidente*, ser. 4:85 (June 1988): 71. [Also in *Habermas y la modernidad* (Mexico City: Cátedra, 1994). Spanish translation of Bernstein book above.]

1984b. "A Reply to Six Critics." *Analyse und Kritik* 6:1 (June): 78–98.

1984c. "Deconstruction and Circumvention." *Critical Inquiry* 11:1 (September): 1–23. (EHO, SS, EKZ)

1984d. "Heidegger Wider den Pragmatisten." *Neue Hefte für Philosophie* 23:1–22. (EHO) [Subsequently partially published in English as 1991i.]

1984e. "The Historiography of Philosophy: Four Genres." In *Philosophy in History: Essays on the Historiography of Philosophy*, ed. Richard Rorty, J. B. Schneewind, Quentin Skinner, 49–75. Cambridge: Cambridge University Press. (TP, RJT)

———. Hungarian translation: in *Magyar Filozofiai Szemle* 3–4 (1986): 495–519.

1984h. [With J. B. Schneewind and Quentin Skinner.] Introduction to *Philosophy in History: Essays on the Historiography of Philosophy*, ed. Richard Rorty, J. B. Schneewind, and Quentin Skinner, 1–14. Cambridge: Cambridge University Press.

1984i. "Solidarity or Objectivity?" *Nanzan Review of American Studies* 6:1–19. (ORT, SO)

———. Reprinted in *Post-Analytic Philosophy*, ed. John Rajchman and Cornel West, 3–19. New York: Columbia University Press, 1985.

———. Also reprinted in *Relativism*, ed. Michael Krausz, 35–50. Notre Dame: University of Notre Dame Press, 1989.

———. French translation: "Solidarité ou Objectivité?" *Critique* 439 (1983): 923–40.

*1985*

1985a. "Comments on Sleeper and Edel." *Transactions of the Charles S. Peirce Society* 21:1 (Winter): 40–48.
1985b. "Philosophy Without Principles." *Critical Inquiry* 11:3 (March): 459–65.
———. Reprinted in *Against Theory: Literary Studies and the New Pragmatism*, ed. W. J. T. Mitchell, 132–38. Chicago: University of Chicago Press, 1985.
1985c. "Le Cosmopolitanisme sans emancipation: Réponse a Jean-François Lyotard." *Critique* 41:456 (May): 569–80, 584. (ORT)
———. Revised version of English original appears in *Modernity and Identity*, ed. Scott Lash and Jonathan Friedman, 59–72. Oxford: Blackwell, 1990.
1985d. "Texts and Lumps." *New Literary History* 17:1 (Autumn): 1–15. (ORT, RJT, HWP)

*1986*

1986a. "The Higher Nominalism in a Nutshell: A Reply to Henry Staten." *Critical Inquiry* 12:2 (Winter): 462–66.
1986b. "Freedom as Higher Than Being." *Working Papers: Critique of Modernity* 1, ed. Robert Langbaum (April): 16–26.
1986c. "The Contingency of Language." *London Review of Books* (April 17), 3–6. [Reprinted as chapter 1 of *Contingency, Irony, and Solidarity.*]
———. Reprinted in *Postmodernism: A Reader*, ed. Patricia Waugh, 170–86. London: E. Arnold, 1992.
———. Also reprinted in *Rhetoric in an Antifoundational World: Language, Culture, and Pedagogy*, ed. Michael Bernard-Donals, 65–85. New Haven, Conn.: Yale University Press, 1998.
———. Polish translation: "Przygodnosc jezyka." In *Postmodernizm i filozofia*, ed. Stanislaw Czerniak and Andrzej Szahaj. Warsaw: IFIS PAN, 1996.
1986d. "The Contingency of Selfhood." *London Review of Books* (May 8), 11–14. [Reprinted as chapter 2 of *Contingency, Irony, and Solidarity.*]
———. Also published as the Seventh Tykociner Memorial Lecture. Urbana: University of Illinois Press, 1986.
———. Also published in *Friedrich Nietzsche*, ed. Harold Bloom, 193–211. New York: Chelsea House Publishers, 1987.
1986e. "The Contingency of Community." *London Review of Books* (July 24), 10–14. [Reprinted as chapter 3 of *Contingency, Irony, and Solidarity.*]
1986f. "Beyond Realism and Anti-Realism." In *Wo Steht die Analytische Philosophie heute?* ed. Richard Heinrich and Ludwig Nagl, 103–15. Vienna: R. Oldenbourg.

————. Italian translation: in *Aut Aut* 217–18 (January–April 1987): 101–49.

1986g. "Comments on Toulmin's 'Conceptual Communities and Rational Conversation.'" *Archivio di Filosofia* 189–93.

1986h. "On Ethnocentrism: A Reply to Clifford Geertz." *Michigan Quarterly Review* 25:525–34. (ORT)

1986i. "Foucault and Epistemology." In *Foucault: A Critical Reader*, ed. D. C. Hoy, 41–49. Oxford: Blackwell.

1986j. "Freud and Moral Reflection." In *Pragmatism's Freud: The Moral Disposition of Psychoanalysis*, ed. William Kerrigan and Joseph H. Smith, 1–27. Baltimore: Johns Hopkins University Press. (EHO, SO)

1986k. "From Logic to Language to Play." *Proceedings and Addresses of the American Philosophical Association* 59:747–53.

————. Spanish translation: "De la logica al lenguaje y al juego." *Cuadernos Americanos* 3:3 (1987): 107–16.

1986l. Introduction to *John Dewey: The Later Works*, vol. 8, 1933–53, ed. Jo Ann Boydston, ix–xviii. Carbondale: Southern Illinois University Press.

1986m. "Philosophie als Wissenschaft, als Metapher, und als Politik." In *Die Krise der Phänomenologie und die Pragmatik des Wissenschaftsfortschritt*, ed. Michael Benedikt and Rudolf Burger, 138–49. Vienna: Österreichischen Staatsdruckeri. [Subsequently published in the English original as 1989i.] (EHO)

————. Italian translation: "Filosofia come scienza, come metafora, e come politica." *Rivista de Estetica* 26:19–20:3–16.

————. Polish translation: "Filozofia jako nauka, jako metafora i jako poltyka." In *Miedzy pragmatyzmem a postmodernizmem: Wokól filozofii Richarda Rorty'ego*, ed. Andrej Szahaj. Wyd. 1. Torun: Uniwersytet Mikolaja Kopernika w Toruniu, 1995.

1986n. "Pragmatism, Davidson, and Truth." In *Truth and Interpretation: Perspectives on the Philosophy of Donald Davidson*, ed. E. LePore, 333–68. Oxford: Blackwell. (ORT, RJT, SS, HZX)

1986o. "Should Hume Be Answered or Bypassed?" In *Human Nature and Natural Knowledge: Essays Presented to Marjorie Grene*, ed. A. Donegan, 341–52. Dordrecht: D. Reidel.

————. Reprinted in *Boston Studies in the Philosophy of Science* 89 (1986): 341–52.


## *1987*

1987a. "Nominalismo e contestualismo." *Alfabeta* 9 (September): 11–12.

1987b. "Thugs and Theorists: A Reply to Bernstein's 'One Step Forward, Two Steps Backward.'" *Political Theory* 15:4 (November): 564–80.

———. French translation: "Brigands et intellectuels." *Critique* 44:493–94 (June–July 1988): 453–72.

1987c. "Non-Reductive Physicalism." In *Theorie der Subjektivität*, ed. Konrad Cramer et al., 278–96. Frankfurt am Main: Suhrkamp. [Initially appeared in Chinese translation in *The Taiwanese Journal for Philosophy and History of Science*.] (ORT, EKZ)

1987d. "Science as Solidarity." In *The Rhetoric of the Human Sciences: Language and Argument in Scholarship and Public Affairs*, ed. Donald N. McCloskey, Allan Megill, and John S. Nelson, 38–52. Madison: University of Wisconsin Press. (ORT, RJT, SS, HZX)

———. Reprinted in *Dismantling Truth: Reality in the Post-Modern World*, ed. Hilary Lawson and Lisa Appignanesi, 6–22. New York: St. Martin's Press, 1989.

———. French translation: "La Science comme solidarité." *Philosophique* 1 (1988): 101–14.

———. Polish translation: "Nauka jako solidarnosc." Trans. A. Chmielecki. *Literatura na Swiecie* 5:238 (1991): 199–218.

1987e. "Unfamiliar Noises: Hesse and Davidson on Metaphor." *Proceedings of the Aristotelian Society*, suppl. vol. 61:283–96. (ORT)

1987f. "Waren die Gesetze Newtons schon vor Newton Wahr?" In *Jahrbuch des Wissenschaftkollegs zu Berlin*: 247–63.

———. Italian translation: "Erano vere le leggi di Newton prima di Newton?" *Intersezioni* 8:1 (1988): 49–64.

## 1988

1988a. "Unger, Castoriadis, and the Romance of a National Future." *Northwestern University Law Review* 82:2 (Winter): 335–51. (EHO)

———. Reprinted in *Critique and Construction: A Symposium on Roberto Unger's "Politics,"* ed. Robin W. Lovin and Michael J. Perry, 29–45. New York: Cambridge University Press, 1990.

———. Spanish translation: "Una esperanza social: Unger, Castoriadis, y el ensueño de un futuro nacional." *Revista de Occidente*, ser. 4:90 (November 1988): 79.

1988b. "That Old-Time Philosophy." Review-article on *The Closing of the American Mind*, by Allan Bloom. *New Republic* (April 4), 28–33.

———. French translation: "Cette bonne vielle philosophie." *Commentaire* 11:42 (1988): 484–91.

1988c. "Representation, Social Practice, and Truth." *Philosophical Studies* 54:2 (September): 215–28. (ORT)

1988d. "Is Natural Science a Natural Kind?" In *Construction and Constraint: The*

*Shaping of Scientific Rationality*, ed. E. McMullin, 49–74. Notre Dame: Notre Dame University Press. (ORT, SS, EKZ, HZX)

1988e. "The Priority of Democracy to Philosophy." In *The Virginia Statue of Religious Freedom*, ed. Merill Peterson and Robert Vaughan, 257–88. Cambridge: Cambridge University Press. (ORT, SO, RJT, HZX)

———. Reprinted in *Prospects for a Common Morality*, ed. Gene Outka and John Reeder, 254–78. Princeton, N.J.: Princeton University Press, 1993.

———. German translation: "Der Vorrang der Demokratie vor der Philosophie." *Zeitschrift für Philosophische Forschung* 42:1 (January–March 1988): 3–17.

———. Polish translation: "Pierwszenstwo demokracji wobec filozofii." Trans. P. Dehnel. *Odra* 7–8 (1992): 22–30.

———. Slovak translation: in *O slobode a spravodlivosti*, trans. Egon Gál. Bratislava: Archa, 1993.


*1989*

1989a. "Comments on Castoriadis' 'The End of Philosophy.'" *Salmagundi* 82–83 (Spring–Summer): 24–30.

1989b. "Education Without Dogma." *Dissent* 36:2 (Spring): 198–204. (PSH, SE)

———. Reprinted as "Education, Socialization, and Individuation" and accompanied by "Replies to Commentators." *Liberal Education* 75:4 (October l989): 28–31.

———. Also reprinted in shortened form as "The Opening of American Minds." *Harper's* (July 1989), 18–20.

———. Polish translation: "Wychowanie bez dogmatu." *Ameryka* 236 (1990): 44–47.

1989c. "Is Derrida a Transcendental Philosopher?" *Yale Journal of Criticism* 2:2 (Spring): 207. (EHO)

———. Reprinted in *Derrida: A Critical Reader*, ed. David Wood, 234–46. Cambridge, Mass.: Blackwell, 1992.

———. Also reprinted in *Working Through Derrida*, ed. Gary B. Madison, 137–46. Evanston, Ill.: Northwestern University Press, 1993.

1989d. "Philosophy and Post-Modernism." Contribution to the symposium "What Is Postmodernism?" *Cambridge Review* 110:2305 (June): 51–53.

1989e. "Wittgenstein e Heidegger: Due percorsi incrociati." *Lettere Internazionale* 22 (October–December): 21–26. (EHO) [Subsequently published in English as 1993i.]

1989f. "The Humanistic Intellectual: Eleven Theses." *Viewpoints: Excerpts from the ACLS Conference on the Humanities in the 1990s*. ACLS Occasional Paper 10. New York: American Council of Learned Societies.

1989g. "Identité morale et autonomie privée." In *Michel Foucault philosophe: Rencontre internationale*, 385–94. Paris: Seuil. [English original appeared as l990b.] (EHO)

———. Spanish translation: in *Michel Foucault: Filósofo*. Barcelona: Gedisa, 1991.

———. Polish translation: "Moralma Tozsamosc a Prywatna Autonomia: przypadek Foucaulta." *Etyka* 26 (1993): 125–32.

1989h. "Two Meanings of 'Logocentrism': A Reply to Norris." In *Redrawing the Lines: Analytic Philosophy, Deconstruction, and Literary Theory*, ed. Reed Way Dasenbrock, 204–16. Minneapolis: University of Minnesota Press. (EHO)

1989i. "Philosophy as Science, as Metaphor, and as Politics." In *The Institution of Philosophy*, ed. Avner Cohen and Marcello Dascal, 13–33. La Salle, Ill.: Open Court. [English original of 1986m.] (EHO, HWP, HZX)

## *1990*

1990a. "Two Cheers for the Cultural Left." *South Atlantic Quarterly* 89 (Winter): 227–34. (EHO)

1990b. "Another Possible World." *London Review of Books* (February 8), 21. (PSH)

———. Reprinted in *Martin Heidegger: Politics, Art and Technology*, ed. Karsten Harries and Christoph Jamme, 34–40. New York: Holmes and Meier, 1994.

———. German translation: "Eine andere mögliche Welt." *Martin Heidegger, Kunst-Politik-Technik*, ed. Karsten Harries and Christoph Jamme, 135–41. Munich: Fink, 1992.

1990c. "Foucault/Dewey/Nietzsche." *Raritan* 9:4 (Spring): 1–8. [English original of 1989g.] (EHO)

1990d. "Truth and Freedom: A Reply to Thomas McCarthy." *Critical Inquiry* 16:3 (Spring): 633–43.

1990e. "The Banality of Pragmatism and the Poetry of Justice." Symposium on the Renaissance of Pragmatism in American Legal Thought. *Southern California Law Review* 63:6 (September): 1811–19. (PSH)

———. Reprinted in *Pragmatism in Law and Society*, ed. Michael Brint and William Weaver, 89–97. Boulder, Colo.: Westview Press, 1991.

1990f. "Consciousness, Intentionality, and Pragmatism." In *Modelos de la mente*, ed. Jose Quiros. Madrid: Universidad Complutense, D.L.

1990g. "The Dangers of Over-Philosophication: Reply to Arcilla and Nicholson." *Educational Theory* 40:1:41–44.

1990h. "Philosophy Without Mirrors" [reprint of chapter 8 of *Philosophy and the Mirror of Nature*]. In *Philosophy: An Introduction Through Literature*, ed. Lowell

Kleinman and Steven Lewis, 75–79. New York: Paragon House.

1990i. "Twenty-five Years After." A postscript to 1967b, published (in Spanish translation) along with 1967b and 1977b, in *El giro lingüístico*, trans. Gabriel Bello. Barcelona: Paidós, UAB, Instituto de Ciencias de la Educación. [Subsequently published in English in *The Linguistic Turn*, 2nd ed.] (SL)

## *1991*

1991a. "Feminism and Pragmatism." *Michigan Quarterly Review* (Spring): 3–14. (TP, CW)

———. Reprinted in *The Tanner Lectures on Human Values*, ed. Grethe B. Peterson, vol. 13. Salt Lake City: University of Utah Press, 1994.

———. Also reprinted in *Postmodernism and Law*, ed. Dennis Patterson. New York: New York University Press, 1994.

———. Also reprinted in *Psychoanalysis, Feminism, and the Future of Gender*, ed. Joseph Smith and Afaf Mahfouz, 42–69. Baltimore: Johns Hopkins University Press, 1994.

———. Spanish translation: "Feminismo y pragmatismo." *Revista Internacional de Filosofía Política* 2 (1993): 37–62.

1991b. "Nietzsche, Socrates, and Pragmatism." *South African Journal of Philosophy* 10:3 (August): 61–63.

1991c. "Intellectuals in Politics." *Dissent* 38:4 (Autumn): 483–90.

1991d. "Comments on Taylor's 'Paralectics.'" In *On the Other: Dialogue and/or Dialectics*, ed. R. P. Scharlemann, 71–78. Working paper 5 of the University of Virginia Committee on the Comparative Study of the Individual and Society. Lanham, Md.: University Press of America.

1991e. Correspondence with Anindita Niyogi Balslev. In *Cultural Otherness: A Correspondence with Richard Rorty*, ed. Anindita Balslev. Indian Institute of Advanced Study. [2nd ed., Atlanta: Scholars Press, 1999.]

1991f. "Inquiry as Recontextualization: An Anti-Dualist Account of Interpretation." In *The Interpretive Turn*, ed. James F. Bohman, David R. Hiley, and Richard Shusterman, 59–80. Ithaca, N.Y.: Cornell University Press. (ORT, HWP)

———. Italian translation: "Ricerca come ricontestualizzazione: Un'analisi anti-dualista." *Paradigmi* 9:25 (1991): 5–29.

———. Czech translation: "Zkoumání jako rekontextualizace: Antidualistické pojetí interpretace." *Filosoficky Casopis* 42:3 (1994): 355–79. [Also published in *Obrat k jazyku: Druhé kolo*, ed. Jaroslav Peregrin (Prague: Filosofia, 1998).]

1991g. "Philosophers, Novelists, and Intercultural Comparisons: Heidegger, Kundera, Dickens." *Culture and Modernity: East-West Philosophic Perspectives*. Papers presented at the Sixth East-West Philosophers' Conference, Honolulu, Hawaii, 1989. Honolulu: University of Hawaii Press. (EHO, EKZ)

———. Polish translation: in *Miedzy pragmatyzmem a postmodernizmem: Wokól filozofii Richarda Rorty'ego*, ed. Andrej Szahaj. Wyd. 1. Torun: Uniwersytet Mikolaja Kopernika w Toruniu, 1995.

———. Russian translation: in *Translators Workshop Almanac* 2:2 (Lviv, Ukraine, 2002).

1991h. "Pragmatismo." *Dicionario do pensiamento contemporanaio.* Ed. Manuel Maria Carrilho. Lisbon: Publiçaoes Dom Quixote.

*1992*

1992a. "The Politicization of the Humanities." *UVa Alumni Journal* (Winter).

1992b. "Love and Money." *Common Knowledge* 1:1 (Spring): 12–16. (PSH)

1992c. "Reply to Andrew Ross' 'On "Intellectuals in Politics."'" *Dissent* 39:2 (Spring): 265–67.

1992d. "The Intellectuals at the End of Socialism." *Yale Review* 80:1–2 (April): 1–16. (TP)

———. An abbreviated version of this article appeared under the title "For a More Banal Politics." *Harper's* (May 1992), 16–21. [A longer version appeared as 1995j.]

———. Italian translation: "Gli intellettuali alla fine del socialismo." *Mulino* 40:338 (1991): 936–49.

———. Polish translation: "Intelektualisci u Kresu Socjalizmu." In *Edukacja wobec zmiany spolecnej*, ed. J. Brzezinski and L. Witkowski. Warszawa-Poznañ-Toruñ: Pañstwowe Wydawnictwo Naukowe, 1993.

1992e. "Nietzsche: Un philosophe pragmatique." *Magazine Litteraire* (April): 28–32.

1992f. "What Can You Expect from Anti-Foundationalist Philosophers? A Reply to Lynn Baker." *Virginia Law Review* 78:3 (April): 719–27.

1992g. "A Pragmatist View of Rationality and Cultural Differences." *Philosophy East and West* 42:4 (October): 581–96. (TP, CW)

———. Italian translation: in *Aut Aut* 251 (September–October 1992): 109–24.

———. Polish translation: "Racjonalnosc i roznica w kulturze: Ujecie pragmatyczne." Trans. L. Witkowski. *Kultura Wspolczesna* 1 (1993): 31–44. [Reprinted in *Miedzy pragmatyzmem a postmodernizmem: Wokól filozofii Richarda Rorty'ego*, ed. Andrej Szahaj. Wyd. 1. (Torun: Uniwersytet Mikolaja Kopernika w Toruniu, 1995).]

1992h. "Dewey entre Hegel et Darwin." *Rue Descartes* 5–6 (November): 53–71. (TP) [English original appeared later as 1994i.]

1992i. "Heidegger, Contingency, and Pragmatism." In *Heidegger: A Critical Reader*, ed. Hubert Dreyfus and Harrison Hall, 209–30. Oxford: Blackwell. (EHO, HWP) [Includes passages from 1984d, an article never published in English.]

1992j. Introduction to *Pale Fire*, by Vladimir Nabokov, v–xxiii. London: Everyman's Library.

1992k. "The Pragmatist's Progress." In *Interpretation and Overinterpretation*, ed. Stefan Collini, 89–108. Cambridge: Cambridge University Press. (PSH, CW)

———. German translation: in *Merkur* 47:12 (December 1993): 1025–36.

———. Italian translation: in *Interpretazione e sovrainterpretazione*, trans. Sandra Cavicchi. Milan: Bompiani, 1995.

———. French translation: in *Interprétation et surinterprétation*, trans. Jean-Pierre Cometti. Paris: Presses Universitaires de France, 1996.

———. Polish translation: "Kariera Pragmatysty." In *Interpretacja i nadinterpretacja*. Kraków: Wydawn, Znak, 1996.

1992l. "Putnam on Truth." *Philosophy and Phenomenological Research* 52:2:415–18. (CT)

1992m. "Réponses de Richard Rorty" [to Jacques Bouveresse, Vincent Descombes, Thomas MacCarthy, Alexander Nehamas, and Hilary Putnam]. In *Lire Rorty*, ed. Jean-Pierre Cometti, 147–250. Paris: L'Eclat.

1992n. "Robustness: A Reply to Jean Bethke Elshtain." In *The Politics of Irony*, ed. David W. Conway and John E. Seery, 219–23. New York: St. Martin's Press.

1992o. "Trotsky and the Wild Orchids." *Common Knowledge* 1:3:140–53. (PSH, CW, CZ)

———. Previously appeared in French translation in *Lire Rorty* [see item 1992m above].

———. Also published in *Wild Orchids and Trotsky: Messages from American Universities*, ed. Mark Edmundson. New York: Viking, 1993.

———. Also published in the *University of Chicago Magazine* (April 1994): 18–23.

———. German translation: in *Real Text: Denken am Rande des Subjektes*. Klagenfurt: Ritter, 1993. [Also in *Neue Rundschau* 109:4 (1998): 113–32.]

———. Polish translation: "Trocki i Dzikie storcyki." *Teksty Drugie* 4 (1994).

*1993*

1993a. "Centers of Moral Gravity: Comments on Donald Spence's 'The Hermeneutic Turn.'" *Psychoanalytic Dialogues* 3:1 (Winter): 21–28.

1993b. "Feminism, Ideology, and Deconstruction: A Pragmatist View." *Hypatia* 8:2 (Spring): 96–103.

1993c. "Putnam and the Relativist Menace." *Journal of Philosophy* 90:9 (September): 443–61. [Previously published in French: see 1992m.] (TP)

————. Italian translation: "Putnam e la minaccia relativistica." *Journal of Philosophy* 90:9 (September 1993): 443–61. [Reprinted in *Il neopragmatismo*, ed. Giancarlo Marchetti, 89–113 (Florence: Nuova Italia, 1999).]

————. Polish translation: "Putnam a Grozba Relatywizmu." In *Miedzy pragmatyzmem a postmodernizmem: Wokól filozofii Richarda Rorty'ego*, ed. Andrej Szahaj. Wyd. 1. Torun: Uniwersytet Mikolaja Kopernika w Toruniu, 1995.

1993d. "An Antirepresentationalist View: Comments on Richard Miller, van Fraassen/Sigman, and Churchland," and "A Comment on Robert Scholes' 'Tlon and Truth.'" In *Realism and Representation*, ed. George Levine, 125–33, 186–89. Madison: University of Wisconsin Press.

1993e. "Human Rights, Rationality, and Sentimentality." In *On Human Rights: The 1993 Oxford Amnesty Lectures*, ed. Susan Hurley and Stephen Shute, 112–34. New York: Basic Books. (TP)

————. A shortened version, without the footnotes, appeared in *Yale Review* 81:4 (October 1993): 1–20.

1993f. "Holism, Intentionality, and the Ambition of Transcendence." In *Dennett and His Critics: Demystifying Mind*, ed. Bo Dahlbom, 184–202. Oxford: Blackwell. (TP)

1993g. "Response to Jacques Bouveresse, 'On Some Undesirable Consequences of Pragmatism.'" *Stanford French Review* 17:2–3:183–95. [Previously appeared in *Lire Rorty*, ed. Jean-Pierre Cometti (Paris: L'Eclat, 1992); reprinted in *Rorty and His Critics*, ed. Robert B. Brandom (Malden, Mass.: Blackwell, 2000).]

1993h. "Wittgenstein, Heidegger, and the Reification of Language." In *The Cambridge Companion to Heidegger*, ed. Charles Guignon, 337–57. Cambridge: Cambridge University Press. (EHO, HWP)

*1994*

1994a. "The Unpatriotic Academy." *New York Times* (February 13), op-ed page. (PSH)

1994b. "Taylor on Self-Celebration and Gratitude." *Philosophy and Phenomenological Research* 54:1 (March): 197–201.

1994c. "Religion as Conversation-Stopper." *Common Knowledge* 3:1 (Spring): 1–6. (PSH)

1994d. "Tales of Two Disciplines." *Callaloo* 17:2 (Summer): 575–607.

————. Reprinted in *Beauty and the Critic: Aesthetics in an Age of Cultural Studies*, ed. James Soderholm, 208–24. Tuscaloosa, Ala.: University of Alabama Press, 1997.

1994e. "Sex, Lies, and Virginia's Voters." *New York Times* (October 13), op-ed page.

1994f. "Does Academic Freedom Have Philosophical Presuppositions?" *Academe* 80:6 (November–December): 52–63. (TP)

———. Reprinted in *The Future of Academic Freedom*, ed. Louis Menand, 21–42. Chicago: University of Chicago Press, 1996.

———. German translation: in *Merkur* 49:1 (January 1995): 28–44.

1994g. "Consciousness, Intentionality, and the Philosophy of Mind." In *The Mind-Body Problem: A Guide to the Current Debate*, ed. Richard Warner, 121–27. Cambridge, Mass.: Blackwell.

1994h. "Dewey Between Hegel and Darwin." In *Modernist Impulses in the Human Sciences*, ed. Dorothy Ross, 46–68. Baltimore: Johns Hopkins University Press. [Previously published in French; see 1992g.] (TP)

———. Reprinted in *Rorty and Pragmatism*, ed. Herman Saatkamp. Nashville, Tenn.: Vanderbilt University Press, 1995. [See 1995h.]

———. German translation: in *Philosophie der Demokratie*, trans. and ed. Hans Jonas. Frankfurt am Main: Suhrkamp, 2000.

1994i. "Does Democracy Need Foundations?" In *Politisches Denken: Jahrbuch 1993* hrsg. *Volker Gerhardt u.a.*, 21–23. Stuttgart: Metzler.

1994j. "Philosophy and the Future" [in Hungarian]. *Magyar Filozofiai Szemle* 5–6:877–84. (PZ)

———. English original published subsequently in *Rorty and Pragmatism*, ed. Herman Saatkamp. Nashville, Tenn.: Vanderbilt University Press, 1995. [See 1995h.]

———. Russian translation: in *Voprosy Filosofii* 6 (1994): 29–34.

———. Polish translation: "Filozofia i Przyszlosc." *Przeglad Filozoficzny* 1 (1996).

1994k. Replies to Burzta and Buchowski, Dziemidok, Gierszewski, Kmita, Kwiek, Morawski, Szahaj, Zeidler, and Zeidler-Janiszewska. *Ruch Filozoficzny* 50:2:178–79, 183–84, 188–89, 194–95, 198–200, 205–7, 209–10, 214–16, 218.

1994l. "Sind Aussagen universelle Geltungsansprüche?" *Deutsche Zeitschrift für Philosophie* 42:6:975–88. (PV)

———. French translation: "Les Assertions experiment-elles des prétensions a une validité universelle?" In *La Modernité en questions*, ed. Francois Gallard, Jacques Poulain, and Richard Shusterman. Paris: Editions du Cerf, 1998.

———. Enlarged version published in English as "Universality and Truth." In *Rorty and His Critics*, ed. Robert B. Brandom, 1–30. Malden, Mass.: Blackwell, 2000.

1994m. "Taylor on Truth." In *Philosophy in an Age of Pluralism: The Philosophy of Charles Taylor in Question*, ed. James Tully, 20–36. Cambridge: Cambridge University Press. (TP)

*1995*

1995a. "Half a Million Blue Helmets?" *Common Knowledge* 4:3 (Winter): 10–13.

1995b. "Movements and Campaigns." *Dissent* 42:1 (Winter): 55–60. [Reprinted as appendix to *Achieving Our Country*.]

———. Spanish translation: "Movimientos y campanas." *Revista de Occidente* 200 (January 1998): 73–78.

1995c. "Remembering John Dewey and Sidney Hook." *Free Inquiry* 16:1 (Winter): 40–42.

1995d. "Is Derrida a *Quasi*-Transcendental Philosopher?" Review-article of *Jacques Derrida*, by Geoffrey Bennington and Jacques Derrida. *Contemporary Literature* 36:1 (Spring): 173–200. (TP)

1995e. "Only Connect: Response to Steven Lukes." *Dissent* 42:2 (Spring): 264–65.

1995f. "Is Truth a Goal of Inquiry? Davidson vs. Wright." Review-article of *Truth and Objectivity*, by Crispin Wright. *Philosophical Quarterly* 45:180 (July): 281–300. [Enlarged version reprinted in TP.]

1995g. "A Spectre Is Haunting the Intellectuals." Review-article of *Spectres of Marx*, by Jacques Derrida. *European Journal of Philosophy* 3:3 (December): 289–98. (PSH)

1995h. "Deconstruction." In *The Cambridge History of Literary Criticism*, vol. 8, *From Formalism to Poststructuralism*, ed. Raman Selden, 166–96. Cambridge: Cambridge University Press. (EHO, CW, HZX)

———. Polish translation: "Deconstrukja." In *Filozofia amerykanska dzis*, ed. Tomasz Komendski and Andrzej Szahaj. Torun: Uniwersytet Mikolaja Kopernika w Toruniu, 1999.

1995i. "The End of Leninism and History as Comic Frame." In *History and the Idea of Progress*, ed. Arthur M. Melzer et al., 211–26. Ithaca, N.Y.: Cornell University Press. [A shortened version of this paper appeared as 1992d.] (TP)

1995j. "Habermas, Derrida, and the Functions of Philosophy." *Revue Internationale de Philosophie* 49:4 (194): 437–60. (TP, PZ)

1995k. Introduction to reprint of *John Dewey: An Intellectual Portrait*, by Sidney Hook, xi–xviii. Buffalo: Prometheus Books.

1995l. Introduction to reprint of "Response to Hartshorne," 29–36; "Response to Lavine," 50–53; "Response to Bernstein," 68–71; "Response to Gouinlock," 91–99; "Response to Hance," 122–25; "Response to Haack," 148–53; "Response to Farrell," 189–96; "Philosophy and the Future," 197–205. In *Contributions to Rorty and Pragmatism*, ed. Herman Saatkamp. Nashville: Vanderbilt University Press. [This volume also includes "Dewey Between Hegel and Darwin," previously published as 1994i.]

*1996*

1996a. "The Necessity of Inspired Reading." *Chronicle of Higher Education* (February 9), A48.

1996b. "Moral Universalism and Economic Triage." *Diogenes* 173 (Spring): 3–15.

———. Reprinted in *Qui sommes-nous? Les Deuxiemes Rencontres philosophiques de UNESCO*. Paris: UNESCO Presse, 1996.

———. Spanish translation: "Quienes somos? Universalismo moral y selección ecónomica." *Revista de Occidente* 210 (November 1998): 93–107.

1996c. "The Ambiguity of 'Rationality.'" *Constellations* 3:1 (April): 73–82.

1996d. "Duties to the Self and Others: Comments on a Paper by Alexander Nehamas." *Salmagundi* 111 (Summer): 59–67.

1996e. "The Inspirational Value of Great Works of Literature." *Raritan* 16:1 (Summer): 8–17. [Reprinted as appendix to *Achieving Our Country*.]

1996f. "What's Wrong with 'Rights'?" *Harper's* (June), 15–18.

1996g. "Fraternity Reigns." *New York Times Magazine* (September 29), 155–58. (PSH)

1996h. "Emancipating Our Culture: A Response to Habermas," 24–30; "Relativism: Finding and Making," 31–47; "On Moral Obligation, Truth, and Common Sense," 48–52; "Response to Kolakowski," 58–66; "The Notion of Rationality," 84–88. In *Debating the State of Philosophy: Habermas, Rorty, and Kolakowski*, ed. Jozef Niznik and John T. Sanders. Westport, Conn.: Praeger.

———. Polish translation: "Relatywizm: Odnajdywanie i tworzenie." In *Habermas, Rorty, Kolakowski: Stan filozofii wspólczesnej*. Warsaw: IFIS PAN, 1996.

———. Serbo-Croat translation of "Relativism: Finding and Making": in *Filozofia* 52:6 (1997): 394–405. (PSH)

———. Spanish translation: in *Debate sobre la situación de la filosofia: Habernas, Rorty, y Kolakowski*. Madrid: Cátedra, 2000.

1996i. "Postmodernism and Antifoundationalism." In *Philosophy, Science, and Ideology in Political Thought*, ed. David Morrice, 172–82. New York: St. Martin's Press.

1996j. "Pragmatism and Law: Response to David Luban." *Cardozo Law Review* 28:1:75–83. (PSH)

———. Reprinted in *The Revival of Pragmatism*, ed. Morris Dickstein, 304–11. Durham, N.C.: Duke University Press, 1998.

1996k. "Religious Faith, Intellectual Responsibility, and Romance." *American Journal of Theology and Philosophy* 17:2:121–40. (PSH)

———. Reprinted in *The Cambridge Companion to William James*, ed. Ruth-Anna Putnam, 84–102. Cambridge: Cambridge University Press, 1997.

———. Also reprinted in *Pragmatism, Neo-Pragmatism, and Religion*, ed. Charley D. Hardwick, 3–21. New York: Lang, 1997.

————. Also reprinted in William James, *Pragmatismus: Eine neue Name für einige alte Wege des Denkens,* ed. Klaus Oehler, 213–33. Berlin: Akademie, 2000.

————. Polish translation: "Wiara religijna, odpowiedzialnosc intelektuelna, romantycsnosc." In *Wspolnotowosc wobec wyzwan liberalizmu,* ed. T. Buksinski. Poznan: Wydawnictwo Naukowe Instytutu Filozofii UAM, 1995.

1996l. "Remarks on Deconstruction and Pragmatism," 13–18; "Response to Simon Critchley," 41–46; "Response to Ernesto Laclau," 69–76. In *Deconstruction and Pragmatism,* ed. Chantal Mouffe. London: Routledge.

## *1997*

1997a. "Back to Class Politics." *Dissent* 44:1 (Winter): 31–34. (PSH, CT)

————. Reprinted as "The People's Flag Is Deepest Red." In *Audacious Democracy: Labor, Intellectuals, and the Social Reconstruction of America,* ed. Steven Fraser and Joshua B. Freeman, 57–63. Boston: Houghton Mifflin, 1997.

1997b. "Intellectuals and the Millennium." *New Leader* (February 24), 10–11.

1997c. "Thomas Kuhn, Rocks, and the Laws of Physics." *Common Knowledge* 6:1 (Spring): 6–16. (PSH, CT)

1997d. "Can Philosophers Help Their Clients?" *New Leader* (April 7), 11–12.

1997e. "Nietzsche and the Pragmatists." *New Leader* (May 19), 9.

1997f. Introduction to "Symposium: Science Out of Context: The Misestimate and Misuse of Natural Sciences." *Common Knowledge* 6:2 (Fall): 20–103.

1997g. "First Projects, Then Principles." *The Nation* (December 22), 18–21.

1997h. "Comments on Michael Williams' 'Unnatural Doubts.'" *Journal of Philosophical Research* 22:1–10.

1997i. "Global Utopias, History, and Philosophy." In *Cultural Pluralism, Identity, and Globalization,* ed. Luiz Soares, 457–69. Rio de Janiero: UNESCO/ISSC/EDUCAM. (PSH)

1997j. Introduction to *Empiricism and the Philosophy of Mind,* by Wilfrid Sellars, 1–12. Cambridge, Mass.: Harvard University Press. [A slightly enlarged version of introductions previously published in French and Italian translations of the same book.]

1997k. "Justice as a Larger Loyalty." In *Justice and Democracy: Cross-Cultural Perspectives,* ed. Ron Bontekoe and Marietta Stepaniants, 9–22. Honolulu: University of Hawaii Press. (PZ, PV)

————. Reprinted in *Cultural Pluralism, Identity, and Globalization,* ed. Luiz Soares. Rio de Janiero: UNESCO/ISSC/EDUCAM.

————. Polish translation: "Sprawiedliwosc jako Poszerzona Logalnosc." *Transit* 3 (1997).

1997l. "Realism, Antirealism, and Pragmatism: Comments on Alston, Chisholm,

Davidson, Harman and Searle." In *Realism/Antirealism and Epistemology*, ed. Christopher Kulp, 149–71. London: Rowman and Littlefield.

1997m. "Relativismus: Finden und Machen." In *Die Wiederentdeckung der Zeit: Reflexionen-Analysen-Konzept*, ed. Antje Gimmler, Mike Sandbothe, and Walters Zimmerli, trans. Andrew Inkpin and Mike Sandbothe, 9–26. Darmstadt: Wissenschaftliche Buchgesellschaft.

1997n. "What Do You Do When They Call You a 'Relativist'?" Part of a symposium on Robert Brandom's *Making it Explicit*. *Philosophy and Phenomenological Research* 57:1:173–77.

## 1998

1998a. "Against Unity." Review-article on *Consilience*, by E. O. Wilson. *Woodrow Wilson Quarterly* 22:1 (Winter): 28–38.

1998b. "Endlich sieht man Freudenthal." *Frankfurter Allgemeine Zeitung* (February 20), 40. [English original subsequently published as 1999k.] (PSH)

———. Also published as *Das Kommunistische Manifest 150 Jahre danach: Gescheiterte Prophezeiungen, glorreiche Hoffnungen*, a "Sonderdruck" from Suhrkamp Verlag. Frankfurt am Main: Suhrkamp, 1998.

1998c. Contribution to "Thinking in Public: A Forum." *American Literary History* 10:1 (Spring): 1–83.

1998d. "Davidson Between Wittgenstein and Tarski." *Critica: Revista Hispano-americana de Filosofía* 30:88 (April): 49–71.

1998e. "The Dark Side of the Academic Left." *Chronicle of Higher Education* (April 3), B4–B6.

1998f. "The American Road to Fascism." *New Statesman* (May 8), 28–29.

1998g. "McDowell, Davidson, and Spontaneity." *Philosophy and Phenomenological Research* 58:2 (June): 389–94.

1998h. "Response to Stuart Rennie's 'Elegant Variations.'" *South African Journal of Philosophy* 17:4 (November): 343–45.

1998i. Contribution to "International Books of the Year." *Times Literary Supplement* (December 4), 9.

1998j. "A Defense of Minimalist Liberalism." In *Debating Democracy's Discontent: Essays on American Politics, Law, and Public Philosophy*, ed. Anita L. Allen and Milton C. Regan, Jr., 117–25. New York: Oxford University Press.

1998k. "Pragmatism." *Routledge Encyclopedia of Philosophy*. Vol. 7. Ed. Edward Craig. New York: Routledge.

———. Polish translation: "Pragmatyzm." In *Filozofia amerykanska dzis*, ed. Tomasz Komendski and Andrzej Szahaj. Torun: Uniwersytet Mikolaja Kopernika w Toruniu, 1999.

1998l. "Pragmatism as Romantic Polytheism." In *The Revival of Pragmatism*, ed. Morris Dickstein, 21–36. Durham, N.C.: Duke University Press. (PV)

1998m. "Vive la Différence." *2B: A Journal of Ideas* 13:79–80.


*1999*

1999a. "Saved from Hypocrisy." *Dissent* 46:2 (Spring): 16–17.

1999b. "Not All *That* Strange: A Response to Dreyfus and Spinosa." *Inquiry* 42:1 (March): 125–28.

1999c. "Mein Jahrhundertbuch: Freud's Vorlesungen zur Einführung in die Psychoanalyse." *Die Zeit* (May 20), 61.

1999d. [With John Searle.] "Rorty v. Searle, at Last: A Debate." *Logos* 2:3 (Summer): 20–67.

1999e. "Comment on Robert Pippin's 'Naturalness and Mindedness: Hegel's Compatibilism.'" *European Journal of Philosophy* 7:2 (August): 213–16.

1999f. Contribution to "International Books of the Year and the Millennium." *Times Literary Supplement* (December 3), 11.

1999g. "Can American Egalitarianism Survive a Globalized Economy?" *Business Ethics Quarterly: Journal of the Society for Business Ethics*. Ruffin Series, special issue 1:1–6.

1999h. "The Communitarian Impulse." *Colorado College Studies* 32:55–61.

1999i. "Coraggio, Europa!" *Iride* 12:27:241–43.

1999j. "Davidson's Mental-Physical Distinction." In *The Philosophy of Donald Davidson*, ed. Lewis Hahn, 575–94. La Salle, Ill.: Open Court.

1999k. "Failed Prophecies, Glorious Hopes." *Constellations* 6:2:216–21. [English original of 1998b.] (PSH)

1999l. "Pragmatism as Anti-authoritarianism." *Revue Internationale de Philosophie* 53:1 (207): 7–20.


*2000*

2000a. "Darwin Versus 'Erkenntnistheorie': Reply to Janos Boros." *Deutsche Zeitschrift für Philosophie* 48:1 (Winter): 149–52.

2000b. "Response to Randall Peerenbloom." *Philosophy East and West* 50:1 (Winter): 90–91.

2000c. "The Overphilosophization of Politics." *Constellations* 7:1 (March): 128–32.

2000d. "Making the Rich Richer." *New York Times* (March 6), op-ed page.

2000e. "Being That Can Be Understood Is Language: On Hans-Georg Gadamer and the Philosophical Conversation." *London Review of Books* (March 16), 23–25. (PZ)

————. German translation: in *Neue Rundschau* III:2 (2000): 103–15.

————. Italian translation: in *L'essere, che puó essere compreso, e linguaggio*, trans. Donatella Di Cesare. Genoa: Il Melangolo, 2001.

2000f. "Is 'Cultural Recognition' a Useful Concept for Leftist Politics?" *Critical Horizons* 1:1:7–20.

2000g. "Keine Zukunft ohne Träume." In *Die Gegenwart der Zukunft*, preface by Klaus Podak, 182–90. Published by the newspaper *Süddeutsche Zeitung* as part of Die Serie der Süddeutschen Zeitung über unsere Welt im neuen Jahrhundert. Berlin: Klaus Wagenbach.

————. Spanish translation: "Sin sueños no hay futuro." *Humboldt* 42:131 (2000): 2.

2000h. "Kuhn." In *A Companion to the Philosophy of Science*, ed. W. H. Newton-Smith, 203–6. Oxford: Blackwell.

2000i. "Lob des Polytheismus: Nietzsches quasi-pragmatische Auffassung der Wahrheit." *Die Zeit* 35, 41.

————. Reprinted in *Was mir Nietzsche Bedeutet*, ed. Patrick Baum and Guenther Seubold, 91–96. Bonn: Denk Mal, 2001.

2000j. "Die moderne analytische Philosophie aus pragmatischer Sicht." Trans. Joachim Schulte. In *Die Renaissance des Pragmatismus*, ed. Mike Sandbothe, 78–95. Göttingen: Velbrueck Wissenschaft. [English original 2003a.]

2000k. "The Moral Purposes of the University: An Exchange [with Julie A. Reuben and George Marsden]." *Hedgehog Review* 2:3 (Fall): 106–20.

2000l. "Pragmatism." *International Journal of Psycho-Analysis* 81:4:819–25.

2000m. "Responses." in *Richard Rorty: Critical Dialogues*, ed. Matthew Festenstein and Simon Thompson, 56–64, 74–80, 87–90, 101–8, 123–28, 146–55, 183–90, 213–19, 236–41, 262–67, 342–50, and 370–77. Cambridge: Polity Press, and Malden, Mass.: Blackwell. [Also includes a reprint of 1997k.]

2000n. "Responses." In *Rorty and His Critics*, ed. Robert B. Brandom. Malden, Mass.: Blackwell.

2000o. *Die Schönheit, die Erhabenheit, und die Gemeinschaft der Philosophen.* Trans. Jürgen Blasius and Christa Krüger. Frankfurt am Main: Suhrkamp. [Also contains "Die Intellektuellen und die Armen."]

2000p. "Die Vorlesungsgast." In *Begegnungen mit Hans-Georg Gadamer*, ed. Günter Figal, 87–91. Stuttgart: Reclam.

### 2001

2001a. Contribution to "What We'll Remember in 2050: Nine Views on Bush v. Gore." *Chronicle of Higher Education* (January 5), 15.

2001b. "Wittgenstein, che separo il naturalismo dell'empirismo." *Reset* 64 (January–February): 84–85.

2001c. "'Postmoderno' e Politica." Trans. Giovanni Battista Clemente. *Paradigmi* 18:55 (January–April): 49–66.

2001d. "An Imaginative Philosopher: The Legacy of W. V. Quine." *Chronicle of Higher Education* (February 2), B7–9.

2001e. "Die Militarisierung Amerikas." Trans. Julia Ritter. *Die Zeit* (September 17), 21.

2001f. Contribution to a collection of thoughts about September 11. *London Review of Books* (October 4).

———. Japanese translation: in a compilation of essays published in *Asahi Shinbunsha*, a Japanese newspaper. Trans. Gen Nakayama. Tokyo: Orion Press, 2002.

2001g. "The Continuity Between the Enlightenment and 'Postmodernism.'" In *What's Left of Enlightenment? A Postmodern Question*, ed. Keith Michael Baker and Peter Hanns Reill, 19–36. Stanford, Calif.: Stanford University Press. [Previously published by De Gruyter (Amsterdam) in a limited-circulation pamphlet containing two Spinoza lectures given at the University of Amsterdam, along with "Spinoza, Pragmatism, and the Love of Wisdom."]

2001h. "Declinul adevarului redemptiv si aparitia unei culturi literare: Drumul pe care au mers intelectualii occidentali." *Postcolonialism si Postcomunism* 1:30–42.

2001i. "Im Dienste der Welterschliessung." In *Was ist ein "philosophisches" Problem?* ed. Joachim Schulte and Uwe Justus Wenzel, 148–54. Frankfurt am Main: Fischer Taschenbuch.

2001j. "Existenzielle Notwendigkeit und kantische Unbedingtheit: Eine Erwiderung auf Harold Koehl." Trans. Joerg Schenuit. *Deutsche Zeitschrift fuer Philosophie* 49:3:459–65.

2001k. "Gefangen zwischen Kant und Dewey: Die gegenwaertige Lage der Moralphilosophie." *Deutsche Zeitschrift fuer Philosophie* 49:2:179–96.

———. Reprinted in *New Essays on the History of Autonomy: A Collection Honoring J. B. Schneewind*, ed. Natlies Brender and Larry Krasnoff, 195–214. Cambridge: Cambridge University Press, 2004.

2001l. "Politica culturala si intrebarea referitoare la existenta lui Dumnezeu." *Postcolonialism si Postcomunism* 1:13–29. [English original published as 2002e.]

2001m. "Redemption from Egotism: James and Proust as Spiritual Exercises." *Telos* 3:3:243–63.

2001n. "Replies." In *Hinter den Spiegeln: Beiträge zur Philosophie Richard Rortys mit Erwiderungen von Richard Rorty*, ed. Thomas Schaefer, Udo Tietz, and Ruediger Zill. Frankfurt am Main: Suhrkamp.

2001o. "Wahrheit und Wissen sind eine Frage der sozialen Kooperation." Trans.

Christa Krueger. *Sueddeutsche Zeitung* (December 4), 14.

———. Italian translation: "La mia religione privata e pragmatica." *Reset* 69 (January–February 2002): 54–58.

———. English original in *Religion After Metaphysics*, ed. Mark A. Wrathall, 37–46. Cambridge: Cambridge University Press, 2003.

———. Also reprinted in *The Future of Religion*, ed. Richard Rorty and Gianni Vattimo. New York: Columbia University Press, 2005.


*2002*

2002a. Contribution to "Die Sprache ist das Licht der Welt: Zum Tod von Hans-Georg Gadamer." *Die Zeit* (March 21), 40.

2002b. "L'Amour de la verité." *Nouvel Observateur* (April–May): 16–18.

2002c. "Comments on Pippin on James." *Inquiry* 45:3:351–59.

2002d. "Cultural Politics and the Question of the Existence of God." In *Radical Interpretation in Religion*, ed. Nancy Frankenberry, 53–77. New York: Cambridge University Press.

2002e. "Fighting Terrorism with Democracy." *The Nation* (October 21), 11–14.

2002f. "Hope and the Future." *Peace Review* 14:2:149–55.

2002g. "Wo ist die charistmatische Internationalist?" Trans. Rudolf Helmstetter. *Merkur* (November): 1034–38.


*2003*

2003a. "Demuetigung oder Solidaritaet?" *Suedeutsche Zeitung* (May 31). [The English original of this piece appeared as "Humiliation or Solidarity?" *Dissent* (Fall): 23–26.]

2003b. "Out of the Matrix" [on Donald Davidson]. *Boston Globe*, Ideas section (October 5), H1.

2003c. "Alcuni usi americani di Hegel." In *Hegel contemporaneo: La ricezione americana di Hegel a confronto con la tradizione europea*, ed. Luigi Ruggiu and Italo Testa, 179–217. Naples: Guerini.

2003d. "Analytic and Conversational Philosophy." In *A House Divided: Comparing Analytic and Continental Philosophy*, ed. C. G. Prado, 17–31. Amherst, N.Y.: Humanity Books.

2003e. "Das Empire der Ungewissheit." In *Empire America: Perspectiven einer neuen Weltordnung*, ed. Ulrich Speck and Natan Sznaider, 240–55. Munich: Deutsches Verlag-Anstalt.

2003f. Foreword to *Knowledge and Civilization*, by Barry Allen, vii–x. Boulder, Colo.: Westview Press.

2003g. "A Pragmatist View of Contemporary Analytic Philosophy." In *The Pragmatic Turn in Philosophy*, ed. William Egginton and Mike Sandbothe, 131–44. New York: State University of New York Press. [Previously appeared in German translation as 2000j.]

2003h. "Was sollen sie denn tun?: Kooperation oder Sabotage? Amerikas widerspruchlich Signale bringen die Iraker in ein Dilemma." *Frankfurter Rundschau* (November 18), 19.

### 2004

2004a. "The Brain as Hardware, Culture as Software." *Inquiry* 47:3 (June): 219–35.

2004b. "Philosophy-Envy." *Daedelus* (Fall): 18–24.

2004c. Two brief memorial tributes to Jacques Derrida. *Die Zeit* (Feuilleton) (October 14); and *Times Higher Education Supplement* (November 12).

2004d. A brief contribution to a symposium on the outcome of the 2004 presidential election. *The Nation* (December 20), 17.

2004e. Afterword to *Sidney Hook Reconsidered*, ed. Matthew J. Cotter, 281–86. Amherst, N.Y.: Prometheus Books.

2004f. Foreword to *Nihilism and Emancipation*, by Gianni Vattimo, ix–xx. New York: Columbia University Press.

2004g. "Philosophy as a Transitional Genre." In *Pragmatism, Critique, Judgment: Essays for Richard J. Bernstein*, ed. Seyla Benhabib and Nancy Fraser, 3–28. Cambridge, Mass.: MIT Press.

2004h. "A Pragmatist View of Contemporary Analytic Philosophy." In *The Pragmatic Turn in Philosophy: Contemporary Engagements Between Analytic and Continental Thought*, ed. William Egginton and Mike Sandbothe, 131–44. Albany: State University of New York Press.

2004i. "Some Inconsistencies in James' Varieties." In *William James and a Science of Religions*, ed. Wayne Proudfoot, 86–97. New York: Columbia University Press.

2004j. "Trapped Between Kant and Dewey: The Current Situation of Moral Philosophy." In *New Essays on the History of Autonomy: A Collection Honoring J. B. Schneewind*, ed. Natlies Brender and Larry Krasnoff, 195–214. Cambridge: Cambridge University Press. [Previously appeared in German as 2001e.]

2004k. "Universalist Grandeur, Romantic Depth, Pragmatist Cunning." *Diogenes* 51:202:129–41.

*2005*

"Comments and Responses." In *Richard Rorty: His Philosophy Under Discussion*, Müenstersche Vorlesungen zur Philosophie 8, ed. Andreas Vieth, 131–47. Heusenstamm: Ontos.

BOOK REVIEWS

*1959*

Review of *Experience and the Analytic: A Reconsideration of Empiricism*, by Alan Pasch. *International Journal of Ethics* 70 (October): 75–77.

*1960*

Review of *Modern Science and Human Freedom*, by David L. Miller. *International Journal of Ethics* 70 (April): 248–49.

Review of *Aristotle*, by John Hermann Randall, Jr., and *Some Assumptions of Aristotle*, by George Boas. *Ethics* 71:1 (October): 54–55.

Review of *John Dewey: His Thought and Influence*, ed. John Blewett. *Teacher's College Record* 62 (October): 88–89.

*1961*

Review of *Introduction to the Philosophy of History*, by Raymond Aron. *The New Leader* (December 25), 18–19.

*1962*

Review of *American Pragmatism: Peirce, James, and Dewey*, by Edward C. Moore. *Ethics* 72:2 (January): 146–47.

Review of *The Value Judgment*, by W. D. Lamont. *Journal for the Scientific Study of Religion* 2:1 (October): 139–40.

*1963*

Review of *Utopian Essays and Practical Proposals*, by Paul Goodman. *Teacher's College Record* 64 (May): 743–44.

Review of *Reason and Analysis*, by Brand Blanshard. *Journal of Philosophy* 60:19 (September 12): 551–57.

Review of *Understanding Whitehead*, by Victor Lowe. *Journal of Philosophy* 60:9:246–51.

*1964*

Review of *Chauncy Wright and the Foundations of Pragmatism*, by Edward H. Madden. *Philosophical Review* 73:2 (April): 287–89.

Review of *Clarity Is Not Enough: Essays in Criticism of Linguistic Philosophy*, by H. D. Lewis. *International Philosophical Quarterly* 4:4 (December): 623–24.

*[1965]*

*1966*

Review of *Charles Peirce and Scholastic Realism: A Study of Peirce's Relation to John Duns Scotus*, by John F. Boler. *Philosophical Review* 75:1 (January): 116–19.

*1967*

Review of *Metaphysics, Reference, and Language*, by James W. Cornman. *Journal of Philosophy* 64:22 (November 23): 770–74.

*[1968]*

*[1969]*

*1970*

Review of *Science and Metaphysics: Variations on Kantian Themes*, by Wilfrid Sellars. *Philosophy* 45 (March): 66–70.

*1971*

Review of *The Origins of Pragmatism: Studies in the Philosophy of Charles Sanders Peirce and William James*, by A. J. Ayer. *Philosophical Review* 80:1 (January): 96–100.

*1972*

Review of *Nihilism*, by Stanley Rosen. *Philosophy Forum* 11:102–8.

*[1973]*

*[1974]*

*[1975]*

*1976*

Review of *On Human Conduct*, by Michael Oakeshott, and *Knowledge and Politics*, by Roberto Mangabiera Unger. *Social Theory and Practice* 4:1 (Fall): 107–16.

"Realism and Necessity." Review of *Nature and Necessity*, by Milton Fisk. *Noûs* 10:3 (September): 345–54.

*[1977]*

*[1978]*

*1979*

"On Worldmaking." Review of *Ways of Worldmaking*, by Nelson Goodman. *Yale Review* 69:2 (December): 276–79.

*1980*

"Kripke vs. Kant." Review of *Naming and Necessity*, by Saul Kripke. *London Review of Books* (September 4), 4–5.

*1981*

"Beyond Nietzsche and Marx." Review of *Power/Knowledge*, by Michel Foucault, *Michel Foucault: The Will to Truth*, by Alan Sheridan, and *Herculine Barbin*, by Oscar Panizza. *London Review of Books* (February 19), 5–6.

"Being Business." Review of *A Heidegger Critique*, by Roger Waterhouse. *Times Literary Supplement* (July 3), 760.

Review of *American Sociology and Pragmatism*, by J. D. Lewis and R. L. Smith, and *The Calling of Sociology and Other Essays*, by Edward Shils. *Review of Metaphysics* 35:1:167–68.

*1982*

"Persuasive Philosophy." Review of *Philosophical Explanations*, by Robert Nozick. *London Review of Books* (May 20), 10–11.

"Brute and Raw Experience." Review of *Philosophy in the Twentieth Century*, by A. J. Ayer. *New Republic* (December 6), 33–36.

## 1983

"The Pragmatist." Review of *A Stroll with William James*, by Jacques Barzun. *New Republic* (May 9), 32–34.

"Against Belatedness." Review of *The Legitimacy of the Modern Age*, by Hans Blumenberg. *London Review of Books* (June 16), 3–5.

"Unsoundness in Perspective." Review of *Nietzsche*, by Richard Schacht, and *Nietzsche and Philosophy*, by Gilles Deleuze. *Times Literary Supplement* (June 17), 619–20.

Review of *Reason, Truth, and History*, by Hilary Putnam. *Critique* 39:439:923–40.

## 1984

"Signposts Along the Way That Reason Went." Review of *Margins of Philosophy*, by Jacques Derrida. *London Review of Books* (February 16), 5–6.

"What's It All About?" Review of *Intentionality*, by John Searle. *London Review of Books* (May 17), 3–4.

"Life at the End of Inquiry." Review of *Realism and Reason: Philosophical Papers III*, by Hilary Putnam. *London Review of Books* (August 2), 6–7.

Review of *The Post-Modern Condition*, by Jean-François Lyotard. *Critique* 40:442:181–97.

## 1985

"Feeling His Way." Review of *The War Diaries of Jean-Paul Sartre: November 1939–March 1940. New Republic* (April 15), 32–34.

Review of *Traditional and Analytical Philosophy: Lectures on the Philosophy of Language*, by Ernst Tugendhat. *Journal of Philosophy* 82:12 (December): 720–29.

"Absolutely Non-Absolute." Review of *Philosophical Papers*, vols. 1–2, by Charles Taylor. *Times Literary Supplement* (December 6), 1379–80.

## 1986

"Sex and the Single Thinker." Review of *Sexual Desire: A Moral Philosophy of the Erotic*, by Roger Scruton. *New Republic* (June 2), 34–37.

## 1987

"Posties." Review of *Der Philosophische Diskurs der Moderne*, by Jürgen Habermas. *London Review of Books* (September 3), 11–12. [French translation: *Sud* 18:78–79 (1988): 173–85.]

*1988*

"Taking Philosophy Seriously." Review of *Heidegger et le Nazisme*, by Victor Farias. *New Republic* (April 11), 31–34.

———. Italian translation: "Prendere sul serio la filosofia." *Aut Aut* 226–27 (July–October): 133–40.

Review of *Derrida*, by Christopher Norris. *The New Leader* (October 3–17), 20–21.

Review of *The Limits of Analysis*, by Stanley Rosen. *Independent Journal of Philosophy* 5–6:153–54.

*1989*

Review of *Connections to the World: The Basic Concepts of Philosophy*, by Arthur C. Danto. *New York Newsday* (March 19), 21.

Review of *In Quest of the Ordinary: Lines of Skepticism and Romanticism*, by Stanley Cavell. *New Republic* (June 19), 38–41.

Review of *Interpreting Across Boundaries*, ed. Eliot Deutsch and G. Larson. *Philosophy East and West* 39:3 (July): 332–37.

*[1990]*

*1991*

Review of *John Dewey and American Democracy*, by Robert Westbrook. *The New Leader* (May 20), 13.

"The Guru of Prague." Review of *Platon et l'Europe et Essais hérétiques*, by Jan Patocka, and *Jan Patocka: Philosophy and Selected Writings*, ed. Ezrahim Kohak. *New Republic* (July 1), 35–40.

"Just One More Species Doing Its Best." Review of *The Later Works, 1925–1953*, vol. 17, by John Dewey; *Dewey*, by J. E. Tiles; *John Dewey and American Democracy*, by Robert Westbrook; and *Beloved Community: The Cultural Criticism of Randolph Bourne, Van Wyck Brooks, Waldo Frank, and Lewis Mumford*, by Casey Blake. *London Review of Books* (July 25), 3–7.

———. German translation: in *Merkur* 46:1 (January 1995): 1–16.

"Blunder Around for a While." Review of *Consciousness Explained*, by Daniel Dennett. *London Review of Books* (November 21), 3–6.

"The Philosopher and the Prophet." Review of *The American Evasion of Philosophy*, by Cornel West. *Transition* 52:70–78.

*1992*

"We Anti-Representationalists." Review of *Ideology: An Introduction*, by Terry Eagleton. *Radical Philosophy* 60 (Spring): 40–42.

"The Feminist Saving Remnant." Review of *The Rise and Fall of the American Left*, by John Patrick Diggins. *The New Leader* (June 1–15), 9–10.

*1993*

"Paroxysms and Politics." Review of *The Passion of Michel Foucault*, by James Miller. *Salmagundi* 97 (Winter): 61–68.

————. Reprinted in *The New Salmagundi Reader*, ed. Robert Boyers and Peggy Boyers, 513–20. Syracuse, N.Y.: Syracuse University Press, 1996.

Review of *The Ethics of Authenticity*, by Charles Taylor. *London Review of Books* (April 8), 3.

Review of *Ideals and Illusions: On Reconstruction and Deconstruction in Contemporary Critical Theory*, by Thomas McCarthy. *Journal of Philosophy* 90:7 (July): 370–73.

*1994*

Review of *Willful Liberalism: Voluntarism and Individuality in Political Theory and Practice*, by Richard Flathman. *Political Theory* 22:1 (February): 190–94.

"Why Can't a Man Be More Like a Woman, and Other Problems in Moral Philosophy." Review of *Moral Prejudices: Essays in Ethics*, by Annette Baier. *London Review of Books* (February 24), 3–6.

"A Leg-Up for Oliver North." Review of *Dictatorship of Virtue: Multiculturalism and the Battle for America's Future*, by Richard Bernstein. *London Review of Books* (October 20), 13–14.

————. A revised version, entitled "Demonizing the Academy," appeared in *Harper's* (January 1995), 13–17.

————. Another version, entitled "The Demonization of Multiculturalism," appeared in the *Journal of Blacks in Higher Education* 7 (Spring 1995): 74–75.

Review of *The Grandeur and Twilight of Radical Universalism*, by Ferenc Feher and Agnes Heller. *Thesis Eleven* 37:119–26.

*1995*

"Two Cheers for Elitism." Review of *The Revolt of the Elites and the Betrayal of Democracy*, by Christopher Lasch. *New Yorker* (January 30), 86–89.

"Untruth and Consequences." Review of *Killing Time*, by Paul Feyerabend. *New Republic* (July 31), 32–36.

"Cranes and Skyhooks." Review of *Darwin's Dangerous Idea: Evolution and the Meanings of Life*, by Daniel Dennett. *Lingua Franca* (August): 62–66.

"Color-Blind in the Marketplace." Review of *The End of Racism: Principles for a Multicultural Society*, by Dinesh d'Souza. *New York Times Book Review* (September 24), 9.

"Consolation Prize." Review of *The Unconsoled*, by Kazuo Ishiguro. *Village Voice Literary Supplement* (October), 13.

## 1996

"The Sins of the Overclass." Review of *The Next American Nation*, by Michael Lind. *Dissent* 43:2 (Spring): 109–12.

Review of *Critical Theory*, ed. David Hoy and Thomas McCarthy. *Ethics* 106:3 (April): 657–59.

"Something to Steer By." Review of *John Dewey and the High Tide of Americal Liberalism*, by Alan Ryan. *London Review of Books* (June 20), 7–8.

Review of *Aramis; or, The Love of Technology*, by Bruno Latour. *Village Voice Literary Supplement* (September), 10.

"Sigmund on the Couch." Review of *Wittgenstein Reads Freud*, by Jacques Bouveresse. *New York Times Book Review* (September 22), 42.

Review of *Pragmatism: An Open Question*, by Hilary Putnam. *Philosophical Review* 105:4 (October): 560–61.

"Knowledge and Acquaintance." Review of *Bertrand Russell: The Spirit of Solitude, 1872–1921*, by Ray Monk. *New Republic* (December 2), 46–52.

## 1997

Review of *When Work Disappears: The World of the New Urban Poor*, by W. J. Wilson. *Dissent* 44:3 (Summer): 111–13.

## 1998

Review of *Martin Heidegger: Between Good and Evil*, by Rudiger Safranski. *New York Times Book Review* (May 3), 12–13.

"Marxists, Straussians, Pragmatists." Review of *Left Out: Pragmatism, Exceptionalism, and the Poverty of American Marxism, 1980–1922*, by Brian Lloyd; *Young Sidney Hook: Pragmatist and Marxist*, by Christopher Phelps; and *Reconstructing America: The Symbol of America in Modern Thought*, by James Caesar. *Raritan* (Fall): 128–36.

*1999*

"Phony Science Wars." Review of *The Social Construction of What?* by Ian Hacking. *Atlantic Monthly* (November), 120.

"I Hear America Sighing." Review of *The Real American Dream*, by Andrew Delbanco. *New York Times Book Review* (November 7), 16.

"Aristotle Had It Right." Review of *The Trouble with Principle*, by Stanley Fish. *The New Leader* (December 13–27), 5–6.

*2000*

"Structures of Deceit." Review of *Papal Sin: Structures of Deceit*, by Garry Wills. *New York Times Book Review* (June 11), 10.

Review of *Happiness, Death, and the Remainder of Life*, by Jonathan Lear. *New York Times Book Review* (October 22), 14.

*2001*

Review of *Idealism as Modernism: Hegelian Variations*, by Robert Pippin. *Ethics* 111:2 (January): 438.

"Studied Ambiguity." Review of *Shaping Science with Rhetoric*, by Leah Ceccarelli. *Science* (September 28), 2399–400.

*2002*

"When Philosophy Is Irrelevant." Review of *Our Posthuman Future*, by Francis Fukuyama. *The New Leader* (May–June), 19.

"To the Sunlit Uplands." Review of *Truth and Truthfulness*, by Bernard Williams. *London Review of Books* (October 31), 13–15.

*2003*

"More Than Compromise." Review of *Law, Pragmatism, and Democracy*, by Richard A. Posner. *Dissent* (Fall 2003): 99–101.

*[2004]*

*2005*

"After Kripke." Review of *Analytic Philosophy in the Twentieth Century*, by Scott Soames. *London Review of Books* (January 20).

Review of *Problems of Rationality*, by Donald Davidson. *Notre Dame Philosophical Reviews* (February 1). http://ndpr.nd.edu/review.cfm?id=1681.

INTERVIEWS

Hudson, Wayne, and Wim van Reijen. "From Philosophy to Post-Philosophy." *Radical Philosophy* 32 (Autumn 1982): 1–4.

Foreman, Joel. "The Humanities: Asking Better Questions, Doing More Things." *Federation Review* 8:2 (March–April 1985): 15–19.

———. "Interview with Richard Rorty." *Journal of Literary Studies / Tydskrif Vir Literatuurwetenskap* 2 (November 1986): 9–13.

———. "I professori sono meglio dei torturatori." *Alfabeta* 10 (March 1988): 5.

Winkler, Karen J. "A Controversial Philosopher States His Case on Politics, Poetry, and Moral Principle." *Chronicle of Higher Education* (May 3, 1989), A7–9.

Olson, Gary. "Social Construction and Composition Theory: A Conversation with Richard Rorty." *Journal of Advanced Composition* 9 (1989): 1–9.

Postel, Danny. "A Post-Philosophical Politics?" *Philosophy and Social Criticism* 15:2 (1989): 199–204.

Kulka, T. "Richard Rorty: Une Interview." *Iyyun* 39:10 (1990): 371–80.

Uzan, Marc. "It's the Real Thing." *The Guardian* (London) (March 14, 1992), 25.

———. "On Democracy, Liberalism, and the Post-Communist Challenge." *Mesotes: Zeitschrift für philosophischen Ost-West Dialog* 4 (1992): 491–500.

———. "Intersubjectividad y libertad." *Theoria: Revista de Filosofía* 1:1 (July 1993): 113–22.

———. "Du pragmatisme en politique." *Le Banquet* 3:2 (1993): 135–47.

Marino, Gordon D. "Shattering Philosophy's Mirror: A Conversation with Richard Rorty." *Commonweal* (May 6, 1994), 11–14.

Oliver, M. "Towards a Liberal Utopia." *Times Literary Supplement* (June 24, 1994), 14.

Borradori, Giovanna. In *Conversazioni americane*. Rome: Laterza, 1991. Trans.: "After Philosophy, Democracy." In *The American Philosopher: Conversations with Quine, Davidson, Putnam, Nozick, Danto, Rorty, Cavell, MacIntyre, and Kuhn*, trans. Rosanna Crocitto, 103–17. Chicago: University of Chicago Press, 1994.

———. "Toward a Post-Metaphysical Culture." *Harvard Journal of Philosophy* (Spring 1995): 58–66.

Knobe, Joshua. "A Talent for Bricolage: An Interview with Richard Rorty." *The Dualist* 2 (1995): 56–71.

Kuehn, G., L. Siliceo-Roman, and J. Salyards. "Interview with Richard Rorty." *Kinesis* 23:1 (1996): 51–64.

———. "Questioning . . . Richard Rorty." *Bochumer Philosophisches Jahrbuch* 2 (1997): 243–52.

Cloquell, Jose Miguel Esteban. "Cómo se un buen pragmatista: Conversación con Richard Rorty." *Debate* 61 (1997): 100–106.

Stanczyk, Zbigniew. "There Is a Crisis Coming: A Conversation with Richard Rorty." *2B: A Journal of Ideas* 11–12 (1997): 18–29. [Reprinted in *Rzeczpospolita*, a major Warsaw newspaper (September 20, 1997).]

Stossel, Scott. "The Next Left." *Atlantic Monthly* (April 23, 1998).

Martin, M. "Richard Rorty: El 'liberal tragico.'" *Revista de Occidente*, ser. 4:90 (November 1998): 103–12.

Baruchello, Giorgio. "Una filosofia tra conversazione e politica." *Iride* 11:25 (1998): 457–82.

Grotker, R., and R. Sonderegger. "Die Armen sind die Grosse Mehrheit [The Poor Are the Overwhelming Majority]." *Deutsche Zeitschrift für Philosophie* 46:6 (1998): 983–90.

Nystrom, Derek, and Kent Puckett. *Against Bosses, Against Oligarchies: A Conversation with Richard Rorty*. Prickly Pear Pamphlets 11. Charlottesville, Va.: Prickly Pear Pamphlets, 1998.

———. Portuguese translation [Brazil]: "Contra os chefes, contra as olgarquias." Trans. Joao Abreu. Rio de Janeiro: DP e A, 2001.

Traval, Jaume. "La apuesta filósofica por la polemica." *Revista Internacional de Filosofia Politica* 11 (1998): 149–54.

Ullrich, Wolfgang, and Helmut Mayer. "Uberreden ist Gut [Convincing Is Good]." *Neue Rundschau* 109:4 (1998): 87–109.

Fosl, Peter. "Note to Realists: Grow Up." *The Philosophers' Magazine* 8 (Autumn 1999): 40–42.

Kunelius, Risto. "Filosofia tänään: Kumousta odoteltaessa [Philosophy Today: Waiting for the Revolution]." *Niin & Näin* 6:2 (1999): 22–27.

Quintanilla, Pablo. "Los régimenes no democráticos colapsan inevitablemente." *Debate* 21:120 (June–August 2000): 33–36.

Auer, Dirk. "Sieben Dollar sind zu wenig." *Frankfurter Rundschau* (August 1, 2000), 19.

Mujkic, Asim. "Filozofski problemi su efemerni." *Odjek* 53:3–4 (2000).

Tamas, Ungar. "A filozofia tronfosztasa." *Hetvege* (May 26, 2001), 28.

Polychroniu, Chronis. "An Exchange: On Philosophy and Politics, the Cold War, and the Left." *New Politics* 8:3 (Summer 2001): 128–40.

"Der Planeten verwestlichen!" *Sueddeutsche Zeitung* (November 20, 2001), 15.

Bauer, Martin, and Christian Esch. "Definitionen spielen hier keine Rolle." *Berliner Zeitung* (November 24–25, 2001), 11.

"Politisch nichts zu lernen." *Frankfurter Rundschau* (November 30, 2001).

Marchetti, Giancarolo. "Un ironico neopragmatismo." *Keiron* 9 (December 2001): 143–49.

Dotzauer, Gregor. "Woher weiss ich, dass ich kein Zombie bin?" *Der Tagesspiegel* (December 1, 2001), 25.

Trifiro, Fabrizio. "Richard Rorty: An Interview." *Arcade* 2 (2001): 96–105.

Deuze, Mark. "Ledereen wordt patriottistisch, als hij wordt aangevallen." *Filosofie Magazine* 11:2 (March 2002): 8–10.

Obermauer, Ralph. "Europa nutzt seine Macht nicht." *Tages-Anzeiger* (April 23, 2002), 57. [Also appeared in the *Frankfurter Allgemeine Zeitung* (April 15, 2002).]

Sjunnesson, Jan. "Filosofernas antifilosof vill ateruppratta den amerikanska vanstern." *Axess* 3 (May 2002): 11–14.

Rapp, E. "Worlds or Words Apart: The Consequences of Pragmatism for Literary Studies." *Philosophy and Literature* 26:2 (October 2002): 369–96.

Lee, Yusun. "Lee-chul-de Lo-ti Kyo-so Wa-ei Dae-Hwa." *Social Philosophy* 3, *Philosophy and Rationality* (2002): 175–86.

Prado, C. G. "A Conversation with Richard Rorty." Symposium in *Journal of the Canadian Society for Hermeneutics and Postmodern Thought* 7:2 (Fall 2003): 227–31.

# Sources

Chapter 1. James Ryerson, "The Quest for Uncertainty: Richard Rorty's Pilgrimage," *Lingua Franca* 10:9 (December 2000–January 2001): 42–52.

Chapter 2. Wayne Hudson and Wim van Reijen, "From Philosophy to Post-Philosophy," *Radical Philosophy* 32 (Autumn 1982): 1–4.

Chapter 3. Danny Postel, "Post-Philosophical Politics," *Philosophy and Social Criticism* 15:2 (1989): 199–204.

Chapter 4. Giovanna Borradori, "After Philosophy, Democracy," in *The American Philosopher: Conversations with Quine, Davidson, Putnam, Nozick, Danto, Rorty, Cavell, MacIntyre, and Kuhn,* by Giovanna Borradori, 103–17 (Chicago: University of Chicago Press, 1994).

Chapter 5. Michael O'Shea, "Toward a Post-Metaphysical Culture," *Harvard Journal of Philosophy* (Spring 1995): 58–66.

Chapter 6. Zbigniew Stanczyk, "There Is a Crisis Coming: A Conversation with Richard Rorty," *2B: A Journal of Ideas* 11–12 (1997): 18–29. [Reprinted in *Rzeczpospolita,* a major Warsaw newspaper (September 20, 1997).]

Chapter 7. Reinhard Kaiser, Helmut Mayer, and Wolfgang Ullrich, "Uberreden ist Gut [Persuasion Is a Good Thing]," *Neue Rundschau* 109:4 (1998): 87–109.

Chapter 8. Chronis Polychroniou, "On Philosophy and Politics," previously unpublished.

Chapter 9. Eduardo Mendieta, "The Best Can Be an Enemy of the Better," previously unpublished.

Chapter 10. Eduardo Mendieta, "On September 11, 2001," previously unpublished.

Chapter 11. Edward Ragg, "Worlds or Words Apart? The Consequences of Pragmatism for Literary Studies," *Philosophy and Literature* 26:2 (2002): 369–96.

Chapter 12. Andrzej Szahaj, "Biography and Philosophy," previously unpublished.

# Index

Cultural Memory | in the Present

Jacob Taubes, *The Political Theology of Paul*

Jean-Luc Marion, *The Crossing of the Visible*

Eric Michaud, *The Cult of Art in Nazi Germany*

Anne Freadman, *The Machinery of Talk: Charles Peirce and the Sign Hypothesis*

Stanley Cavell, *Emerson's Transcendental Etudes*

Stuart McLean, *The Event and its Terrors: Ireland, Famine, Modernity*

Beate Rössler, ed., *Privacies: Philosophical Evaluations*

Bernard Faure, *Double Exposure: Cutting Across Buddhist and Western Discourses*

Alessia Ricciardi, *The Ends Of Mourning: Psychoanalysis, Literature, Film*

Alain Badiou, *Saint Paul: The Foundation of Universalism*

Gil Anidjar, *The Jew, the Arab: A History of the Enemy*

Jonathan Culler and Kevin Lamb, eds., *Just Being Difficult? Academic Writing in the Public Arena*

Jean-Luc Nancy, *A Finite Thinking*, edited by Simon Sparks

Theodor W. Adorno, *Can One Live after Auschwitz? A Philosophical Reader*, edited by Rolf Tiedemann

Patricia Pisters, *The Matrix of Visual Culture: Working with Deleuze in Film Theory*

Andreas Huyssen, *Present Pasts: Urban Palimpsests and the Politics of Memory*

Talal Asad, *Formations of the Secular: Christianity, Islam, Modernity*

Dorothea von Mücke, *The Rise of the Fantastic Tale*

Marc Redfield, *The Politics of Aesthetics: Nationalism, Gender, Romanticism*

Emmanuel Levinas, *On Escape*

Dan Zahavi, *Husserl's Phenomenology*

Rodolphe Gasché, *The Idea of Form: Rethinking Kant's Aesthetics*

Michael Naas, *Taking on the Tradition: Jacques Derrida and the Legacies of Deconstruction*

Herlinde Pauer-Studer, ed., *Constructions of Practical Reason: Interviews on Moral and Political Philosophy*

Jean-Luc Marion, *Being Given That: Toward a Phenomenology of Givenness*

Theodor W. Adorno and Max Horkheimer, *Dialectic of Enlightenment*

Ian Balfour, *The Rhetoric of Romantic Prophecy*

Martin Stokhof, *World and Life as One: Ethics and Ontology in Wittgenstein's Early Thought*

Gianni Vattimo, *Nietzsche: An Introduction*

Jacques Derrida, *Negotiations: Interventions and Interviews, 1971-1998*, edited by Elizabeth Rottenberg

Brett Levinson, *The Ends of Literature: The Latin American "Boom" in the Neoliberal Marketplace*

Timothy J. Reiss, *Against Autonomy: Cultural Instruments, Mutualities, and the Fictive Imagination*

Hent de Vries and Samuel Weber, editors, *Religion and Media*

Niklas Luhmann, *Theories of Distinction: Re-Describing the Descriptions of Modernity*, edited and Introduction by William Rasch

Johannes Fabian, *Anthropology with an Attitude: Critical Essays*

Michel Henry, *I am the Truth: Toward a Philosophy of Christianity*

Gil Anidjar, *"Our Place in Al-Andalus": Kabbalah, Philosophy, Literature in Arab-Jewish Letters*

Hélène Cixous and Jacques Derrida, *Veils*

F. R. Ankersmit, *Historical Representation*

F. R. Ankersmit, *Political Representation*

Elissa Marder, *Dead Time: Temporal Disorders in the Wake of Modernity (Baudelaire and Flaubert)*

Reinhart Koselleck, *The Practice of Conceptual History: Timing History, Spacing Concepts*

Niklas Luhmann, *The Reality of the Mass Media*

Hubert Damisch, *A Childhood Memory by Piero della Francesca*

Hubert Damisch, *A Theory of /Cloud/: Toward a History of Painting*

Jean-Luc Nancy, *The Speculative Remark: (One of Hegel's bon mots)*

Jean-François Lyotard, *Soundproof Room: Malraux's Anti-Aesthetics*

Jan Patočka, *Plato and Europe*

Hubert Damisch, *Skyline: The Narcissistic City*

Isabel Hoving, *In Praise of New Travelers: Reading Caribbean Migrant Women Writers*

Richard Rand, ed., *Futures: Of Jacques Derrida*

William Rasch, *Niklas Luhmann's Modernity: The Paradoxes of Differentiation*

Jacques Derrida and Anne Dufourmantelle, *Of Hospitality*

Jean-François Lyotard, *The Confession of Augustine*

Kaja Silverman, *World Spectators*

Samuel Weber, *Institution and Interpretation: Expanded Edition*

Jeffrey S. Librett, *The Rhetoric of Cultural Dialogue: Jews and Germans in the Epoch of Emancipation*

Ulrich Baer, *Remnants of Song: Trauma and the Experience of Modernity in Charles Baudelaire and Paul Celan*